FLAVOURS
of Cooper's Cove Guesthouse

by Angelo Prosperi-Porta

photographs by Andrei Fedorov

TouchWood
Editions

TouchWood Editions
www.touchwoodeditions.com

Library and Archives Canada Cataloguing in Publication
Prosperi-Porta, Angelo
    Flavours of Cooper's Cove Guesthouse / by Angelo Prosperi-Porta ; photographs by Andrei Fedorov.

Includes index.
ISBN 978-1-926741-01-7

1. Cookery—British Columbia—Sooke. 2. Cooper's Cove Guesthouse. I. Title.

TX715.6.P83 2010   641.5'0971128   C2010-905105-2

Recipes and food styling: Angelo Prosperi-Porta
Photographer: Andrei Fedorov
Additional photography: Gary McKinstry, inside title page, Sandy Reber, pages 52, 114, 120, 146, 248
Book design and layout: Reber Creative, Victoria, BC

We gratefully acknowledge the financial support for our publishing activities from the Government of Canada through the Book Publishing Industry Development Program (BPIDP), Canada Council for the Arts, and the province of British Columbia through the British Columbia Arts Council and the Book Publishing Tax Credit.

Mixed Sources
Cert no. SW-COC-001271
© 1996 FSC
FSC

1 2 3 4 5 13 12 11 10

PRINTED IN CANADA

Contents

About the Recipes 1

Breakfast 2
    Side Dishes 4
    Breakfast Baking 8
    Breakfast Main Course 18

Hors d'Oeuvres 38

Soups 52

Starters & Salads 72

Side Dishes 114

Pasta & Risotto 120

Sorbetti & Graniti 138

Main Course 146
    Fish & Shellfish 148
    Poultry 164
    Meats 176

Desserts 198

Breads 238

Basics 248

Index 264

Acknowledgements

First of all, I want to thank my parents for the invaluable lessons on the importance of food and family in our day-to-day lives. I learned through action rather than words that the growing, preparation and sharing of food is not only for sustenance but an act of love and nurturing that binds families together. Food creates a natural edible history that we all carry with us and makes us forever grateful.

This book is dedicated to the efforts of my parents and others like them, and especially to the memory of my mother, Armandina Prosperi-Porta, who without knowing inspired my love, appreciation and approach to the preparation of food.

I would also like to thank my "Team" for their dedication and enthusiasm in putting my first book together. Thanks to Sandy Reber and her staff at Reber Creative for the design, layout and first reading of the book. Thanks to Andrei Fedorov for his beautiful photography and input. And thanks to Elizabeth Levinson and my sister, Yole Mallory, for their inspired help. I would also like to thank Villeroy & Boch, Victoria BC, for the use of their elegant dinnerware displayed in our photos.

My biggest thank-you is for my biggest fan, Ina Haegemann, for her never-ending encouragement, love and support, without which our second career together would not have been possible.

Foreword

"Who eats like us? Nobody – not even kings."

My father, Ferruccio Prosperi-Porta, said that every night when our family sat down for dinner. It was not meant as a comparison to what other families may or may not have had, but rather as an expression of just how fortunate and privileged we were to have what we had. In retrospect, that time-honoured phrase helped to kindle my appreciation of food, and it always reminds me of the significance of the everyday family dinner.

Food and family. The two are intrinsically bound, in my case by the traditions with which I was raised. It is difficult to overstate the role that food plays in the daily life of an Italian family. Everything revolves around what you last ate, what you are eating now and what you are going to eat. This is not to say that we were always eating, but it was always important to know.

Wherever we lived, we always had a large edible garden. Most of what we ate came from our own harvest. From vegetables to fruit to livestock, we lacked nothing. My parents dried, froze and canned fruits and vegetables. They made cheese from goat's milk and cured their own meats: sausages, prosciutto, pancetta. My mother made head cheese from the pigs' heads and a sweetened version of blood sausage that contained walnuts and raisins – a good memory, which I can still taste.

My mother, Armandina, was an excellent cook. She was a little adventurous also. Besides all her great Italian dishes, I fondly remember her chow mein (believe it or not), her rhubarb upside-down cake, her berry and fruit pies. She passed her love of cooking to my sister and me. So, long before I decided to become a chef, I was interested in cooking.

Even during my first career working at the local pulp mill in Powell River, I loved to cook for my friends. We would gather in my garden and roast a pig or a side of baby veal on a spit for 30 or 40 people. I enjoyed pleasing friends and family with my food and I do to this day.

One year, a friend opened a restaurant. I went to work for her a couple of evenings a week while still holding down my day job at the mill. That experience led me to take the cook's training program at Malaspina College in Nanaimo, British Columbia. In addition to earning my chef's papers, I caught the competition bug. I won several recipe contests and was honoured to compete as a member of Culinary Team Victoria (1990 and 1992) and Culinary Team Canada (1994), bringing home gold and silver medals.

My culinary career began at Murchie's Tearoom in Victoria where I worked in a pastry kitchen that was open to the restaurant. When the tearoom closed, I moved to the Oak Bay Beach Hotel and then to Whistler to run the pastry kitchen at the Delta Mountain Inn. There I met Ina Haegemann, the woman who would influence and make possible the second part of my culinary career.

We both wanted a change of surroundings and a new direction in our careers. We both preferred a mild climate. So in 1994, the idea was born for Cooper's Cove Guesthouse and Angelo's Cooking School in Sooke on Vancouver Island, a place where we could have personal contact with our guests and where we could showcase our individual talents.

We are delighted to have chosen this path. Guests have the opportunity to spend an afternoon in our professional kitchen, watching their meal prepared and interacting with the chef. I've been able to develop a productive kitchen garden so we harvest many varieties of edible flowers, herbs, vegetables, fruits and berries to use in the kitchen. Many of these plants are descendants from my family's gardens – quince grafted from my father's tree, *mintucia* from my uncle's garden in Italy, and of course, many fig trees.

My guests ask how I come up with new recipes and decide on flavour combinations. Often, I look to what is ready in my garden, and I consider the three main flavourings: salt, sweet, and tart or sour. If I look at those characteristics in creating a dish or a taste, the idea of freshly smoked spring salmon on a slice of ripe peach from my tree with a few drops of authentic Aceto Balsamico makes sense.

Such a combination is the essence of the recipes that I create in my interactive dinners and cooking classes and share here with you: fresh, quality ingredients simply prepared. And with recipes like these, it is hard to imagine kings eating as well as us.

Angelo Prosperi-Porta

About the Recipes

I have created the majority of recipes in this book over the ten years of operating at Cooper's Cove Guesthouse. A few were created during my previous years working in various restaurants and hotels and some, mostly in the "Basics" section near the back of the book, are pastry, sauce and similar recipes that are parts of the main recipes. A few of these basic recipes are traditional, such as some of the doughs, which have been passed on by other cooks and chefs and have proven themselves over the years. The "Basics" in this book refer to my recipes, although they can certainly be used in your own new creations.

For the most part, the recipes have been kept simple, with a few exceptions, and are easy to follow. Some of the recipes may look difficult at first but once read through they can be broken down into their various parts and executed with time and a little patience. A common refrain heard in my cooking classes is "READ YOUR RECIPES!"

The ingredients are usually common and relatively easy to find, with an emphasis on freshness. I always recommend that if a certain ingredient, whether it be fish, meat, vegetable, spice or herb, is not available or is not of the desired quality, there is always a substitute. After all, I believe that the recipes are about technique and ideas rather than a rigid adherence to ingredients. I take inspiration from the Italian approach to preparing food and that is to always try to obtain the best quality that is available, and treat it simply. Note that all recipes serve eight unless otherwise stated.

Amounts in the recipes are given in imperial measures. Listed below are easy conversions for those who prefer to use metric measurements. Be aware that the metric conversions are meant to be replacement values and not exact equivalents.

Measuring by weight instead of volume is a more accurate method of measurement, therefore I have used weight measures for items in recipes where the accuracy is more important to the outcome of the recipe such as in the sorbetto, granita, ice cream, baking and dessert recipes. Proteins, such as meat and fish, are also portioned by weight.

Although measuring by weight is less common in North America, a small investment in a kitchen scale that measures in ounces and grams will make measuring easier and quicker once one has grown accustomed to the change. Most department and kitchen stores stock digital scales. A digital readout scale that displays in 1/4-ounce or 5-gram increments will provide accurate results.

Measuring by Volume		Liquid Measurements			Measuring by Weight			
1/4 tsp.	1 ml	1 tbsp.	1/2 oz.	15 ml	Sugar	1 c.	6 oz.	180 grams
1/2 tsp.	2 ml	2 tbsp.	1 oz.	30 ml	Flour	1 c.	5 oz.	150 grams
1 tsp.	5 ml	1/4 c.	2 oz.	60 ml	Sifted flour	1 c.	4 oz.	120 grams
1 tbsp.	15 ml	1/3 c.	2 2/3 oz.	85 ml	Sifted flour	4 c.	16 oz. (1 lb.)	450 grams
1/4 c.	60 ml	1/2 c.	4 oz.	125 ml				
1/2 c.	120 ml	1 c.	8 oz.	250 ml	Whole wheat flour	3 3/4 c.	16 oz.	450 grams
1/3 c.	80 ml	4 c.	1 quart	1 litre less 50 ml	Large eggs (5)	1 c.	9 oz.	250 grams
2/3 c.	160 ml				Large egg white (1)	2 tbsp.	1 oz.	30 grams
3/4 c.	180 ml	1 litre	34 oz.	1 quart plus 2 oz.	Large egg yolk (1)	1 tbsp.	1/2 oz.	15 grams
1 c.	250 ml				Butter	1/2 c.	4 oz.	125 grams
					Butter	2 tbsp.	1/2 oz.	15 grams
					Nuts	1 c.	5 oz.	150 grams
					Frozen berries	1 c.	5 oz.	150 grams

Honey

I use honey as a flavouring ingredient as well as a sweetener in many of my recipes. I also use honey a lot in dessert recipes and to balance flavours in savoury sauces and dressings.

The colour, flavour and textures of honey vary greatly from region to region with each area having its own distinct characteristics. The consumption of local honey is reputed to have health benefits in boosting the immune system and may assist in protecting against allergies. If nothing else, honey certainly adds flavour and texture to dishes that sugar or other sweeteners do not.

breakfast side dish

Fresh Berries with Honey and Mint	4
Fresh Fruit Salad with Ginger and Cinnamon	4
Soft Goat Cheese with Toasted Pine Nuts and Honey	5
Rhubarb and Berry Compote	5
Poached Dried Figs in Riesling Wine	6
Apricot and Sunflower Seed Yogurt Cheese	6
Quince in Vanilla Syrup	7

breakfast baking

Fresh Berry and Almond Tarts	8
Sour Cherry Tarts	9
Chocolate Crescents	10
Apple Turnovers	11
Pear and Almond Strudel	12
Hazelnut Cinnamon Rolls	13
Rosemary, Honey and Cornmeal Scones	14
Breakfast Focaccia	15
Chocolate Fig Bread	16

breakfast main course

Baked Eggs with Pancetta and Mushrooms	19
Ricotta Flan with Prosciutto Wrapped Asparagus	20
Individual Sausage, Potato and Onion Frittata	22
Poached Egg, Fennel Sausage and Roasted Potatoes	25
Rolled Smoked Salmon and Swiss Chard Omelet	26
Savoury French Toast with Smoked Chicken-Scrambled Eggs and Honey Balsamic Vinegar Syrup	29
Warm Apple Crêpe with Caramel Orange Sauce	30
Dessert or Breakfast Crêpes	30
Ricotta and Fresh Fruit Crêpe with Yellow Plum Sauce	33
French Toast with Plum Compote	34
Seedy Little Pancakes with Sour Cherry Sauce	37

Recipes clockwise from top right: Soft Goat Cheese with Toasted Pine Nuts, Fresh Fruit Salad with Ginger and Cinnamon, Fresh Berries with Honey and Mint, Rhubarb and Berry Compote, Poached Figs in Riesling Wine, Apricot and Sunflower Seed Yogurt Cheese.

See section on Breads for a variety of breads to serve at breakfast or any time of day.

breakfast

Fresh Berries with Honey and Mint

Sweet local honey, freshly picked mint and a handful of seasonal berries. Does it get any simpler?

Berries are one of my favourite foods. I think the best way to eat them is fresh off the plant, preferably in the morning while they are still slightly cool. This recipe is the second way.

Fresh berries are very perishable so pick them as close to serving as possible. Local growers often grow a variety of berries, some of which are hybrids of raspberries and blackberries. They are well worth seeking out.

2 c. fresh seasonal berries such as strawberries, raspberries, blackberries or blueberries
2 tbsp. honey
1 tbsp. slivered fresh mint

Place the berries in a bowl.

Warm the honey if necessary to make it flow, and drizzle over the berries.

Add the slivered mint and toss very carefully so as not to crush the berries. Don't worry if some do not get coated with honey.

Serve for breakfast or as a quick dessert.

Fresh Fruit Salad with Ginger and Cinnamon

This is more an idea than a recipe. The fruit of course can vary with the season. Choose a variety of fruit that is at its peak and that provides interesting colours and textures. Added sugar is an option but I find it unnecessary if the fruit is of good quality.

The pomegranate seeds add colour, crunch and a little tartness. Fresh berries when available are also a nice addition.

Serve this salad immediately for the best flavour. If you plan to keep it for a time before serving, add a small amount of lemon juice to keep the fruit from discolouring.

2 medium oranges, sectioned
1 apple
1 ripe but firm pear
1 ripe but firm banana
2 kiwi
2-3 ripe plums
1 c. seedless red or green grapes
1 tbsp. peeled, grated fresh ginger
1/2-3/4 tsp. ground cinnamon
1 1/2 tsp. pure vanilla extract
1 tbsp. sugar (optional)
1/4 c. pomegranate seeds

To section the oranges place on a cutting board. Slice off the stem end about 1/4 inch.

Repeat with the opposite end and set the orange flat on the board.

Following the contour of the orange, cut off the peel including the white pith to expose the orange sections.

Working over a bowl, cut in between the membrane to release the sections into the bowl.

When all the sections have been removed, squeeze the juice out of what is left on the orange into the bowl.

Quarter and core the apple and pear and slice thinly into the bowl. Toss lightly to coat with the orange juice.

Peel and slice the banana and add.

Peel, halve and slice the kiwis and add.

Remove the pits from the plums, cut the fruit into 6-8 pieces and add.

Add the grapes, grated ginger, cinnamon, vanilla extract and sugar (if using).

Toss gently to combine and place in a serving bowl or individual serving dishes.

Top with the pomegranate seeds and serve.

Soft Goat Cheese with Toasted Pine Nuts and Honey

Try this spread on toasted sourdough. The tart cheese and sour edge from the bread balance well with the honey and nuts. The orange sugar can be omitted but it adds an interesting subtle background.

Place the goat cheese in a bowl. Set aside 2 tbsp. of the pine nuts and add the rest to the bowl with the orange sugar (if using). Stir to combine.

Place a 10 x 12-inch piece of waxed paper or parchment or plastic wrap on a flat surface.

Spoon the mixture onto the paper and spread with a spoon or knife into a roughly 6-inch-long log.

Pick up the edge of the paper closest to you and roll the cheese into a cylinder, enclosing it in the paper. Twist and tuck the ends underneath and refrigerate.

Remove from the refrigerator at least 30 minutes before serving to allow the cheese to soften.

Place on a serving tray or slice into individual portions.

Drizzle with the honey and sprinkle the reserved pine nuts on top.

*For the orange sugar

Remove the zest of one orange in strips using a sharp paring knife or vegetable peeler. Cut into strips and place in a warm spot to dry for a day.

Place in a food processor or blender with 1 cup of granulated sugar and blend until fine.

Store in a covered container.

6 oz. soft, unripened goat cheese, room temperature
1/2 c. toasted pine nuts
1 tsp. orange sugar* (optional)
2 tbsp. honey

Rhubarb and Berry Compote

A good way to use seasonal fruit. This compote can also be enjoyed year-round using frozen fruit. Dried figs, prunes, raisins or cranberries all make great additions.

Serve at breakfast with granola and yogurt. If using frozen fruit, adjust the cooking time accordingly.

Place the rhubarb, orange zest, orange juice, sugar and spices into a saucepan and bring to a simmer.

Cook over medium heat for 5-6 minutes until the rhubarb begins to soften.

Add the apple and cook a few minutes more. Be careful not to overcook the rhubarb.

Remove from the heat and cool slightly.

Place the berries into a heatproof bowl, pour in the rhubarb mixture and mix gently with a rubber spatula.

When the mixture has cooled, cover and refrigerate.

3 c. fresh rhubarb cut into 3/4- to 1-inch pieces
grated zest of one orange
1/2 c. orange juice
1/3 c. brown sugar
1 tsp. ground cinnamon
2 tsp. ground ginger
1/4 tsp. ground cloves
1/4 tsp. freshly grated nutmeg
1 apple, cored, quartered and diced
1 c. each fresh or frozen blackberries, blueberries and raspberries

Poached Dried Figs in Riesling Wine

Figs are rich in vitamins A, B, and C and are a good source of fibre. They also happen to be my favourite summertime fruit. They are at their best when picked and eaten straight from the tree. Dried figs cooked using the following method make a delicious breakfast fruit or dessert topping.

12 oz. whole dried figs, trimmed
2 c. Riesling wine
1/2 c. water
1/4 c. honey
6 whole cloves
2 whole star anise
2 cinnamon sticks
zest of one orange
zest of one lemon

With a sharp paring knife or vegetable peeler remove the zest from the orange and lemon and cut into 1/4-inch-wide strips.

Place all the ingredients in a medium-sized pot and bring to a simmer.

Cook gently for 60 minutes until the figs are tender when pierced with a fork.

With a slotted spoon remove the figs to a container and continue to simmer the syrup until it has reduced to about 1 cup.

Pour the syrup over the figs and cool to room temperature.

Cover and refrigerate.

Use as a breakfast fruit or dessert topping.

Apricot and Sunflower Seed Yogurt Cheese

A healthy, low-fat alternative spread for your morning bread or bagel. The slight tang from the yogurt is well balanced by the honey. I find the flavour to be more interesting with the lesser amount of honey but it can be adjusted to personal taste.

For best results use a full-fat natural yogurt, usually between 3.5 and 4 per cent milk fat. Try to find one that contains only bacterial culture and milk products without any thickeners or preservatives.

4 c. full-fat all-natural yogurt
1 c. minced dried apricots*
2/3 c. toasted unsalted sunflower seeds*
grated zest of one orange
1-2 tbsp. honey

Place a fine meshed sieve over a deep bowl and line with a double thickness of cheesecloth or a clean kitchen towel.

Pour the yogurt into the strainer and fold the cheesecloth over the top to cover.

For a firmer yogurt place a small bowl or plate with a 1- to 2-lb. weight on top of the yogurt.

Refrigerate for several hours or overnight.

Discard the liquid that has collected in the bowl.**

Remove the yogurt from the cheesecloth and combine in a bowl with the rest of the ingredients.

Place in a clean container, cover and refrigerate. The mixture will keep 1-2 weeks.

* For an interesting variation, substitute dried figs for the apricots and toasted, coarsely chopped hazelnuts for the sunflower seeds.

**If you are like me and have a problem throwing out something that you are "sure" there is a use for, the liquid could be used as the liquid in a favourite bread recipe. It will give the bread a pleasant sourdough-like edge. The liquid could also be used as a base for a summertime fruit soup.

Quince in Vanilla Syrup

Quince is an unusual fruit that is a member of the apple family. They are a very hard, pear shaped, fuzzy fruit that must be cooked before eating. Quince is usually used in preserves, jellies, baked whole like apples or poached in a syrup as in this recipe. The tart flavour is reminiscent of apple, pear and pineapple.

In a large wide pot combine the water and sugar and bring to a simmer.

Using a vegetable peeler or sharp paring knife cut the zest in strips off the lemons and the orange, leaving the bitter white pith. Add the zest to the syrup.

With a paring knife split the vanilla beans down the middle, scrape out the seeds and add the beans and seeds to the syrup. (If using vanilla extract add it to the syrup at the end of the cooking.)

Wash the quince and rub off the fuzz with a cloth or your fingers.

With a sharp vegetable peeler remove the skin and cut the quince into 6-8 wedges. Remove the core with a paring knife. When all the quince are done you should have 2^{1}/$_{2}$-3 lbs.

Add the fruit to the simmering syrup, making sure it is all covered. If not, add boiling water.

Simmer the fruit gently until tender when tested with a knife. Individual pieces may cook at different rates.

As the fruit becomes tender remove the pieces to a bowl.

When all the fruit is done increase the heat and reduce the syrup to about 2 cups.

Pour the syrup over the cooked quince and allow to cool to room temperature.

Cover and refrigerate overnight.

Serve for breakfast or as a quick dessert with whipped cream. It can also be used as a filling for a tart using a favourite shortcrust dough.

3 c. water
3 c. sugar
2 large lemons
1 large orange
2 whole vanilla beans or 2 tsp. pure vanilla extract
4 lbs. fresh quince

TIP
To extract more flavour from a vanilla bean after its initial use, just rinse it, let it dry, then store in a jar of sugar to make vanilla sugar. You can also add it to your favourite cooking liqueur. I like to add it to grappa; great for sipping with dessert or in zabaglione.

Fresh Berry and Almond Tarts

A great way to use fresh berries in season. Frozen berries also work well but they will bleed into the filling as they bake. This may bother some; it doesn't bother me. For a variation, use the fresh berries for topping the baked tarts by pressing them into the filling and glazing with a little warmed fruit jelly for a different look. If you don't have tart tins or metal rings (page 248), a muffin pan works well. This recipe makes approximately thirty 2 1/2-inch tarts.

1 recipe Shortcrust Dough (page 263)
1 recipe Almond or Hazelnut Filling (page 262)
about 2 c. fresh or frozen berries such as blueberries, raspberries, blackberries or any firm ripe berries in season
icing sugar for dusting
extra berries for decorating

Roll the shortcrust to 1/8-inch thick.

With a round cutter cut 4-inch circles and line greased tart tins.

Spoon 2 tbsp. of filling into the bottom of each tart and top with some of the berries, pressing them into the filling.

Bake in a preheated 350°F oven 15-18 minutes or until the edges of the pastry are lightly browned and the filling is slightly firm.

Remove and cool on baking tray before removing the tarts from the tins.

Top with a few fresh berries, dust with icing sugar and serve.

Sour Cherry Tarts

Makes 36 tarts

A quick easy-to-prepare tart for a special breakfast treat, which can be made ahead and frozen for later. Once frozen, they are best when baked directly from the freezer and served immediately.

Frozen sour cherries are preferable but sour cherries in syrup are a good substitute. If using sour cherries in syrup make sure to drain well before using.

Lay one sheet of phyllo pastry on a work surface and brush with approximately 1 tbsp. of the melted butter.

Sprinkle with 1 tbsp. of spiced sugar and top with another sheet of pastry. (Keep the unused pastry covered with a slightly damp cloth.)

Brush again with butter and sprinkle with spiced sugar.

Using a sharp knife or pastry cutter, cut the phyllo into 3 strips lengthwise and then into 4 crosswise to form 12 squares. It is not crucial that they be exact.

Working with one square at a time, fold the corners into the middle of each piece and then press the pastry into a muffin cup to form a tart shell about 2/3 of the depth of the pan. Repeat with the rest of the squares.

Spoon 1 heaping tbsp. of almond mixture into each shell, then press in 4-5 sour cherries.

If freezing, carefully pry out the tarts, place side by side on a nonstick baking sheet and freeze.

Repeat with the rest of the pastry and fillings. Any extra Almond Filling can be frozen for a later use.

To bake, preheat oven to 375°F. Bake the tarts in the muffin pan for 18-20 minutes until the pastry is golden and crisp.

Remove the tarts from the pan and place on a rack to cool slightly. Dust with icing sugar and serve slightly warm.

6 sheets phyllo pastry
1/2 c. melted unsalted butter
Spiced Sugar (page 262)
Almond Filling (page 262)
2 c. frozen sour cherries
one 12-portion standard muffin pan for shaping the tarts

Chocolate Crescents

Makes 16 crescents

These little goodies are best eaten while still warm and you can no longer wait.

1 tbsp. dry yeast
1 c. warm milk
3 tbsp. sugar
1/2 tbsp. salt
3 eggs
1 lb. 5 oz. (4-41/2 c.) bread flour
31/2 oz. softened butter
4 oz. semi-sweet chocolate pieces
2 oz. semi-sweet chocolate, melted
icing sugar for dusting

Dissolve the yeast in the warm milk. Add the sugar, salt and 2 beaten eggs. Reserve a few ounces of the flour and stir in the remainder.

Mix in the butter and adjust the dough with the remaining flour to make a dough stiff enough to roll out.

Knead the dough until smooth and elastic, cover and let rest until doubled in size.

Divide the dough in half and shape each piece into a 10- to 12-inch circle.

With a pastry cutter or sharp knife cut each circle into 8 wedges.

Whisk the remaining egg with 1 tbsp. water and brush the top of the dough.

Evenly distribute the chocolate pieces onto the wide end of each wedge.

Fold the wide edge over to enclose the chocolate and roll into a crescent, tucking the pointed end underneath.

Place on a parchment-lined baking tray and let rise until half-doubled in size. Bake at 375°F for 8-10 minutes.

Cool slightly, then drizzle with the melted chocolate and dust with the icing sugar.

Apple Turnovers

This makes approximately 2 dozen small turnovers. They freeze well unbaked. For those who don't want raisins and walnuts they can easily be omitted. (I mean the raisins and walnuts, not the people who don't like them.)

After cutting rounds, carefully layer the trims on top of each other and re-roll to cut more.

Combine all ingredients for the filling in the bowl of a food processor. Process to an even, coarse mixture and set aside.

Using just enough flour to keep the pastry from sticking, roll the dough to 1/8-inch thick.

Cut out 4-inch rounds or squares and brush lightly with some of the beaten egg.

Place 1 1/2 tbsp. of filling in the centre of each piece.

Fold circles in half or squares into triangles and press firmly to seal.

Brush the tops with more egg and sprinkle with cinnamon sugar.

With a floured fork, prick holes in the tops and bake in a 375°F oven for 15-18 minutes until lightly browned.

These are best served warm.

1 recipe Basic Pie Dough (page 263)
2 c. peeled, cored and diced tart cooking apple
1/4 c. brown sugar
1 tbsp. cornstarch
1 tsp. cinnamon
1/4 tsp. ground nutmeg
1/2 tsp. ground ginger
1/4 c. raisins (optional)
1/4 c. chopped walnuts (optional)
1 well-beaten egg
1/2 c. Cinnamon Sugar (page 262)

Pear and Almond Strudel

A quicker version of the classic. Phyllo pastry is available in most grocery stores in the frozen food section. Most brands come in a 1 lb. box containing about 18-20 sheets. Thaw the pastry in the refrigerator overnight. Dried fruits and other spices can be substituted or added to make your own filling. The finished product, before baking, freezes well. Just bake directly from the freezer.

Serve for breakfast or for dessert with whipped cream.

For the filling
3 c. peeled, cored and diced firm ripe
    pear (about 3 whole pears)
1/4 c. sugar
2 tbsp. cornstarch
grated zest of 1 lemon
1/2 c. Spiced Sugar (page 262)

For the strudel
6 sheets phyllo pastry, thawed
1/3 c. melted unsalted butter
1/3 c. whole almonds, toasted and
    coarsely ground
1 well-beaten egg
icing sugar for dusting

Combine the pears, sugar, cornstarch, lemon zest and 1 tbsp. of the spiced sugar.

Place one sheet of phyllo pastry on a work surface, brush lightly and evenly with some of the melted butter.

Sprinkle with 1 tbsp. of spiced sugar and top with one more sheet.

Repeat to make three layers. Brush again with butter and spread half the almonds on top.

Spread half the filling onto the prepared pastry to within 1 1/2 inches from each end.

Roll up the filling into the pastry to form a tight cylinder and tuck the ends under to secure.

Place on a baking tray, brush with the beaten egg and sprinkle with spiced sugar.

Repeat with the rest of the ingredients to make another strudel.

Before baking make 1/2-inch-deep cuts into the top of the strudels to release steam as they bake and to make slicing easier.

Bake in a preheated 375°F oven for 20-25 minutes until lightly browned and crisp.

Cool slightly and cut into portions. Dust with icing sugar and serve warm.

Hazelnut Cinnamon Rolls

Who doesn't like cinnamon rolls? These are enhanced with the addition of a rich, buttery hazelnut filling. The recipe makes approximately 32 small rolls but they can be made larger if preferred. If you don't want to bake them all, freeze one pan for a later use. They can be frozen for up to two weeks without any effect on the yeast. Remove from the freezer and thaw in the refrigerator overnight, then place in a warm spot to rise.

Combine the warm milk, yeast and sugar and place in a warm spot.

When the yeast is dissolved and creamy,s add the salt, eggs and 1/3 of the flour.

Beat with an electric mixer using a dough hook, or wooden spoon if working by hand, until smooth.

Beat in the butter a little at a time and then the rest of the flour until you have a smooth, elastic dough that does not stick to the sides of the bowl.

Remove from the bowl and knead by hand for 3-4 minutes, then place in a buttered bowl.

Cover with a damp towel or plastic wrap and set aside in a warm spot until doubled in size.

Divide the dough into two pieces. Put one piece back in the bowl and cover.

On a lightly floured board, roll the second piece out to a 10 x 16-inch rectangle with the long end closest to you.

Spread a 1/4-inch layer of Hazelnut Filling over the surface, leaving a 1-inch strip at the far end.

Sprinkle evenly with 1/4 cup cinnamon sugar.

Starting with the long edge closest to you, roll the dough into a cylinder, stopping short of the far edge.

Brush the edge with water or eggwash made by whisking egg with 1 tbsp. water, and press to seal.

With a sharp knife, cut the roll into 16 pieces, or fewer larger pieces if you like, and place them in a well-greased 9 x 12-inch pan.

Repeat with the second piece of dough.

Cover and set aside in a warm spot until slightly less than doubled in size.

Sprinkle with extra cinnamon sugar, dot with extra butter and bake in a preheated 375°F oven for 12-14 minutes.

1 tbsp. dry yeast
1 1/4 c. warm milk
3 tbsp. sugar
1/2 tsp. salt
2 eggs, room temperature, plus 1 egg for eggwash
1 lb. 5 oz. (4-4 1/2 c.) bread flour
3 1/2 oz. unsalted butter, room temperature
Hazelnut Filling (page 262)
3/4 c. Cinnamon Sugar (page 262)

Rosemary, Honey and Cornmeal Scones

The texture of these scones is very different than most. The extra yolk gives it a cake-like crumb and the cornmeal adds a bit of a crunch. These are best served while still warm from the oven. A little extra honey drizzled over the top doesn't hurt either.

The scones will spread a little as they bake. To get a higher, lighter result, bake the scones in a ring mold (page 248) or create one using aluminum foil and a paper clip.

10 oz. (2 c.) all-purpose flour
1/4 tsp. salt
4 tsp. baking powder
6 oz. (1 c.) white or yellow cornmeal
1 tbsp. minced fresh rosemary
1 whole egg, plus 1 egg separated
3 tbsp. honey
3/4 c. milk
1/4 c. olive oil

Sift together the flour, salt and baking powder into a bowl, then add the cornmeal and rosemary.

Whisk together the egg, egg yolk, honey, milk and olive oil.

Pour the egg mixture into the dry ingredients and mix with a wooden spoon until combined. A few spots of unmixed flour are fine. Be sure not to overmix or the scones will be tough.

Place the dough on a lightly floured board, knead it slightly and divide in two.

Shape each piece into a 6-inch round and place on a non-stick baking sheet. Cut each round into 6 wedges, but do not separate.

Whisk the extra egg white with 1 tbsp. water and brush each round lightly. Sprinkle with a little extra cornmeal and bake at 350°F for 20-25 minutes.

Serve warm with honey and unsalted butter.

Breakfast Focaccia

A simple creative way to use seasonal fruit. Substitute fresh berries, apples, pears or almost any fresh fruit you have available. The mascarpone cheese adds a nice richness. This recipe makes four 8-inch breads but it can easily be divided and made into several small individual breads or one or two large ones. They also freeze well before baking. Thaw overnight in the refrigerator, bring to room temperature and bake as directed.

Combine the warm milk, yeast and 1 tbsp. sugar in a mixing bowl.

Place in a warm spot until dissolved and frothy.

Add the egg and egg yolk, 2 tbsp. olive oil and beat in the flour. Add more flour if necessary to form a soft dough.

Turn out on a lightly floured board and knead 5-6 minutes until smooth. Place in a lightly oiled bowl, then cover and allow to rise until doubled in size.

Remove the dough from the bowl and place on a lightly floured surface. Divide into four pieces.

With your hands or a rolling pin form each piece into an 8-inch circle. Whisk the extra egg white with 1 tbsp. water and brush top lightly.

Sprinkle evenly with the anise seeds and coarse salt.

Spread the grapes over the dough and press in slightly.

Drizzle with the remaining 1 tbsp. olive oil and top with the remaining sugar.

Set aside for 15 minutes to allow the bread to rise slightly, then bake at 350°F for 12-15 minutes.

Remove and cut into wedges. Serve warm with the mascarpone cheese on the side.

1 c. warm milk
1 tbsp. dry yeast
2 tbsp. granulated sugar
1 whole egg, plus 1 egg separated
3 tbsp. olive oil
14 oz. (3 c.) all-purpose or bread flour
1 tbsp. anise seed
1 tsp. coarse salt
1½ c. seedless grapes
2 c. room temperature mascarpone cheese or cream cheese whipped with an equal amount of heavy cream (optional)

Chocolate Fig Bread

This dough works well in many different shapes. There is enough to make three standard 9 x 5 inch loaves or 5-6 half-sized loaves, approximately 4 x 5 inches. For a more interesting presentation, bake the fig bread in fluted brioche molds.

2 tsp. dry yeast
1 1/2 c. warm milk
2 tbsp. honey
2 eggs, plus 1 egg for eggwash
1 c. dark cocoa powder, sifted
1 tsp. salt
2 tbsp. minced orange zest
1 lb. 14 oz. (5 1/2 c.) flour
1/2 c. softened butter
1/3 c. good quality dark chocolate pieces
2/3 c. diced dried figs

In a mixing bowl dissolve the yeast and honey with the warm milk.

Cover and place in a warm spot 5-10 minutes until frothy.

Beat in 2 eggs, the cocoa powder, salt, orange zest and about half the flour.

Continue to beat until smooth, then beat in the softened butter.

Add the rest of the flour 1/2 cup at a time until you have a dough that does not stick to the sides of the bowl.

Turn out onto a lightly floured work surface, add the chocolate pieces and diced figs and knead for 8-10 minutes, adding more flour, 1 tbsp. at a time, if necessary, until the dough is smooth and elastic.

Place the dough in a lightly oiled bowl, cover and place in a warm spot until doubled in size. Divide into pieces, shape into loaves and press into loaf pans.*

Cover with plastic wrap and place in a warm spot until about 1 1/2 times in size.

Whisk together the third egg with 1 tbsp. water for the eggwash. Brush the top of the loaves with eggwash, being careful not to let it run down the sides or the baked breads will stick to the mold.

Bake in a pre-heated 375°F oven for 20-25 minutes.

Remove the breads from the molds and cool on a rack.

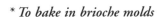

* To bake in brioche molds

Divide the dough into 16 pieces. From each piece take off another piece about the size of a walnut.

Roll the large pieces into balls and place in 16 well-buttered 4-inch brioche molds, pressing the dough firmly into the bottom.

Brush the tops with eggwash.

Roll the remaining pieces into balls and form a point on one end.

With a floured finger press a hole in the centre of the dough in the mold. Dip the pointed ball in the egg and then press the ball, pointed end down, into the hole in the dough.

Baked Eggs with Pancetta and Mushrooms

This recipe can be adjusted for an endless variety of flavours. Add blanched spinach, precooked vegetables, cheese, your favourite seafood, etc. Wild mushrooms are also a great addition.

Serve hot from the oven in their own dishes. I like to serve crisp large croutons fried in extra virgin olive oil on the side. It also makes a great light lunch or brunch dish that can be prepared ahead of time and baked at the last minute.

Using 2 tbsp. of the olive oil, coat the insides of eight 4-oz. ramekins. Place in an ovenproof pan with 2-inch sides and set aside.

Heat a sauté pan on medium and add the remaining tbsp. of oil and the pancetta.

Cook until browned and beginning to crisp.

Add the diced onion, cook for 1-2 minutes and add the mushrooms.

Cook until the mushrooms are soft, remove the pan from the heat and stir in the tomato and chopped parsley.

Season the mixture to taste and divide evenly among the 8 ramekins.

Make a small indentation in the centre of the mixture (to keep the egg centred) and break one egg into each ramekin.

Add about 1 1/2 tbsp. cream to each cup and season the tops lightly with salt and freshly ground black pepper.

Pour enough boiling water into the pan to come halfway up the sides of the ramekins and bake in a preheated 325°F oven for 20-25 minutes to desired doneness.

*To avoid spilling hot water place the pan in the oven before pouring.

3 tbsp. extra virgin olive oil
4 oz. pancetta, thinly sliced and slivered
1/2 c. diced red onion
1 c. sliced mushrooms
1/2 c. diced Roma tomato
1/4 c. chopped Italian parsley
salt and freshly ground black pepper
  to taste
8 large eggs
3/4 c. cream
boiling water*

Ricotta Flan with Prosciutto Wrapped Asparagus

Save this elegant dish for a special morning. It takes a bit more planning but is well worth the effort. It would also make a good brunch or light lunch course.

1 c. ricotta cheese
1/4 c. grated Parmigiano Reggiano
2 eggs, lightly beaten
1/4 c. heavy cream
1/4 tsp. salt
4 tbsp. extra virgin olive oil
boiling water
16 asparagus spears
8 slices prosciutto
2-3 slices coarse Italian-style or
    sourdough bread
8 oz. fresh baby spinach, washed and
    spun dry
grated zest of one lemon
freshly ground black pepper
24 grape or cherry tomatoes
minced chives
minced parsley

Preheat oven to 325°F.

Place the ricotta, Parmigiano Reggiano, eggs, cream and salt in a mixing bowl, and combine well.

Coat the insides of 8 ramekins using 1 tbsp. of the olive oil or a non-stick vegetable spray.

Divide the cheese mixture into the 8 ramekins and place in an ovenproof dish with 2-inch sides. Place the dish on the middle rack of the preheated oven and pour in enough boiling water to come 3/4 up the sides of the ramekins.

Cover the dish loosely with tin foil or a lid and bake 25 minutes or until the flans are slightly firm in the centre. Remove the dish from the oven and let the flans rest in their ramekins in the water for 5-10 minutes to set.

Trim the asparagus spears to about 5 inches.

Cut the prosciutto slices in half lengthwise and wrap each asparagus with a half, leaving about 1 1/2 inches exposed on either end, and set aside.

With a 2-inch round cutter, cut 8 rounds from the bread slices.

Heat a non-stick pan with 2 tbsp. olive oil and brown the bread on both sides. Remove and set aside.

Add the asparagus to the pan and cook 3-4 minutes on medium heat, turning to brown evenly. Remove from the pan and keep warm.

When ready to serve, add the spinach to the pan and toss until wilted. Add the grated lemon zest and turn off heat.

To assemble, place a toasted bread round in the centre of a plate and top with some of the spinach.

Run a sharp knife around the inside edge of the ramekin and carefully turn out the flan onto the spinach.

Place two of the asparagus spears on the flan. Drizzle with a little extra virgin olive oil and garnish with grape tomato halves, chives and parsley.

TIP
Large asparagus can be made more tender by peeling the lower 2/3 with a vegetable peeler. This also will help to cook them more evenly.

Individual Sausage, Potato and Onion Frittata

This recipe requires eight 3 x 1-inch metal rings (page 248), or it can also be made in a 10-inch pan and cut into wedges. Serve for breakfast or a light lunch.

1/2 c. extra virgin olive oil

12 oz. fresh Italian sausage sliced
   1/2-inch thick

11/2 lbs. small potatoes, sliced about
   1/4-inch thick

2 c. thinly sliced onion

6 large eggs

1/2 c. fresh oregano leaves

1 c. fresh diced tomato

1/2 c. chopped green onion

1 tsp. salt

1 tsp. freshly ground black pepper

1/4 c. grated Parmigiano Reggiano

1/2 c. grated smoked provolone cheese

In a heavy 10- to 12-inch skillet heat the 3 tbsp. olive oil until slightly smoking.

Add the sausage and cook 1-2 minutes on each side, then remove from the pan and set aside.

Add the potatoes to the pan and turn them to coat with the oil. Season with a little salt and pepper.

Cook potatoes, turning them occasionally until lightly browned. Remove and set aside.

Add the onions to the pan, season with a little salt and pepper and cook about 5 minutes until tender. Remove and set aside.

Whisk the eggs together, and stir in the herbs, tomato, green onion and the cheeses.

To assemble, place eight 3-inch metal rings on a flat baking sheet and coat the insides with olive oil or a nonstick vegetable spray.

Divide the cooked potatoes into the rings and top with the onions.

Place in a 400°F oven for 5 minutes.

Remove the tray from the oven and while still very hot pour the egg mixture into the rings and top with pieces of the cooked sausage.

Immediately place back into the oven and reduce heat to 350°F.

Bake 5-8 minutes or until the egg is firm on top. Remove from oven.

Carefully remove the rings and place on individual serving dishes.

....

To make one large frittata

Cook the sausage, potato and onion as directed.

Place the potato and onion back into a well-oiled, ovenproof nonstick skillet on medium-low heat.

Add the egg mixture, shaking the pan gently to allow the egg to reach the bottom.

Top with the sausage pieces and place in a 350°F oven.

Bake approximately 10-12 minutes or until firm.

Cool slightly and cut into wedges.

Poached Egg, Fennel Sausage and Roasted Potatoes

The key to keeping poached eggs from spreading in the water is by using the freshest eggs possible. Another hint is to add a little vinegar to the water which helps to firm the egg white before it spreads. Eggs can also be poached using small stainless steel rings (page 248) to contain the individual eggs, which is my preferred method.

Combine 3 tbsp. olive oil, the chopped parsley, fennel, chives, balsamic vinegar, tomato and 1/2 tsp. each salt and pepper and set aside.

Heat a pan with 1 tbsp. olive oil and add the sausages. Turn occasionally to brown evenly and cook for a total of about 20 minutes.

Slice the potatoes with the skins into 4-5 slices each and coat with 2-3 tbsp. olive oil, the chopped sage and rosemary and 1/2 tsp. each salt and pepper.

Place on a greased baking tray and roast in a preheated 375°F oven for 20 minutes or until tender.

While the sausage and potatoes are cooking, coat the bottom of an 8-inch pot with 1 tbsp. olive oil and fill with water to about 2 inches.

Grease four 2 x 2-inch stainless steel rings (if using) and place them in the pan with the water.

Season water with 1 tsp. salt and 1 tbsp. of white wine vinegar. Bring to a boil and reduce to a very slight simmer.

Crack the eggs one at a time into the individual rings and cook 4-5 minutes depending on the degree of doneness desired.

To serve, place a stack of potato slices onto a plate, then place a small mound of the tomato mixture to one side.

Remove the rings from the pot with tongs and with a slotted spoon lift the eggs from the water. Drain before placing on top of the potatoes.

Place a sausage on top of the tomato mixture and serve.

6 tbsp. extra virgin olive oil
2 tbsp. chopped parsley
2 tbsp. chopped fresh fennel or dill
1 1/2 tbsp. chopped fresh chives
1 tbsp. balsamic vinegar
2 medium Roma tomatoes, seeded and diced
1 tsp. salt
1 tsp. freshly ground black pepper
4 fennel-flavoured pure pork sausages, preferably homemade* (page 190)
2-3 medium potatoes
3 tbsp. chopped fresh sage
2 tbsp. chopped fresh rosemary
1 tbsp. white wine vinegar
4 large eggs

....

* To make your own fennel-flavoured pork sausage, you will need 2 lb. minced pork shoulder or leg, 2 tbsp. whole fennel seeds, and 1/2 tsp. each salt and freshly ground black pepper. See page 190 for tips on how to make homemade sausage.

TIP

For poached eggs always use the freshest eggs possible. The yolk will stand up firm and the white will not spread out as much. A little lemon juice or vinegar in the water helps the white firm up more quickly. For hard boiled, use eggs that are not as fresh; they will peel easier.

Rolled Smoked Salmon and Swiss Chard Omelet

Serves 4

This is one of my most popular breakfast dishes. Try substituting other cooked seafood such as shrimp or crab. It also works well with thinly sliced smoked meats such as chicken or ham with the addition of a small amount of cheese.

5 large eggs
4 tbsp. chopped fresh parsley
3 tbsp. chopped fresh fennel or dill
3 tbsp. minced fresh chives
1 tbsp. cold water
1 tsp salt
1 tsp. freshly ground black pepper
2 medium-sized Roma tomatoes, cored, seeded and diced
5 tbsp. extra virgin olive oil
2 tbsp. balsamic vinegar
3 large Swiss chard leaves
8 slices of lox-style cold-smoked salmon

Crack the eggs into a bowl and add half the fresh herbs, water, 1/2 tsp. salt and 1/2 tsp. freshly ground pepper.

Whisk lightly to combine and set aside.

Combine the rest of the fresh herbs with the chopped tomato, 3 tbsp. of the extra virgin olive oil, the vinegar and the remaining salt and pepper and set aside.

In a pot of boiling salted water cook the Swiss chard leaves until the stems begin to get tender. Remove and drain on a clean cloth or paper towel.

Remove the stems, chop them into 1/4- to 1/2-inch dice and add to the egg mixture.

Heat an 11-inch square nonstick griddle pan on medium low and add the remaining 2 tsp. extra virgin olive oil.

Pour half the egg mixture into the pan and spread evenly.

Lay one Swiss chard leaf on top of the raw egg, then turn it over and press it into the egg to coat both sides. This will help hold the finished omelet together.

Place 4 slices of the smoked salmon on top of the chard in an overlapping pattern.

As the egg just begins to set, lift one edge of the omelet with a long spatula and roll in a jelly roll fashion into a cylinder.

With the omelet still in the pan, repeat the process with the remaining ingredients, rolling the first omelet into the second to form one large omelet.

Place the omelet in a preheated 325°F oven 5-10 minutes to heat through.

Take four heated plates and place a heaping spoonful of the tomato mixture into the centre of each.

Remove the omelet from the oven and slice on a bias into 12 slices.

Fan 3 slices onto each mound of tomato mixture, then drizzle the remaining tomato mixture around the sliced omelet.

Garnish with fresh herb sprigs and edible flowers.

TIP
Keep fresh herbs in the refrigerator with their stems in water. Basil, however, is cold sensitive and is best kept in water at room temperature.

Savoury French Toast with Smoked Chicken-Scrambled Eggs and Honey Balsamic Vinegar Syrup   *Serves 4*

For the syrup

Heat a small saucepan on low heat and add the balsamic vinegar. Remove from the heat, stir in the honey to combine, then whisk in 1 tsp. of the unsalted butter and set aside.

For the French toast and scrambled eggs

In a small bowl whisk together 1 egg, the milk, 1/4 tsp. salt, 1/4 tsp. ground black pepper, 1 tbsp. each chopped thyme, oregano and parsley and set aside.

In another bowl combine the remaining eggs and the smoked chicken and set aside.

Heat two 10-inch nonstick skillets on medium heat.

Into one pan add 1 tbsp. of the extra virgin olive oil, and the pepper, onion and zucchini. Cook, stirring, for 3-4 minutes until tender but not soft. Season with the remaining salt and ground black pepper and remove from the pan, keeping warm.

Reduce the heat to low. Into each pan add 1 tbsp. extra virgin olive oil and 1 tbsp. unsalted butter.

Dip the bread rounds into the egg and herb mixture and add to one pan on medium heat, cooking approximately 2-3 minutes on each side until firm and lightly browned.

While the toasts are browning add the egg and chicken mixture to the other pan on low heat and cook, stirring, until the eggs begin to set.

Stir in the cooked vegetable mixture and the remaining herbs, keeping 2 tbsp. of chopped parsley aside.

Cook until the eggs have set but are still moist. Remove from the heat.

To serve, place one French toast on each of four plates and divide the scrambled eggs onto each.

Top with half the shredded cheese, another French toast, then the rest of the shredded cheese.

Drizzle 1-2 tsp. of the honey balsamic vinegar syrup around the dish, sprinkle with the remaining chopped parsley and serve.

* See directions for how to quick-smoke chicken (page 257).

For the syrup
4 tbsp. balsamic vinegar
2 tbsp. honey
1 tsp. unsalted butter

For the French toast and scrambled eggs
5 large eggs
1/3 c. milk
1/2 tsp. salt
1/2 tsp. ground black pepper
2 tbsp. chopped fresh thyme leaves
2 tbsp. chopped fresh oregano
6 tbsp. chopped fresh Italian parsley
3 oz. boneless, skinless smoked chicken*, diced
3 tbsp. extra virgin olive oil
1/3 c. finely diced red pepper
1/3 c. finely diced red onion
1/3 c. finely diced zucchini
2 tbsp. unsalted butter
four 1/2 inch-thick slices sourdough bread cut into eight 2 1/2-inch rounds
1/2 c. shredded smoked provolone cheese or smoked Gruyère

Warm Apple Crêpe with Caramel Orange Sauce

4 medium-sized cooking apples
2 tbsp. fresh lemon juice
3/4 c. sugar
4 tbsp. unsalted butter
1 tsp. each ground cinnamon and
   ginger
1/2 tsp. grated nutmeg
1/4 tsp. ground allspice
1/2 c. orange juice concentrate
1/2 c. plus 1 tbsp. water
2 tbsp. minced orange zest
2 tsp. cornstarch
1/2 tsp. vanilla extract
8 breakfast crêpes (recipe below)
1/2 c. fruit jam or preserves

Peel and core the apples and slice into 1/4-inch thick wedges. Toss in the fresh lemon juice and set aside.

Pour the sugar into a heavy-bottomed pan and heat on medium heat. As the sugar begins to melt tilt the pan to spread the sugar evenly but do not stir.

Continue to melt the sugar and watch carefully as it begins to colour.

When all the sugar has melted and has become golden brown add 2 tbsp. butter, the apples and spices. Toss carefully and let the apples brown slightly. Cook until the apples are tender but still maintain their shape.

With a slotted spoon lift out the apple slices and place in a strainer over a bowl to drain.

Add the orange juice concentrate, 1/2 cup water and orange zest and simmer, stirring occasionally. Cook a few minutes to reduce slightly.

Combine the cornstarch and 1 tbsp. water. Add to the pan and cook 1 minute or until the sauce becomes clear. Add the liquid that has drained from the apples.

Pour the sauce into a bowl and whisk in the remaining butter and vanilla extract and set aside.

Lay out the crêpes on a work surface and spread 1 tbsp. of preserves in a thin layer over each crêpe.

Divide the apple pieces among the 8 crêpes, then starting from the edge nearest you, roll each crêpe into a tight cylinder.

Cut in half, place on individual serving plates and serve with the reserved sauce.

Dessert or Breakfast Crêpes

When making crêpes the first one is always a test. To make a very thin crêpe, the batter must be thin also. If the first crêpe is too thick adjust the batter with a bit of extra milk until the desired consistency is achieved. This recipe makes about twenty-four 8-inch crêpes that can be used with an endless variety of fillings.

In a bowl large enough to hold all the ingredients whisk the eggs with the sugar, then stir in the milk and vanilla extract.

Whisk in the flour 1/2 cup at a time until smooth.

Stir in the orange and lemon zest and the vegetable oil. Set the batter aside for 20-30 minutes before making the crêpes.

Heat an 8-inch nonstick pan on medium heat. Coat lightly with oil or vegetable spray and pour about 1 1/2 oz. of batter into the pan, swirling the pan to coat the bottom.

Cook until the edges of the crêpe begin to brown, then using a thin-bladed spatula flip the crêpe over and cook another 10-15 seconds.

Remove to a plate and repeat with the rest of the batter, stacking the crêpes on top of each other as they are made. The crêpes will not stick together and can also be frozen in stacks to be used at another time.

6 eggs
1/2 c. sugar
2 1/4 c. milk
1 tsp. vanilla extract
2 c. all-purpose flour
minced zest of 1 orange
minced zest of 1 lemon
1/4 c. vegetable oil

TIP
Once you have mastered the technique for flipping crêpes, save time by using two pans at once.

Ricotta and Fresh Fruit Crêpe with Yellow Plum Sauce

Ricotta is an Italian cheese similar to cottage cheese that can be used in a variety of sweet and savoury fillings. The name translates to "cooked again" referring to the fact it is made from the leftover whey from cheese making.

Yellow plums are very juicy and sweet yet maintain a slight tartness in the skin which helps to balance the flavour of the sauce. If using other plums or fruits, adding a little fresh lemon juice would have the same effect.

For the yellow plum sauce

Combine all the ingredients in a heavy-bottomed saucepan and bring to a simmer.

Stir to dissolve the sugar and increase the heat to medium. Cook until the fruit is very soft.

Press through a fine sieve and set aside to cool.

For the crêpe filling

Whip the cream to soft peaks and set aside.

Beat the ricotta with the sugar, then beat in the rest of the ingredients.

Fold in the whipped cream and set aside.

To fill the crêpes

Place eight 8-inch crêpes on a work surface and divide the filling among them.

Spread the filling to cover the bottom 3/4 of the crêpe with the edge furthest away from you left bare.

Divide the sliced fruit or berries onto the crêpes, then starting from the edge nearest you, roll the crêpe into a firm cylinder.

Place on a serving dish, garnish with additional fresh fruit and the yellow plum sauce.

Dust with cinnamon and icing sugar and serve.

For the yellow plum sauce
4 c. pitted and quartered fresh yellow plums or other available plums
1 1/2 c. sugar
1/4 c. water
2 tbsp. grated fresh ginger

For the crêpes
8 breakfast crêpes (page 30)
1/2 c. heavy cream
2 c. ricotta at room temperature
2 tbsp. sugar
minced zest and juice of 1 orange
minced zest of 1 lemon
1/2 tsp. ground cinnamon
1/4 tsp. ground nutmeg
1 tbsp. Marsala wine
1/4 tsp. vanilla extract
2 1/2 c. (approx.) mixed freshly sliced seasonal fruit or berries
cinnamon and icing sugar for dusting

French Toast with Plum Compote

Use firm-fleshed plums for this delicious compote. My preference is prune plums.

If you have an abundance of fruit, the compote can also be frozen for a rainy day or a cool winter morning. The mascarpone cheese is a slightly sweet Italian style of cream cheese. It adds a special richness to the toast.

For the plum compote

2¹/2 c. plums halved and cut into 3/4-inch pieces

1/2 c. honey

1/2 c. raspberry-flavoured or favourite fruit-flavoured liqueur

1/2 tsp. ground cinnamon

1/2 tsp. grated whole nutmeg

1 tbsp. grated fresh ginger

grated zest of half an orange

grated zest of half a lemon

For the plum compote

Combine all the ingredients for the compote in a pot and bring to a simmer.

Cook gently until the plum pieces are tender but still hold their shape.

With a slotted spoon remove the plums to a bowl.

Increase the heat and reduce the syrup by half. Pour the syrup over the plums and set aside.

For the French toast

eight 3/4-inch thick slices French baguette, cut on a bias

2 eggs

1 c. milk

1/4 c. sugar

1/2 tsp. ground cinnamon

1/2 tsp. grated whole nutmeg

2 tsp. grated fresh ginger

grated zest of half an orange

grated zest of half a lemon

1 tsp. vanilla extract

1 tbsp. unsalted butter

1 tbsp. vegetable oil

3/4 c. mascarpone cheese at room temperature

For the French toast

Cut each slice of baguette in two to form two pointed pieces each.

Combine all the ingredients for the French toast except the bread, butter, oil and mascarpone cheese. Pour into a wide shallow bowl or tray and set aside.

Soak the bread slices in the egg mixture.

Heat a nonstick griddle on medium to medium high and add the butter and oil.

When the butter mixture is hot and the foam has subsided place the soaked bread slices on the hot griddle and brown well on both sides.

Serve with the plum compote and small spoonfuls of the mascarpone cheese.

Seedy Little Pancakes with Sour Cherry Sauce

For the pancake batter

In a large bowl, whisk together the dry ingredients.

In a separate smaller bowl, whisk the egg and add the rest of the ingredients.

Add the liquid mixture to the dry mixture and, with a wooden spoon or spatula, stir to combine. Cover and set aside for 15 minutes.

For the sour cherry sauce

In a saucepan combine the cherries, orange juice concentrate, brown sugar and 1/4 cup water.

Bring to a simmer and cook 4-5 minutes until the cherries begin to soften but still hold their shape.

Combine the cornstarch with 2 tbsp. water and stir into the mixture. Bring to a simmer and cook 1 minute or until the sauce becomes clear.

Pour the mixture into a bowl and gently stir in the butter and vanilla extract.

To serve

Heat a griddle or flat pan on medium and add 1-2 tbsp. vegetable oil or a combination of unsalted butter and oil to coat.

Spoon the pancake mix onto the hot griddle to form small 2- to 2 1/2 inch round pancakes.

Flip with a spatula when small bubbles begin to form.

Make layered stacks of three pancakes with cherries in between and serve with the sour cherry sauce.

For the pancakes
1 c. all-purpose flour
1/4 c. ground flax seeds
2 1/2 tsp. baking powder
1 tbsp. toasted sesame seeds
1 tbsp. flax seeds
1 tbsp. toasted pumpkin seeds
1 tbsp. toasted sunflower seeds
1 tbsp. poppy seeds
1 egg
1/2 c. milk
2 tbsp. vegetable oil or melted butter
2 tsp. toasted sesame oil
1/2 tsp. vanilla extract
extra oil and/or butter for cooking

For the sour cherry sauce
2 c. pitted sour cherries, fresh or frozen
1/2 c. orange juice concentrate
1/2 c. brown sugar
1/4 c. plus 2 tbsp. water
2 tsp. cornstarch
2 tbsp. unsalted butter
1 tsp. vanilla extract

TIP

For a more decorative presentation, thin a bit of yogurt or sour cream with milk to the same consistency as the sauce. Place a few drops in the sauce and draw the tip of a knife or toothpick through them.

Cooking With Fresh Herbs

The use of fresh herbs is an easy, effective way to raise the flavour level of the simplest dishes.

Eggs and fresh herbs go hand in hand. Garnish your favourite omelet or poached eggs with a fresh Roma tomato salsa. Take two ripe Roma tomatoes, cut them in half, squeeze out the seeds and chop into half-inch pieces. Combine with 1 tbsp. minced green onion, 1 tbsp. minced parsley, 2 tbsp. roughly chopped basil, 1 tbsp. chopped oregano, 2 tbsp. extra virgin olive oil, 1 tbsp. balsamic vinegar, salt and freshly ground black pepper to taste.

For a quick baked fish, take a 6 ounce wild salmon fillet, rub with minced garlic, salt and freshly ground pepper. Top with a mixture of 1 tbsp. minced parsley, 1 tbsp. minced chives and 1 tbsp. minced fresh dill or fennel. Drizzle with extra virgin olive oil and bake 6-8 minutes at 375°F. When done to your liking, drizzle with a little more extra virgin olive oil and a squeeze of fresh lemon juice and enjoy.

Stronger herbs like rosemary, sage and thyme go well with grilled and roasted meats and vegetables.

The possibilities with fresh herbs are endless. Combinations can be adjusted to suit your personal taste. Let your imagination be your guide as you experiment with fresh herbs!

hors d'oeuvres

Pickled Wild Mushrooms	40
Citrus Marinated Salmon and Tuna	41
Salmon, Fennel and Goat Cheese Tarts	41
Poached Prawn with Cucumber and Parsley Pesto	43
Candied Trout with Seared Apple and Fresh Mint	43
Deep Fried Olives	44
Salmon Fillet with Baccala Salad	44
Mushroom, Ricotta and Sun-dried Tomato Strudel	47
Polenta Crostini	48
Leek and Potato Tarts	49
Curried Chicken Pancake	51

Photo: Citrus Marinated Salmon and Tuna

hors d'oeuvres

Pickled Wild Mushrooms

I love wild mushrooms. Like many European immigrants, my father would gather wild mushrooms in the forests surrounding our home in Powell River. He limited himself to a few varieties that he was familiar with from his hometown in Italy, and we usually had them simply fried in olive oil with a little fresh garlic, sage and rosemary. My mother would also pickle the mushrooms to use on an antipasto platter. She used mostly chanterelle mushrooms. Since then I have become familiar with many more varieties and include several in my pickle mix when they are available. This is a very satisfying method of preserving the flavours of fall, even if just for a short time.

Wild mushrooms are often available in larger urban markets in the fall. A variety of very good cultivated mushrooms, such as shiitake, oyster and portobello, are usually available year round.

In a stainless steel pot combine half the oil and vinegar with the salt, pepper, herbs and chili flakes (if using).

Bring to a simmer and add the mushrooms. Reduce heat to very low and toss gently for 2 minutes until the mushrooms are cooked through.

Spoon into a sterilized jar and top with the rest of the oil and vinegar.

Cool to room temperature and cover with the lid.

Refrigerate and allow 24-48 hours for the flavours to develop before tasting. These will keep for several weeks in the refrigerator.

Makes one 24-oz. jar or several smaller ones.

1 c. extra virgin olive oil
1 c. white wine vinegar
1 1/2 tsp. salt
1 tsp. black peppercorns coarsely crushed with the back of a knife
3 tbsp. whole Italian parsley leaves
four to five 3-inch long sprigs of fresh rosemary, leaves only
2-3 large sage leaves, slivered
pinch of crushed red chili flakes (optional)
1 lb. fresh assorted mushrooms

Citrus Marinated Salmon and Tuna

photo, page 39

Simple and quick with an interesting presentation that allows guests to help themselves. You will need about 18 Chinese soup spoons – the ceramic or pottery type with the flat bottom that will sit flat on a tray.

For the fish

Combine all the ingredients for the marinade and then add the fish.

Refrigerate for 2-3 hours.

For the salad

Combine the cabbage, carrot, half the sesame seeds and 1 tsp. sesame oil. Season with salt and pepper.

Place about 1 tbsp. of the cabbage mixture on each of the Chinese soup spoons.

Top the cabbage mixture with about 1 tbsp. of the salmon and tuna mixture.

Garnish the top with a cilantro leaf and a sprinkle of the remaining sesame seeds.

Serve the spoons on a tray and allow guests to help themselves.

For the fish
4 oz. diced fresh salmon
4 oz. diced fresh tuna
1 tbsp. each grated fresh lemon and lime zest
juice of one lemon and one lime
1 tbsp. grated fresh ginger
1 tbsp. grated fresh garlic
2 tbsp. minced green onion, white and green part
1 tbsp. minced jalapeño pepper
3 tbsp. minced sweet red pepper
2 tbsp. olive oil
1/4 c. minced fresh cilantro or Chinese parsley

For the salad
1 tbsp. sesame oil
1/4 tsp. each salt and ground black pepper
1/4 c. toasted sesame seeds
1/4 c. finely shredded Chinese cabbage
1/4 c. grated carrot

Salmon, Fennel and Goat Cheese Tarts

photo top, page 42

You will need two mini 12-muffin pans or use one and bake the tarts in two batches.

Sauté the fennel in 2 tbsp. of the olive oil and set aside to cool.

Beat the goat cheese until light, then add in the yolks one at a time to incorporate. Fold in the salmon, chives, green onions, and salt and pepper.

Whip the egg white to soft peaks and fold into the mixture.

Coat the insides of the muffin cups with a little olive oil or spray with a nonstick spray.

Combine the fennel seeds and chili flakes on a cutting board and crush with the back of a heavy knife. This can also be done in a small spice grinder.

Lay one phyllo sheet on a work surface and brush with some of the oil. Season with salt and ground pepper and 1/2 of the fennel seed mixture.

Top with one more sheet, brush with oil and repeat with the rest of the fennel seed mixture. Top with the third sheet and brush with oil.

Cut the phyllo lengthwise into 3, then cut across in 6 to form 18 pieces. Line each muffin cup with a piece of the pastry, folding in the edges so there is no overhang.

Spoon in filling to 3/4 full and bake at 350°F for 15-20 minutes, on the lower shelf, until the pastry is golden and the filling is slightly firm to the touch.

When the baked tarts come out of the oven remove them from the pan to prevent the pastry from absorbing moisture.

The tarts can be served immediately or they can be baked ahead and placed back in the oven before serving.

1 1/2 c. thinly sliced fresh fennel bulb
1/2 c. olive oil
3 oz. goat cheese, room temperature
2 egg yolks
8 oz. diced fresh salmon
3 tbsp. minced chives
1/3 c. minced green onions
1 tsp. salt
1/2 tsp. freshly ground black pepper
1 egg white
1 tsp. fennel seeds
1 tsp. (or to taste) chili flakes
3 sheets phyllo pastry

Poached Prawn with Cucumber and Parsley Pesto

photo middle, page 42

This recipe also works well with large sea scallops.

For the prawns

Combine all the ingredients in a medium-sized saucepan except the prawns and bring to a simmer.

Add the prawns and turn off the heat. Cover with a lid and leave for 3-4 minutes.

Remove prawns from the poaching liquid and cool. Strain the liquid and reserve the lemon zest and garlic slices.

For the pesto

Combine ingredients in the bowl of a food processor and blend to a coarse paste. Set aside.

For the cucumber

Trim the ends, peel and cut the cucumber into sixteen 3/4-inch rounds.

With a medium-sized melon baller, scoop out the seeds from the centre of each slice, leaving a thin layer on the bottom.

To finish

Spoon some of the pesto into the cucumber and top with a prawn.

Garnish with the reserved poached lemon zest and garlic and drizzle with olive oil.

For the prawns
11/4 c. water
1/2 c. dry white wine
slivered zest of one lemon
2 garlic cloves sliced very thin
salt and ground black pepper to taste
16 medium-sized peeled raw prawns

For the pesto
1 c. loosely packed Italian parsley leaves
1 garlic clove
1 tbsp. grated lemon zest
1 tbsp. orange zest
1/4 c. toasted pine nuts
2-3 tbsp. extra virgin olive oil
salt and freshly ground black pepper
   to taste

For the cucumber
1 long English cucumber

Candied Trout with Seared Apple and Fresh Mint

photo bottom, page 42

Candied trout or salmon is smoked fish that has been placed in an extra-sweet brine. The result is a much sweeter smoked fish with a chewy, moist texture. Substitute other smoked fish if the candied type is not available.

Heat a nonstick sauté pan on medium heat and add 1-2 tbsp. or just enough olive oil to coat the bottom.

Carefully add the apple slices and sear both sides for about 20 seconds, being careful not to overcook.

Season with salt and pepper, remove from the pan and cool.

Cut the smoked fish into thin strips.

Top each crouton with three slices of apple, some of the chopped mint and then some of the candied trout.

Drizzle with extra virgin olive oil and garnish with mint leaves and fresh apple slices.

extra virgin olive oil
2 medium-sized tart apples, peeled,
   cored and thinly sliced (you will need
   48 good slices)
salt and freshly ground black pepper
4 oz. candied trout or substitute candied
   salmon
1/2 c. fresh chopped mint
sixteen 2-inch round croutons (page 255)
mint leaves and apple slices to garnish

Deep Fried Olives

photo, top

You will need a small deep fryer or 3-quart sauce pan and a candy or deep-fry thermometer.

24 large pitted green olives
2 oz. Asiago cheese cut into twenty-four
    1/4-inch slivers
1/3 c. blanched ground almonds
1/3 c. fine white breadcrumbs
1/4 c. flour
1 egg, beaten with 1 tbsp. water
1/2 tsp. salt
1/2 tsp. freshly ground pepper
2 c. vegetable oil for frying

Pat the olives dry. Stuff each one with a piece of the Asiago cheese.

Combine the almonds and breadcrumbs and season with the salt and pepper.

Roll the olives in the flour and shake off the excess.

Roll them in the egg mixture and then in the almond and breadcrumb mixture to coat evenly.

Deep fry the olives in 350-360°F oil until golden.

Drain on paper towels and serve hot.

Salmon Fillet with Baccala Salad

photo, bottom

Baccala is an Italian word for salted, dried cod. The filling for this hors d'oeuvre was inspired by the salt cod salad my mother used to make. It is a traditional salad we always had at Christmas and special times of the year. I have added a little minced preserved lemon to the original recipe to enhance the lemon flavour. For the salmon fillet you will need a piece that is 1 1/4-1 1/2 inches thick by approximately 10 inches long.

For the baccala salad
12 oz. bone-in salt cod, soaked and
    cooked (see method in Codfish Cakes,
    page 104)
1 tbsp. fresh lemon juice
2 tbsp. chopped fresh parsley
1 garlic clove, peeled and finely minced
2 tbsp. minced preserved lemon
    (page 250)
1-2 tbsp. extra virgin olive oil
salt and ground black pepper to taste

For the salmon fillet
one 1 1/2-lb. piece boneless, skinless fresh
    salmon fillet

TIP
To help the salmon hold together, slice while still wrapped in plastic, then remove plastic carefully before serving.

Place the cooked baccala in a bowl. After preparing the salt cod, you will have about 5 oz. cooked fish. Break up the cod with a fork or spoon into small pieces.

Add the rest of the ingredients, mix well and set aside.

For the salmon

Lay the salmon on a cutting board and trim if necessary to obtain a fillet of relatively equal thickness throughout. Cut the fillet lengthwise down the middle to make two equal-sized pieces approximately 10 inches long.

Working with one piece at a time make a horizontal cut along one side of the salmon fillet to form a pocket, leaving a 1/2-inch wall.

Spread the fillet open and press gently to flatten.

Season the inside with salt and ground black pepper. Place approximately half of the baccala filling in the pocket, pressing firmly to spread the filling to within 1 inch of the fillet's edges.

Fold the fillet closed and gently press with your hands to reshape the piece. Repeat with the second piece and season both with salt and pepper.

Place on a nonstick baking sheet and bake in a preheated 450°F oven for 6-8 minutes. Remove from the oven and set aside to cool enough to handle.

With a long spatula carefully lift the pieces and place on individual sheets of plastic wrap.

Wrap tightly in the plastic wrap and refrigerate.

When ready to serve, remove from the refrigerator and cut with a sharp, thin-bladed knife into 8-10 pieces each.

Mushroom, Ricotta and Sun-dried Tomato Strudel

photo top, page 46

Wild mushrooms would make this a great fall hors d'oeuvre. An alternative is to cut the strudel slightly larger and serve as an accompaniment to meat dishes.

Heat a nonstick sauté pan on medium and add 2-3 tbsp. olive oil.

Add the mushroom and onion slices and cook 2 minutes.

Add the garlic, sage, rosemary and a little salt and ground black pepper. Cook stirring until the mushrooms and onion are tender and the moisture has evaporated.

Remove from the pan and cool.

In a separate bowl combine the ricotta, flour, lemon zest and a little salt and ground black pepper. Set aside.

To finish

Place a sheet of phyllo pastry on a work surface with the short end facing you.

Brush lightly with about 1 tbsp. olive oil, season with salt and ground black pepper, and sprinkle with 2-3 tbsp. Parmigiano Reggiano.

Lay 1/3 of the cooled mushroom mixture in a line across the phyllo about 2 inches from the edge closest to you, leaving about 1 1/2 inches on the left and right edges.

Top with 1/3 of the ricotta mixture, then with 1/3 of the minced tomato.

Carefully lift the edge of the pastry, roll up the filling into a long, tight cylinder and tuck the ends underneath.

Place the cylinder on a parchment-lined baking sheet and brush lightly with olive oil.

Sprinkle with a little more Parmigiano Reggiano.

With a sharp serrated knife score the pastry on the diagonal into 6 portions. This will make the pastry easier to slice once it is baked.

Repeat with the rest of the pastry and filling and bake in a 375°F oven for 20-25 minutes or until crisp and browned.

Remove from the oven and portion while still hot.

1/2 c. extra virgin olive oil
2 medium portobello mushrooms, sliced 1/8-inch thick
1/2 c. onion, thinly sliced
3 large garlic cloves, thinly sliced
3 tbsp. minced fresh sage
1 tbsp. minced fresh rosemary
salt and freshly ground black pepper
3/4 c. ricotta cheese
1 tbsp. flour
grated zest of 1 lemon
1/2 c. minced sun-dried tomatoes
3 sheets phyllo pastry
3/4 c. grated Parmigiano Reggiano

TIP
When working with phyllo, be sure to work on a dry surface and keep unused sheets covered with a damp cloth. Phyllo will keep in the refrigerator for up to 2 weeks.

Polenta Crostini

photo bottom, page 46

An easy do-ahead appetizer. Crostini is a Tuscan term used for any type of bread base, toasted or untoasted, with a variety of toppings. In this recipe, I've used polenta as the base. You can vary the topping with almost any vegetable or add seafood or minced roasted meats.

For the polenta squares
1 1/2 c. water
1 tsp. salt, or to taste
1/2 tsp. ground black pepper
1/2 c. yellow cornmeal
2 tbsp. minced chives
2 tbsp. extra virgin olive oil
1/4 c. grated Parmigiano Reggiano

For the topping
2 tbsp. extra virgin olive oil
1/4 c. minced onion
1 garlic clove, finely minced
1/4 c. small diced cauliflower tops
2 tbsp. each minced red and yellow
  pepper
1/4 c. small diced mushrooms
1 tbsp. tomato paste dissolved in
  2 tbsp. water
1/4 c. fresh or frozen baby peas
1/4 c. small diced fresh asparagus
1/2 c. cooked small white beans
salt and freshly ground black pepper
  to taste
Parmesan Crisps to garnish (page 255)

For the polenta squares

Bring the water to a boil in a 1-quart pot and add the salt and pepper.

While whisking, pour the cornmeal into the boiling water in a steady fine stream.

Lower the heat and continue to whisk the mixture smooth.

Switch to a wooden spoon if the mixture becomes too thick. Stir occasionally for 10-15 minutes more until the mixture begins to pull away from the sides of the pot.

Stir in the chives, olive oil and cheese and remove from the heat.

Pour the mixture into an oiled 8-inch square pan and smooth the top. Set aside to cool.

Turn the polenta out of the pan onto a cutting board. Trim the edges and cut the polenta into sixteen squares.

For the topping

Heat a pan on medium heat and add the olive oil. Add the onion and cook until soft.

Stir in the garlic and cook 30 seconds, then add the cauliflower, peppers, mushrooms and tomato paste dissolved in water.

Stir to combine and cook 3-4 minutes until the vegetables start to become tender, then stir in the peas and asparagus. Cook 2-3 minutes more until tender and the liquid has evaporated.

Mash about 1/3 of the beans with a fork and add to the pan with the rest of the beans. Season to taste.

To finish, spoon the topping onto the individual polenta squares. Place the crostini into a preheated 375°F oven for 8-10 minutes until heated through, remove and top with Parmesan Crisps.

The crostini can also be served cold.

TIP
For very finely minced garlic, roughly chop 2-3 large cloves, sprinkle with a half teaspoon of salt, then with the flat of a chef's knife grind into a fine paste. The salt acts as an abrasive.

Leek and Potato Tarts

photo top, page 50

For these little tarts you will need two mini 12-muffin pans or use one and bake the tarts in two batches. The recipe will make 16 tarts.

Place a medium sauté pan on medium to low heat and add the diced bacon and 1 tbsp. of olive oil. Cook stirring until the bacon is crisp.

With a slotted spoon remove the bacon and reserve.

Add the diced potato, leek, garlic and water. Cook on low heat, stirring occasionally to prevent sticking.

When the potatoes are tender and the moisture has evaporated, remove the mixture and place in a bowl to cool.

Combine the egg, cream and nutmeg. Add to the cooled leek mixture along with the chives, grated cheese and a little salt and freshly ground black pepper.

Coat the mini-muffin pans with oil or nonstick spray and set aside.

Lay one phyllo sheet on a work surface with the long end facing you.

Brush 2/3 of the sheet with olive oil and season with salt and ground black pepper.

Fold the dry third of the pastry over the middle third and then the last third over top of the first.

Brush with oil and cut into 4 equal pieces.

Line 4 of the muffin cups with the pastry and repeat with the other 3 sheets.

Place approximately 1 tbsp. of filling into each cup and bake in a 350°F oven for 15 minutes.

Remove from the pans and garnish the tops with sour cream, the reserved bacon and chives.

2 slices thick-cut smoked bacon cut into small dice
1/4 c. extra virgin olive oil
1 c. peeled and diced yellow-fleshed potato
1 c. finely chopped leek, white and light green part only
1 tbsp. minced garlic
3-4 tbsp. water
1 egg
3 tbsp. cream
1/4 tsp. fresh grated nutmeg
1/4 c. minced chives or green onion
3 oz. grated smoked Cacciocavallo cheese or other smoked cheese
4 sheets phyllo pastry
salt and ground black pepper
1/4 c. sour cream

Curried Chicken Pancake

photo bottom, page 50

For the filling

Heat a medium sauté pan on medium heat and add 2 tbsp. olive oil.

Lay the chicken breast flat on a cutting board and slice horizontally into 3 thin pieces.

Cut across the grain into slivers and add to the hot pan.

Stir briefly and add the onion, garlic, ginger, turmeric, coriander, cumin, salt and ground black pepper.

Cook stirring for a few minutes until the chicken is cooked through, then add the coconut milk and reduce until thickened.

Remove from the heat and stir in the chopped cilantro. Set aside to cool.

For the pancakes

In a small bowl whisk together the egg, milk and 3 tbsp. olive oil.

In another bowl whisk together the flour, salt and pepper, baking powder and cilantro.

Add the egg mixture to the flour and whisk to combine.

Cover and set aside for 15 minutes.

Heat a nonstick pan on medium heat and add 1 tbsp. olive oil to coat lightly.

Drop spoonfuls of the batter to form 2- to 2$1/2$-inch diameter pancakes.

Cook until lightly browned, flip and cook 30 seconds more.

Repeat with the rest of the batter, which should make about 16-20 pancakes.

Cool on a tray and keep covered to prevent the pancakes from drying out.

To fill the pancakes

Take one pancake in hand and place about 1 tbsp. of chicken filling in the middle.

Fold in half and skewer with a toothpick or stiff herb stalk to hold it closed.

Set the filled pancakes on an ovenproof tray and place in a 350°F oven for 10-12 minutes to heat through.

Top with diced papaya and serve warm.

For the filling
2 tbsp. olive oil
8 oz. boneless, skinless chicken breast
$1/4$ c. thin sliced onion
2 large garlic cloves, minced
1 tbsp. fresh ginger, minced
$1/2$ tsp. ground turmeric
$1 1/2$ tsp. ground coriander
$1 1/2$ tsp. ground cumin
salt and freshly ground black pepper
3 tbsp. coconut milk
2 tbsp. chopped fresh cilantro (Chinese parsley)
$1/2$ c. small diced fresh papaya

For the pancakes
1 whole egg, plus 1 egg white
$3/4$ c. milk
5 tbsp. olive oil
$3/4$ c. all-purpose flour
pinch of salt and freshly ground black pepper
$1 1/2$ tsp. baking powder
2 tbsp. chopped fresh cilantro
16-20 stiff herb stalks or sturdy toothpicks

Parmesan and Pecorino Cheese

There are two basic types of parmesan cheese. In my pasta and risotto recipes I call for grated Parmigiano Reggiano, probably the best-known of any type of parmesan. Parmigiano Reggiano is produced in a strictly defined area of Northern Italy between Parma (where Prosciutto de Parma comes from), Modena, Reggio-Emilia, Bologna and Mantua. It is aged for a minimum of 24 months, becoming pale golden with a slightly flaky granular texture and mild, nutty, salty flavour that improves with further aging. This also makes a wonderful table cheese eaten with fruit and a good red wine.

The other type of parmesan is Grana Padano which, although produced using the same method as Parmigiano Reggiano, is considered an inferior cheese in flavour and texture. The milk used comes from other regions and the cheese is aged only 18 months, resulting in a cheese that is sharper and saltier with a grainy texture. Both cheeses can be used in the same way for cooking.

All Italian cheeses made from ewe's milk are referred to as Pecorino. Pecorino is thought to be the oldest of the Italian cheeses. The cheese can vary greatly in texture and flavour, from soft and mild to hard and strong. The best-known types are Romano from Lazio and Sardo from Sardinia, both favourites of my parents. They are hard, aged cheeses with a sharp, salty flavour, becoming sharper the longer they are aged.

Aged Pecorino can be used grated in cooking the same way as parmesan. It has a stronger flavour, which blends well with spicy pasta dishes. It may be too strong for milder dishes but this can be left to personal preference.

soups

Chilled Fava Bean Soup with Snow Pea and
Preserved Lemon Salad   54

Prosciutto and Melon Soup   57

Mushroom Broth with Chicken Gorgonzola Dumplings   58

Roasted Butternut Squash Bisque   59

Smoked Tomato Soup with Gorgonzola Vegetable Dumplings   61

Crab and Corn Soup with Sorrel and Roasted Garlic Oil   62

Mussel, Clam and Roasted Corn Chowder   65

Oyster Soup with Fresh Mint   67

Saffron Gnocchi in a Seafood Broth   68

Parsnip Soup with Chanterelle Mushrooms   71

Photo: Mushroom Broth with Chicken Gorgonzola Dumplings

soups

Chilled Fava Bean Soup with Snow Pea and Preserved Lemon Salad

A refreshing, flavourful soup for those late spring or early summer days. If fava beans are not available, green peas make a good substitute. Follow the same procedure and cook the peas half the time.

For the soup

3 c. water
1/2 c. roughly chopped onion
1 c. roughly chopped celery
4 large garlic cloves, peeled
2 lb. fresh fava beans in the pod
1/4 c. each finely diced red and yellow pepper
5 oz. fresh spinach leaves
1/2 tsp. salt
1/4 tsp. freshly ground black pepper
8 oz. soft tofu
1/2 c. fresh mint leaves

For the salad

1 c. fresh snow peas
1/3 c. slivered Preserved Lemons (page 250)
1/4 c. slivered fresh mint leaves
2 tbsp. extra virgin olive oil
freshly ground black pepper to taste

For the soup

In a 2- to 3-quart pot combine the water, onion, celery and garlic cloves and bring to a simmer. Cook 30-40 minutes.

In a separate pot, bring more salted water to a boil.

While the water comes to a boil, remove the fava beans from their pods and set aside.

Have ready at the side a large bowl of ice water that will contain the beans after they are blanched.

Add the fava beans to the boiling salted water and cook 1 minute only. Immediately remove the beans with a slotted spoon and drop them into the ice water to cool. This will preserve the colour of the beans. Remove the beans from the ice water when cooled and set aside.

Place the diced peppers in a sieve and immerse briefly in the boiling water.

Remove and immerse peppers in the ice water to cool. Remove and set aside in the refrigerator.

When the onion, celery and garlic mixture has simmered 30-40 minutes or when the vegetables are soft, remove from the heat and stir in the spinach leaves to wilt them.

Pour the mixture into a bowl and cool quickly. Add the fava beans, salt, pepper, tofu and the mint leaves and purée in a blender or food processor.

Strain through a fine sieve, cover and refrigerate until needed.

For the salad

Remove the stem end of the snow peas and cut on a sharp bias into thin slivers. Combine in a bowl with the preserved lemon, mint, olive oil and salt and pepper.

To serve

Ladle about 4 oz. of the chilled soup into well-chilled soup bowls or cups.

Place a heaping spoonful of the salad in the centre of the soup and sprinkle some of the red and yellow pepper around the soup. Drizzle with a little more extra virgin olive oil and serve.

Prosciutto and Melon Soup

A little twist on the classic Italian appetizer. Prosciutto is an air-dried cured ham that is seasoned with salt, pepper and sometimes red pepper. The traditional way to have prosciutto is with slices of fresh melon.

This is a refreshing light starter for lunch or dinner on a warm summer day. Look for melons that have a bit of give when squeezed. A softer melon will have more flavour and will purée more smoothly. When making the melon soups it is important they are the same consistency so they stay separate in the bowl when poured in together. The consistency can be adjusted by using more of the honey syrup.

For the honey syrup

Place the honey and water in a saucepan and warm on medium heat. Stir until combined, remove to a bowl and set aside to cool.

For the honey syrup
3/4 c. honey
1/2 c. water

For the mint oil

Bring a large pot of water to a boil, adding about 1 tbsp. salt for each quart. Add the mint leaves and blanch about 15 seconds. Immediately remove and immerse leaves in a bowl of ice water to cool thoroughly. Squeeze the mint as dry as possible and place half in a blender with the sunflower seed oil. Blend for 1 minute. If the mixture does not move well in the blender add a little more oil. Add the rest of the mint and blend 1 more minute. Remove from the blender and place in a bowl. Cover and refrigerate overnight. The next day pour the mixture into a strainer lined with 2 layers of cheesecloth and allow to drip through. To keep the oil clear do not press or squeeze the mixture. Set aside.

For the mint oil
3 c. packed fresh mint leaves
3/4 c. sunflower seed oil

For the cantaloupe soup

With a small melon baller (3/8- to 1/2-inch diameter), scoop out 1/3 cup of small melon balls from the firmer part of the cantaloupe and set aside in the refrigerator. Peel and roughly chop the remainder of the cantaloupe, approximately 2 1/2 cups, and place in a blender. Add the fresh lemon juice, salt and 1/4 cup of the honey syrup. Blend until smooth and pass through a fine strainer. Place in a jug that has a pouring spout and refrigerate.

For the cantaloupe soup
1 medium cantaloupe melon
2 tbsp. fresh lemon juice
1/4 tsp. salt
1/4 c. honey syrup

For the honeydew soup

With the same melon baller, scoop out 1/3 cup of small melon balls from the firmer part of the honeydew. Peel and roughly chop the remainder of the honeydew, approximately 2 cups, and place in a blender with the pear, ginger, lemon juice, salt and 1/4 cup honey syrup. Blend until smooth and pass through a fine strainer. Place in a jug with a pouring spout and refrigerate.

For the honeydew soup
1 medium honeydew melon
1 soft ripe pear, peeled and cored
2 tbsp. roughly chopped peeled fresh ginger
2 tbsp. fresh lemon juice
1/4 tsp. salt
1/4 c. honey syrup

To serve

With the melon baller, scoop out 1/3 cup of small melon balls from the watermelon and combine with the reserved cantaloupe and honeydew melon balls. Season with a little salt. Place a 1 1/2 x 1 1/2-inch diameter ring in the centre of a chilled soup bowl and fill with some of the melon ball mixture, pressing it in firmly with the back of a spoon. With a jug of each soup in each hand, simultaneously pour about 2 oz. of each soup into the bowl. Remove the ring and place a bit of prosciutto on top of the melon balls. Drizzle about 2 tsp. of the mint oil around the centre of the bowl and garnish with mint leaves.

To serve
3 oz. prosciutto, cut into spoon-sized slivers
watermelon

Mushroom Broth with Chicken Gorgonzola Dumplings   *photo, page 53*

For the basic broth
1 lb. chicken bones
2 carrots
2 celery sticks
2 medium onions
1 parsnip
6 whole peeled garlic cloves, flattened
four 4- to 5-inch sprigs fresh rosemary
8 c. cold water

For the dumplings
6 oz. chicken thigh meat
1 egg white
1/4 c. cream
1 1/2 oz. Gorgonzola cheese
1/4 tsp. freshly ground pepper
2 tbsp. minced fresh chives

To finish the broth
4 oz. thick-cut pancetta or bacon, slivered
1 tbsp. extra virgin olive oil
6 oz. fresh mushrooms, thinly sliced
2 oz. dried shiitake mushrooms, soaked
    in hot water 30 minutes, stems
    removed, thinly sliced
4 large garlic cloves, peeled and thinly
    sliced
1/3 c. dry sherry
3-4 green onions, white part only, thinly
    sliced on a bias
4 cherry tomatoes, thinly sliced

For the basic broth

Place the bones in a roasting pan and roast in a preheated 400°F oven for 45-60 minutes, and brown the bones well, stirring frequently.

Add the carrots, celery, onions, parsnip and 6 whole garlic cloves and roast 15 minutes until soft and beginning to brown.

Remove from the oven and scrape the contents of the roasting pan into a stock pot. Add the rosemary and cold water and bring to a simmer.

Cook at least 3-4 hours or up to 6 hours.

Strain through several layers of cheesecloth and set aside. You should have 5-6 cups of broth.

The broth can be made one day ahead and refrigerated until needed.

For the dumplings

In the bowl of a food processor, purée the chicken and egg white until smooth.

Add the cream and pulse to combine, being careful not to overmix.

Pulse in the cheese and pepper, then gently blend in the chives.

Refrigerate until needed.

To finish the broth

Heat the oil and pancetta in a soup pot and cook until the pancetta begins to crisp.

Add the mushrooms and cook stirring for 2-3 minutes, then add the sliced garlic. Cook one minute, add the reserved broth and bring to a simmer.

Take the chicken mixture from the refrigerator and using two small spoons dipped in water, form the mixture into small pointed ovals, dropping them into the simmering broth as you go.

When you have used all the mixture, simmer 5 minutes, add the sherry and season to taste with salt and ground black pepper.

Serve the broth with the dumplings, garnished with the sliced green onions and tomatoes.

Roasted Butternut Squash Bisque

Dice the squash into 1-inch cubes and toss with the honey.

Spread on a roasting pan and roast in a 450°F oven for 20 minutes.

Heat the olive oil in a soup pot and add the onion and garlic. Cook stirring for 1 minute.

Add the roasted squash, the candied ginger and stock to cover, adding water if needed.

Cook until the squash is very soft, about 15 minutes.

Remove from heat and purée the soup until it is very smooth (using a food processor or blender).

Strain into a clean pot and add the buttermilk.

Bring the bisque to a low simmer. Do not allow to boil – this may curdle the buttermilk.

Season to taste and serve garnished with slivered candied ginger, toasted pumpkin seeds and Coriander Chips.

2 lbs. peeled butternut squash
2 tbsp. honey
2 tbsp. olive oil
1 c. chopped onion
4-5 garlic cloves, sliced
1/2 c. chopped candied ginger plus extra for garnish
4 c. chicken or vegetable stock (page 256)
1 1/2 c. buttermilk
1 tsp. salt
1/4 c. toasted pumpkin seeds
Coriander Chips to garnish (optional) (page 254)

Smoked Tomato Soup with Gorgonzola Vegetable Dumplings

Since the tomatoes are the star of this soup it is important to get the best, most flavourful ones possible. Late summer and early fall, when the best tomatoes are still available, is a good time to make this soup. If you have an abundance of your own harvest you can freeze whole tomatoes for a later use. Just thaw the tomatoes, drain excess water (and save to add back later), then proceed as directed. For a vegetarian version, substitute vegetable stock or water.

For the soup

Smoke the tomatoes, onion and sun-dried tomatoes following the procedure for Quick Smoked Trout (page 257).

Instead of placing the ingredients directly on the grill place them on a dinner plate with the sun-dried tomatoes on the bottom. This way they will absorb the juices from the fresh tomatoes and will not dry out. Smoke for 30 minutes.

In a 2- to 3-quart pot heat the olive oil on medium and add the garlic and paprika.

Cook stirring for 1-2 minutes, then add the smoked ingredients, any excess water from the plate and the chicken stock.

Season lightly with salt and pepper and simmer for 20-30 minutes.

In 2-3 batches, purée the soup in a blender, strain through a fine sieve and return to a clean pot. Keep the soup warm while you make the dumplings.

For the soup
2 lb. ripe tomatoes, halved
1 medium onion, peeled and quartered
3 oz. sun-dried tomatoes
2 tbsp. extra virgin olive oil
6-8 large garlic cloves minced
2 tbsp. paprika
3-4 c. chicken stock (page 256)
salt and freshly ground pepper to taste
1/2 c. heavy cream (optional)
1/2-3/4 c. diced fresh tomatoes to garnish

For the dumplings

Place the potato and enough water to cover in a small pot and simmer until tender.

Mash the potato with a fork or a potato masher and set aside, keeping warm.

Heat the olive oil in a sauté pan and add the onion, carrot, celery and squash. Cook stirring until tender. Combine with the mashed potato, Gorgonzola and minced chervil, and season with salt and pepper.

To serve, ladle some soup into a warm bowl.

Dip two soup spoons in water and take some of the dumpling mixture in one spoon.

Using both spoons, shape the mixture into a pointed oval and place in the centre of the soup.

Whisk the cream until thickened but still runny. Season to taste with salt and pepper and drizzle a spoonful around the dumpling and into the soup.

Garnish with diced fresh tomato and serve.

For the dumplings
1 c. peeled diced potato
1 tbsp. extra virgin olive oil
1/4 c. finely minced red onion
1/2 c. finely minced carrot
1/2 c. finely minced celery
1/2 c. finely minced firm squash
1 oz. Gorgonzola cheese, room
    temperature
1/2 c. minced fresh chervil
salt and freshly ground pepper to taste

Crab and Corn Soup with Sorrel and Roasted Garlic Oil

For the sorrel and roasted garlic oil
1/2 c. washed and dried fresh sorrel leaves
1 tbsp. roasted garlic*
2 tsp. honey
1 c. extra virgin olive oil

For the crab stock
1 cooked 11/2 lb. fresh Dungeness crab,
    shelled, with the meat and shells
    reserved separately
1 c. each minced carrot, celery and onion
2-3 crushed fresh garlic cloves
handful minced Italian parsley, including
    stems
5 c. cold water

For the soup
2 tbsp. extra virgin olive oil
4 c. fresh or frozen corn kernels
1/2 c. minced onion
2 tbsp. minced garlic
1/2 tsp. chili flakes
1/2 tsp. ground turmeric
4 c. crab stock
1 roasted red bell pepper (page 107),
    peeled, seeded and diced
1/2 c. heavy cream
reserved crab meat
2 tbsp. minced fresh chives
salt and freshly ground pepper to taste

For the sorrel and roasted garlic oil

Combine ingredients in a blender and purée until very smooth. Strain through a fine sieve and season to taste with salt and pepper. Set aside.

For the crab stock

Keep all the shell pieces and liquid that may have collected and discard the lungs and inner parts of the crab.

Break the shells into small pieces, place them in a pot with the minced carrot, celery and onion, crushed garlic and handful of fresh parsley.

Cover with the water, bring to a simmer and cook for 30-40 minutes. Strain through cheesecloth and set liquid aside.

For the soup

In a large pot heat 1 tbsp. olive oil on medium and add the corn. Cook for 4-5 minutes, stirring occasionally until the kernels begin to colour slightly.

Remove 1/3 of the corn and set aside.

Add the onion, garlic, chili flakes and turmeric and cook stirring until soft.

Add the crab stock, bring to a simmer and cook for 5 minutes. Remove from the heat and purée in a blender.

Strain through a fine sieve and return to the pot.

Add the roasted red pepper and the cream and warm the soup on low heat while you make the crab topping.

To make the topping, combine the crab meat with the reserved corn kernels, minced chives, and 1 tbsp. olive oil.

Season the soup with salt and pepper if necessary and ladle about 4 oz. into warm bowls. Top with the corn and the crab mixture.

Drizzle with the sorrel and roasted garlic oil and serve.

***TIP**
To roast whole heads of garlic use a serrated knife and cut off the root end; this makes it easier for the individual cloves to pop out later. Place in tin foil, drizzle with a little olive oil, add some dry white wine and close up into a pouch. Roast in a 275-300°F oven until tender, about 2-21/2 hours.

TIP
To cut fresh corn off the cob first cut the stem end flat, then stand the cob inside a plate with a raised edge. A quiche plate works well. This will keep the kernels from scattering as they are cut off.

Mussel, Clam and Roasted Corn Chowder

The jalapeño pepper gives a mild spice to the chowder and can be adjusted to your liking. The Coriander Chips make a tasty garnish.

Heat a large nonstick sauté pan on medium to high heat with the olive oil until a slight haze forms above the oil.

Add the corn and cook, stirring occasionally, until it has coloured and taken on a roasted appearance. Remove from the heat and set aside.

Scrub the mussels and clams lightly and remove the beards from the mussels. This is the fibrous, stringy material that mussels use to attach themselves to rocks.

Place the mussels and clams in a stock pot with the wine and cover. Place on high heat and cook until the shells begin to open. Remove the mussels and clams as they open. The clams may take a little longer than the mussels.

Cool and remove the meat from the shells. Strain the broth that is left in the pot and set aside.

Heat the butter in a 3- to 4-quart stock pot and add all the vegetables except the corn.

Sauté 3-4 minutes and add the cumin, black pepper and flour, stirring to coat the vegetables. Cook for 1-2 minutes.

Add the reserved broth, fish stock and cream, stirring as the liquid is added.

Add the roasted corn and bring to a simmer. Cook for 10 minutes and add the mussel and clam meat.

Season to taste and serve with Coriander Chips.

2 tbsp. extra virgin olive oil
3 c. fresh or frozen corn kernels
1 1/2 lb. fresh mussels
1 1/2 lb. fresh small clams
1/2 c. dry white wine
1/4 c. unsalted butter
1/4 c. minced onion
2 tbsp. minced garlic
2 tbsp. minced jalapeño pepper
1/2 c. minced red bell pepper
1/2 c. diced carrot
1/2 c. diced celery
1 tbsp. ground cumin
1 tsp. freshly ground black pepper
1/4 c. all-purpose flour
4 c. fish stock (page 256)
1/2 c. heavy cream
Coriander Chips to garnish (page 254)

TIP

Save prawn, shrimp and lobster shells in your freezer. When you have enough you can make a flavourful stock to use for seafood soups or to add great flavour to sauces.

Oyster Soup with Fresh Mint

A quick and easy soup that captures the briny flavours of fresh oysters.

If possible try to shuck the oysters yourself so you have the juices to add to the soup. Although large oysters would work fine in this recipe, try to choose small to medium oysters that are not as strongly flavoured and will cook quickly.

In a wide saucepan or soup pot, heat 2 tbsp. of the olive oil on low to medium heat and add the onion, garlic and potato.

Cook, gently stirring, until the potato begins to soften without colouring.

Add the vermouth, heavy cream, milk and mascarpone cheese and bring to a simmer, stirring all the while to incorporate the cheese.

Add the oysters and their juices and cook until the edges of the oysters begin to curl.

Stir in the chili flakes and season to taste with the salt and pepper.

In a separate pan heat the rest of the olive oil on medium and add the spinach. Turn the spinach in the oil and cook only until wilted.

Add the chives, parsley and mint to the soup and simmer 1 minute.

Divide the wilted spinach among 8 heated serving bowls and top with the shredded vegetables. Top with 3-4 oysters and ladle the soup around the greens.

Serve with plenty of crusty bread.

---

3 tbsp. extra virgin olive oil

2 tbsp. finely minced red onion

1 tbsp. very thinly sliced garlic

1 large potato, peeled and cut into 1/4-inch dice (about 1 1/2 c.)

2 tbsp. dry vermouth

1 c. heavy cream

1 c. whole milk

1/4 c. mascarpone cheese (Italian-style cream cheese)

24-32 small to medium fresh shucked oysters, with their juices

1/2 tsp. chili flakes

salt and freshly ground pepper to taste

10 oz. fresh baby spinach leaves

2 tbsp. chopped fresh chives

2 tbsp. chopped fresh Italian parsley

4 tbsp. chopped fresh mint

1/4 c. each shredded carrot, zucchini and celery

Saffron Gnocchi in a Seafood Broth

The amount and types of fish or shellfish for this dish can vary depending on availability and appetite. Add more of your choice, including vegetables, to make this a more substantial first course or light meal.

The periwinkle in this recipe may be difficult to find in your area. You can substitute with available shellfish.

For the gnocchi

1¹/2 lbs. baking potatoes (e.g., Idaho, Russet)

1 egg

¹/2 tsp. saffron threads, dissolved in 2 tbsp. hot water

1-1¹/4 c. all-purpose flour

2 tbsp. chopped fresh cilantro

1 tsp. salt

For the broth

4 c. well-flavoured fish stock, preferably from white fish bones (page 256)

24 steamed mussels and their liquor

24 steamed clams and their liquor

24-30 periwinkles (optional)

1-2 tsp. toasted sesame oil

8 oz. white fish (e.g., snapper, halibut, sole) cut into 16 pieces

¹/2 c. each finely julienned carrots, celery and zucchini combined

¹/2 c. green onions, sliced thin on a bias

about 40 whole fresh cilantro leaves

For the gnocchi

Place the unpeeled potatoes in a pot and cover with water. Bring to a simmer and cook until they are tender. Drain and allow to cool slightly.

While still warm, peel the potatoes and purée them, preferably through a potato ricer. (Do not use a food processor; this will make the potatoes gluey.)

Let the potatoes cool a little and make a well in the centre. Whisk in the egg, then add the dissolved saffron, flour, chopped cilantro and salt.

Mix well, remove from the pot and knead gently to form a smooth dough, using only enough extra flour to keep the dough from sticking to the work surface.

Divide the dough into four pieces and roll each piece into a rope about ³/4-inch thick.

Cut the ropes into pieces ³/4- to 1-inch long and dust with flour, keeping them separate to prevent sticking. Set aside (or freeze) until ready to cook.

Bring a pot of well-salted water to a rapid boil and drop the gnocchi in a few at a time, removing them with a slotted spoon as they float to the top. In the meantime prepare the broth and shellfish.

For the broth

Bring the fish stock and the shellfish liquor to a simmer and add the sesame oil along with the fish pieces and periwinkles. Poach for 3-4 minutes, then add the mussels and clams and simmer 1-2 minutes more to heat through.

To serve, put a mound of the mixed vegetables into the centre of 8 warm soup bowls, place 4 or 5 cooked gnocchi on top of each mound and divide the seafood among the bowls.

Season the broth to taste and ladle 3-4 oz. into each bowl. Sprinkle with the sliced onions and garnish with the cilantro leaves.

Parsnip Soup with Chanterelle Mushrooms

The ingredients for this soup are purposely kept very simple. The natural sweet flavour of the parsnips comes through because I use only a small amount of stock and water, which also helps to keep the soup white. The balsamic vinegar and honey syrup also provides a good balance to the sweetness of the parsnips.

For the balsamic vinegar and honey syrup

Combine ingredients in a small saucepan over low heat. Heat the mixture and reduce, without boiling, to about 1/3 cup. This may take about 90 minutes. Remove from heat and set aside.

For the soup

Warm the olive oil in a pot over medium heat and add the parsnip, onion and garlic. Cook stirring for 3-4 minutes to soften. Be careful not to brown the mixture.

Add the stock, water, salt and pepper and simmer until the vegetables are soft.

Remove from heat and in a food processor or blender purée the mixture and strain through a fine sieve.

Return to the pot and over low heat stir in the buttermilk. Thin to desired consistency with more buttermilk if necessary and keep warm.

For the mushrooms

Place the olive oil and sliced garlic in a pan and heat together on medium heat until the garlic begins to brown. This technique helps to flavour the oil more.

Add the minced onion and cook stirring for 1-2 minutes, then add the mushrooms, herbs, salt and pepper.

Raise the heat and cook 2-3 minutes until thoroughly cooked and there is no moisture in the pan. Season if necessary.

To serve

Place a 2-inch cookie cutter or other ring in the centre of a heated soup bowl and fill with some of the mushroom mixture.

Ladle the soup around the cookie cutter, then carefully remove the cutter.

Drizzle approximately 1 tsp. of the balsamic honey syrup around the mushrooms, garnish with Crispy Parsnip Strips and serve.

For the balsamic vinegar and honey syrup
1/2 c. balsamic vinegar
1/2 c. red wine
2 tbsp. honey

For the soup
3 tbsp. extra virgin olive oil
11/2-2 c. parsnip, peeled and thinly sliced
3/4 c. minced onion
6 large garlic cloves, peeled and crushed
1 c. chicken stock (page 256)
2 c. water
1/2 tsp. salt
1/2 tsp. ground black pepper
1 c. buttermilk
Crispy Parsnip Strips (page 254) to garnish

For the mushrooms
2 tbsp. extra virgin olive oil
3 garlic cloves, peeled and sliced
1/4 c. minced onion
16 oz. sliced chanterelle mushrooms
2 tbsp. minced fresh rosemary
2 tbsp. minced fresh sage
1/4 tsp. salt
1/4 tsp. freshly ground black pepper

Edible Flowers

Growing up I had little consideration for the wide variety of flowers that are not only edible but also contribute flavour to a dish either as an ingredient or as a garnish. As is common in Italy and other European countries squash blossoms were a regular summer treat, simply coated with flour and egg and either shallow fried or baked. As kids my cousins and I would spend a lot of time in the woods picking berries and other things or hiking, and in the spring we would sometimes come across Oregon grape plants in bloom. The bright yellow flowers grew in long grape-like clusters and, contrary to the tart ripe berries, were quite sweet. That was the extent of my edible flower repertoire.

Throughout this book you will see an extensive use of edible flowers as garnishes for my dishes. Some dishes also have flowers as an ingredient, such as the Flower Petal Confetti for the Roasted Beet Salad.

Edible flowers vary greatly in flavour and texture. They can be pungent and have a perfume-like flavour as with lilac and lavender or sharp and peppery like nasturtium and arugula. The petals of yucca and fuscia can be quite succulent and crisp. The small yellow flowers of plants from the cabbage and broccoli family all have a delicious, slightly milder flavour than the vegetable.

Mixing a variety of blossoms gives a range of colour, textures and flavours. All the flowers used in this book are ones we have been using for years and are sure to be safe. You should not eat flowers from a nursery or an unknown source. Eat only organically grown flowers.

As with wild mushrooms or wild food of any kind you should never use a flower on a plate that you are not 100% sure is edible even if intended solely as a garnish. Although considered safe, some flowers may have varying effects on people; therefore consume flowers in small amounts when eating them for the first time.

starters & salads

Seafood Pâté with Fresh Baby Greens and Nasturtium Vinaigrette 74

Prosciutto Wrapped Prawns 75

Herb-Crusted Goat Cheese with Rainbow Tomato Salad 77

Smoked Trout and Green Bean Salad 78

Roasted Beet Salad with Fresh Greens and Goat Cheese 81

Prawn and Tuna Cocktail 82

Crab and Mascarpone Parfait 85

Island Spot Prawns with Prawn Roe Emulsion and Swiss Chard Flan 86

Grilled Prawns with Beet and Orange Slaw and Pickled Red Onion 88

Oyster Turnover with Fennel and Mascarpone Cream 91

Spiced Scallops in a Smoked Salmon Broth 92

Smoked Salmon Crêpe 95

Sea Asparagus Salad 95

Salmon Cakes with Dungeness Crab Salad 96

Tuna Carpaccio with Fennel and Black Olive Salad 99

Seared Tuna Medallions with Pickled Summer Squash, Cucumber and Sea Asparagus 100

Smoked Sablefish and Mascarpone Pâté with Warm Potato Arugula Salad 103

Codfish Cakes with Fresh Coriander and Mint 104

Aioli 104

White Beans with Prosciutto and Roasted Pepper Salad 107

Roasted Eggplant and Fennel Tart with Fresh Goat Cheese and Thyme-Scented Honey 108

Smoked Pork Hock, Rabbit and Chervil Terrine 110

Apple Frisée Salad 110

Grilled Summer Vegetable Terrine 113

Photo: Seafood Pâté with Fresh Baby Greens and Nasturtium Vinaigrette

starters & salads

photo, page 73

Seafood Pâté with Fresh Baby Greens and Nasturtium Vinaigrette

Nasturtiums have a very nice, nutty, peppery flavour similar to watercress or arugula. The flowers, leaves and even unripe seed pods are edible. The green seed pods can be pickled and used as a "poor man's caper."

For the pâté
5 oz. boneless, skinless halibut
5 oz. boneless, skinless salmon fillet
5 oz. boneless, skinless red snapper fillet
2 tbsp. soft unsalted butter
1 large whole egg, plus 1 egg white
1 tbsp. anise- or fennel-flavoured liqueur
1/4 c. heavy cream
4 oz. scallops cut into 1/2-inch cubes
4 oz. peeled prawns or shrimp cut into cubes
1 1/2 tsp. finely minced fresh garlic
1/4 c. minced fresh Italian parsley
1/4 c. minced fresh fennel leaves
1/2 tsp. salt
1/2 tsp. freshly ground black pepper
25-30 fresh steamed mussels, 16 of the best left on the half shell and set aside

For the nasturtium vinaigrette
1 tsp. whole grain mustard
1 tbsp. fresh lemon juice
1 tbsp. honey
3 tbsp. Nasturtium Vinegar (page 253)
1/2 c. extra virgin olive oil
salt and freshly ground black pepper

For the greens
approximately 3 c. fresh baby greens, washed and dried
1/3 c. assorted edible flower petals

For the pâté

Have all the ingredients and the bowl and metal blade of a food processor chilled before starting.

Cut the halibut into 1- to 1 1/2-inch cubes and place in the bowl of the food processor fitted with the metal blade. Cut the salmon and red snapper fillets into 8 strips each, measuring approximately 1/2 x 1/2 x 3 inches. Set aside and cube the rest of the salmon and red snapper and add to the bowl with the halibut.

Process until smooth, then blend in the butter followed by the whole egg, egg white and liqueur. Blend in the cream, adding a little at a time until it is all absorbed. Transfer the mixture to a mixing bowl.

Fold in the cubed scallops, prawns, garlic, parsley, fennel, salt and ground pepper.

Lay an approximately 11 x 16-inch piece of plastic wrap flat on a work surface. Spread a quarter of the pâté mixture onto the middle of the plastic in a 2 x 8-inch rectangle.

Take half of the mussels and lay them in a row down the middle of the pâté mixture and press them in slightly.

Lay 2 salmon strips down each side of the mussels and press in. Lay 2 red snapper strips next to the salmon and press in.

Top with another quarter of the pâté mixture and form into a cylinder.

Fold the edge of the plastic wrap closest to you over the pâté and tightly roll it up to enclose it.

Tie a knot on each end, either with the excess plastic wrap or with kitchen string, then wrap the pâté in aluminum foil, twisting the ends to keep it tight. This will help keep the cylindrical shape of the pâté.

Repeat the procedure to make a second pâté with the remaining ingredients.

Fill a roasting pan with 2 inches of hot, not boiling, water and add the wrapped pâtés. Cook in a preheated 250°F oven approximately 45-55 minutes until firm. Remove from the water bath and place in a flat pan, top with ice to cool quickly, then remove from the ice and refrigerate.

For the nasturtium vinaigrette

Combine the mustard, lemon juice, honey and Nasturtium Vinegar in a small bowl. Whisk in the oil, season with salt and pepper to taste and set aside.

To serve

Arrange a mixture of the baby greens into a small bouquet and place slightly above centre on each plate. Drizzle with 1-2 tbsp. of the vinaigrette.

Unwrap the chilled pâté and with a sharp thin-bladed knife take three 3/8- to 1/2-inch slices and place next to the greens. Drizzle the plates with a little more of the vinaigrette. Garnish with two of the reserved cooked mussels on the half shell and sprinkle the plates with the edible flower petals.

Prosciutto Wrapped Prawns

These spiced-up prawns make a good starter course simply served on a bed of fresh greens or they can also make a great finger food to serve with cocktails. I like to serve them as a starter with Fresh Egg Noodles with Tomatoes and Fresh Herbs.

16 medium to large prawns
2 tsp. fennel seed
2 tbsp. finely minced garlic
3/4 tsp. crushed chili
3 tbsp. chopped fresh mint
3 tbsp. chopped parsley
1 tbsp. chopped fresh rosemary
2 tsp. freshly ground black pepper
1 tbsp. extra virgin olive oil
8 slices prosciutto
16 toothpicks or 3-inch lengths of firm
    rosemary stalk

Peel and de-vein the prawns, then combine with all the other ingredients except the prosciutto.

Slice the prosciutto in half lengthwise. Wrap each prawn with a strip of prosciutto and hold in place with a toothpick or rosemary stalk. Set aside until ready to cook.

Just before serving, cook the prawns at medium high to high heat on a grill or in a skillet 2-3 minutes on each side, depending on the size of the prawns.

Serve on a bed of Fresh Egg Noodles with Tomatoes and Fresh Herbs (page 130) and drizzle with Chive and Rosemary Garlic Oil (page 253).

Herb-Crusted Goat Cheese with Rainbow Tomato Salad

A simple, elegant first course using the best tomatoes you can find. Summer farmers' markets are the best places to find the variety of tomatoes used in this salad.

For the cheese

Place the bread crumbs in the bowl of a food processor and add the herbs. Process using the pulse button until the herbs are minced and well combined. This method will give the mixture a light green colour. Set aside in a bowl.

Divide the goat cheese into 8 pieces. Roll each piece into a ball and flatten. Coat with flour and set aside.

Dip the cheese pieces one at a time into the egg to coat and then roll in the crumb mixture. Repeat the process with the egg and crumbs to ensure a coating that will keep the cheese from breaking through. Refrigerate the coated cheese pieces until ready to serve.

For the rainbow tomato salad

Quarter or slice the tomatoes depending on size and place in a bowl.

Add the torn basil leaves, toss gently with the Basil Pesto, and season with salt and ground black pepper if necessary. Set aside. Do not chill the mixture – it is much more flavourful at room temperature.

To serve

Pour enough olive oil into a deep pot to about 2 inches deep. Heat to between 350-360°F.

Gently lower the cheese pieces into the oil and fry until crisp and lightly browned, about 3-4 minutes. Drain on a clean cloth.

While the cheese pieces are frying, place a mound of the salad in the centre of each plate. Top each mound with the fried cheese.

Add a little extra olive oil to the remaining pesto in the salad bowl and drizzle a little pesto around each plate. Garnish with extra basil leaves and serve while cheese is still warm.

For the cheese
1 1/2 c. fresh white bread crumbs
1/4 c. fresh Italian parsley
1/4 c. minced fresh basil
2 tbsp. minced fresh mint
salt and freshly ground pepper to taste
6 oz. soft goat cheese
1/3 c. all-purpose flour
2 eggs beaten
olive oil for frying

For the rainbow tomato salad
2 1/2-3 c. tomatoes of various colours and sizes
1/2 c. torn fresh basil leaves
1/2 c. fresh Basil Pesto (page 252)
extra olive oil

TIP
To make a more uniform mound, press the tomato salad into a 2 x 2-inch ring, removing carefully before topping with cheese.

Smoked Trout and Green Bean Salad

16 oz. fresh green beans, trimmed and cut on a sharp bias into thin 2-inch pieces

4 medium-sized leeks, white and pale green part only, sliced on a sharp bias into $1/8$-inch pieces and rinsed well

12 red radishes, trimmed, halved and sliced thin

4 tbsp. small fresh mint leaves

6 tbsp. fresh chervil leaves plus extra to garnish

2 egg yolks

2 tbsp. fresh lemon juice

3 tbsp. freshly grated horseradish or $1^1/2$ tbsp. pickled horseradish

$1/3$ c. extra virgin olive oil

salt and freshly ground black pepper to taste

6 smoked trout fillets (page 257), cut into sixteen $1^1/2$-inch (approx.) squares, refrigerated with any trims until needed

$1/2$ c. peeled, seeded tomato cut into $1/4$-inch dice

Chive and Rosemary Garlic Oil for the plate (optional) (page 253)

Bring a large pot of water to a boil, season well with salt and add the beans.

Cook just until tender, 4-5 minutes, then immediately remove with a slotted spoon and drop into a bowl of ice water. Let them chill thoroughly and then drain well.

Repeat this procedure with the leeks.

Pat the leeks and beans dry with a clean kitchen towel.

Combine with the radishes, mint and chervil leaves and refrigerate until needed.

In the bowl of a food processor or blender combine the egg yolks, lemon juice and horseradish.

Turn on the machine and very slowly at first, drizzle in the olive oil, adding it a little faster as the mixture comes together and thickens to a thin mayonnaise consistency.

Season to taste with salt and pepper and fold the mixture into the beans, along with any trimmings from the trout, adding only enough dressing to coat lightly.

To plate the salad, place a piece of trout in the centre of a serving plate then top with a heaped spoonful of the bean mixture. Top with another piece of trout and more salad.

Repeat with the rest of the trout and salad to make 8 servings, then garnish the tops with a small bunch of the extra chervil.

Garnish the plates with diced tomato and a drizzle of Chive and Rosemary Garlic Oil or plain extra virgin olive oil.

Roasted Beet Salad with Fresh Greens and Goat Cheese

For the beets

Wash and dry the beets and rub with the 2 tbsp. olive oil. Place in a small roasting pan and roast in a preheated 375°F oven for 1¹/₂-2 hours until tender when pierced with a knife.

Remove and set aside. When cool enough to handle, peel and cut into ¹/₂-inch cubes and set aside.

For the vinaigrette

In a large bowl, whisk together all the ingredients except the olive oil. While continuing to whisk slowly, pour in the oil. Taste and season with more salt and pepper if necessary, then add the cubed beets. Refrigerate.

For the greens

Divide ingredients into 8 bunches and lay on a damp cloth. Cover with another damp cloth and refrigerate.

For the phyllo rings

Lay one sheet of phyllo pastry on a flat work surface and brush with 1 tbsp. of the oil.

Season with salt and ground black pepper and sprinkle with the parmesan cheese and herbs.

Place the second sheet on top and smooth to press out excess air. Brush with 1 tbsp. extra virgin olive oil.

Cut the sheet across the width into eight 2-inch strips.

Rub the outside of the ring molds with a little oil or spray them lightly with nonstick spray.

Wrap a pastry strip around a ring and place on a nonstick baking sheet pastry side down with the seam on the bottom.

Repeat with the rest of the pastry and rings and bake at 375°F for 6-8 minutes until evenly browned.

Set aside to cool, then carefully remove the pastry from the rings.

To serve

Place a phyllo ring in the centre of each plate and place one bunch of the greens in each.

Place a few of the beets around the base of the rings and top with small spoons of the cheese.

Drizzle the greens with the vinaigrette and sprinkle with the petals.

For the beets
4 medium-sized red beets
2 tbsp. extra virgin olive oil

For the vinaigrette
2 tsp. finely minced fresh garlic
¹/₂ tsp. salt
¹/₂ tsp. freshly ground black pepper
3 tbsp. balsamic vinegar or
   red wine vinegar
1 tbsp. honey
¹/₂ c. extra virgin olive oil

For the greens
3 c. mixed baby greens, washed and
   dried
¹/₂ c. assorted fresh edible flower petals
3-4 oz. soft goat cheese

For the phyllo rings
2 sheets phyllo pastry
2 tbsp. extra virgin olive oil
salt and freshly ground black pepper
¹/₄ c. freshly grated parmesan cheese
2 tbsp. chopped fresh herbs of choice
eight 2 x 2-inch ring molds (page 248)
oil or nonstick spray for the ring molds

Prawn and Tuna Cocktail

For the prawns

1¹/2 c. orange juice
¹/2 c. dry white vermouth
grated zest of 1 lemon
2 tbsp. fresh lemon juice
6 garlic cloves, peeled and thinly sliced
¹/2 c. minced red onion
1 tbsp. fresh grated ginger
1 tsp. salt
16 medium to large prawn tails, peeled,
   with the tips left on
2 tbsp. extra virgin olive oil

For the couscous

³/4 c. instant couscous
¹/4 tsp. salt
¹/4 tsp. freshly ground black pepper
³/4 c. boiling water
¹/4 c. reserved poaching liquid
reserved solids from the poaching liquid
3 tbsp. olive oil
¹/4 c. chopped fresh Italian parsley
¹/4 c. chopped fresh chives

For the tuna

1 tbsp. whole fennel seed
1 tbsp. whole cumin seed
2 tsp. whole coriander seed
1 tsp. whole black peppercorns
2 tsp. coarse salt
1 piece tuna loin, approximately
   2 x 2 x 10 inches

To finish

2 c. loosely packed fresh arugula or
   watercress

In a saucepan large enough to hold the prawns in one layer combine the first 8 ingredients, keeping 1 tbsp. lemon juice aside.

Heat on a low simmer for 10 minutes to develop the flavours.

Add the prawn tails and cook 2 minutes or until opaque.* Remove from the poaching liquid and set aside to cool.

Strain the poaching liquid and reserve the solids.

Remove ¹/4 cup of the poaching liquid, set aside and return the rest to the pan.

On low heat reduce the liquid to about ¹/2 cup, pour into a small bowl and set aside to cool.

For the couscous

Place the first 7 ingredients in a bowl. Stir briefly to combine, cover with plastic wrap and set aside for 5 minutes.

After 5 minutes remove the cover and fluff the couscous with a fork. Set aside to cool.

For the tuna

Place all the seeds and salt into a coffee grinder or mortar and crush very coarsely. (This can also be done on a cutting board using the bottom of a heavy pan.) Set aside.

Place the tuna loin on a cutting board and slice in half lengthwise.

Coat the tuna on all sides with the crushed seed and salt mixture.

Heat a heavy-bottomed sauté pan on medium high, add the olive oil and sear the loins approximately 1 minute on each side.

Remove from the pan and set aside to cool.

To finish

Add the chopped parsley and chives to the couscous and season with salt and pepper if necessary.

Divide among 8 stemmed martini glasses.

Cut the arugula into 1- to 2-inch pieces and pile on top of the couscous.

Place 2 prawns to one side of the glass and then 3 thin slices of the seared tuna in front of the prawns.

Whisk 1 tbsp. of lemon juice and 2 tbsp. of olive oil into the reduced poaching liquid. Season if necessary and drizzle a little of the liquid over each cocktail.

Garnish as desired and serve.

* For presentation purposes you can keep the prawns from curling
  as they cook by inserting a wooden skewer through the centre.

Crab and Mascarpone Parfait

Combine the cucumber, tomato and 1 tbsp. salt and place in a strainer over a bowl to allow moisture to drain. Keep chilled.

Combine the crab meat with the minced garlic, 1tbsp. chopped dill, 1 tbsp. lemon juice, olive oil and salt and pepper to taste. Keep chilled.

Combine the mascarpone cheese and 1 tbsp. lemon juice and beat with a wooden spoon or hand mixer until smooth and fluffy.

Whip the cream to soft peaks and fold into the cheese with the lemon zest and 1 tbsp. chopped dill. Season to taste with salt and freshly ground black pepper.

To assemble the parfaits

Rinse and gently pat dry the cucumber and tomato.

Combine in a bowl and add 1 tbsp. chopped dill, freshly ground pepper to taste and salt if necessary.

Place the oiled metal or plastic ring molds on individual plates.

Divide the shredded radicchio into the bottom of each ring and press firmly.

Repeat with the cucumber and tomato mixture, pressing firmly.

Repeat with the cheese mixture, reserving about 1/3 of the mixture.

Top with the crab meat and press firmly.

Gently remove the ring and place a small spoonful of the remaining cheese mixture on top of the crab.

Sprinkle more chopped dill around the plate, then drizzle with a little extra virgin olive oil and any liquid from the crab mixture.

Garnish with a fresh dill sprig and serve.

---

1 1/2 c. peeled and seeded cucumber, cut into 1/4-inch dice

1 c. fresh Roma tomato, cut into 1/4-inch dice

1 tbsp. salt

12 oz. fresh crab meat

1 large garlic clove, very finely minced

3 tbsp. chopped fresh dill

juice and grated zest of 1 lemon

2 tbsp. extra virgin olive oil

1/3 c. mascarpone cheese at room temperature

1/3 c. heavy cream

2 c. shredded radicchio lettuce or other red leaf lettuce

salt and freshly ground pepper to taste

eight oiled 2 x 2-inch ring molds (page 248)

Island Spot Prawns with Prawn Roe Emulsion and Swiss Chard Flan

The prawns caught around Vancouver Island and along the British Columbia coast have a beautiful firm texture and distinctive, briny flavour. I may be a little biased (just a little), but I believe due to the deep cold waters off our coast they are the most flavourful prawns available. The prawns are quite often harvested with their roe, or eggs, which inspired this recipe. If the prawns you purchase do not contain roe, salmon or other fish roe is usually available at most fish markets.

For the Swiss chard flan
1/4 c. minced onion
2 heads roasted garlic (page 62)
3/4 c. blanched Swiss chard, squeezed dry
    and coarsely chopped
1/4 c. peeled seeded fresh tomato
3 eggs
3/4 c. milk or cream
1/4 tsp. grated nutmeg
1/2 tsp. salt
1/2 tsp. freshly ground black pepper

For the prawn roe emulsion
1/2 c. extra virgin olive oil
1/4 c. minced onion
1 garlic clove, finely minced
2 tbsp. dry white wine
1/4 c. prawn roe or red caviar (salmon or
    lumpfish)
2 large egg yolks
1 tsp. Dijon mustard
1 tbsp. fresh lemon juice
salt and freshly ground black pepper

For the spot prawns
2 tbsp. extra virgin olive oil
1 1/2 lb. spot prawns with roe
1 garlic clove, finely minced
4 tbsp. dry white wine
3 tbsp. finely diced peeled and seeded
    fresh tomato
2 tbsp. each minced chives
2 tbsp. slivered fresh basil
salt and freshly ground black pepper

For the Swiss chard flan

Combine all ingredients for the flan.

Coat eight 3-oz. ramekins liberally with olive oil or nonstick spray and place in a deep ovenproof dish. Divide the mixture into the ramekins and pour enough hot water into the dish to come 3/4 up the sides of the ramekins.

Place in a 275°F oven and cover loosely with foil or parchment paper.

Bake 25-35 minutes or until slightly firm in the centre.

Remove from the oven. Take the ramekins out of the water and cool flans slightly while finishing the prawns and emulsion.

Run a sharp knife around the inside edge of the ramekins and turn the flans out onto individual serving plates.

For the prawn roe emulsion

Heat 2 tbsp. olive oil in a small sauté pan, add the onion and cook 1-2 minutes.

Add the garlic and cook stirring for 30 seconds until it becomes aromatic.

Add the white wine and prawn roe and cook until the roe has turned pink (if using salmon roe, cook the onion, garlic and wine a minute longer and add the caviar to it after it has cooled).

Remove from the heat and place in a small bowl or plate and cool the mixture.

Place the mixture in a blender and add the egg yolks, mustard and lemon juice.

With the blender running, drizzle in the rest of the olive oil, very slowly at first, until the mixture is thickened and has formed an emulsion.

Refrigerate until needed.

For the spot prawns

Heat the olive oil and add the prawns.

Sauté for 15-20 seconds, add the garlic and sauté another 15-20 seconds. Add the white wine, tomato and fresh chives and basil.

Toss to coat evenly (the wine should have almost disappeared), season to taste and serve the prawns on top of the flans with the emulsion spooned over the top.

Grilled Prawns with Beet and Orange Slaw and Pickled Red Onion

For the pickled red onion
1/2 c. white wine vinegar
1 tsp. salt
1 tbsp. honey
1 large red onion, peeled and thinly sliced

For the beet and orange slaw
2 c. grated raw red beets
zest of one large orange
2 large oranges, sectioned
2 tbsp. extra virgin olive oil
1/4 c. chopped fresh Italian parsley
4 tsp. pickle juice from the onions
salt and ground black pepper to taste

For the prawn tails
24 medium tiger prawn tails in the shell
1 tbsp. minced fresh garlic
3 tsp. dry oregano leaves
2 tsp. dry thyme leaves
1 tsp. crushed red chili flakes
1 tbsp. plus 1 tsp. honey
1 c. honey ale or favourite beer
1/2 c. fresh orange juice
4 tbsp. extra virgin olive oil

For the garnish
3 tbsp. pickled capers
3 tbsp. extra virgin olive oil

For the pickled red onion

In a small saucepan combine the vinegar, salt and honey.

Bring to a simmer and add the sliced onion. Cook on low heat for 2-3 minutes.

Place in a bowl and chill.

For the beet and orange slaw

Place the grated beets in a bowl. Add the orange zest, olive oil, pickle juice and parsley.

Season to taste with salt and black freshly ground black pepper. Set aside.

For the prawn tails

Slit the prawns down the back and remove any trace of black vein. Set aside.

In a separate bowl combine all the other ingredients, using 2 tbsp. of olive oil, and add the prawn tails. Set aside to marinate for 15 minutes.

Remove the prawns from the marinade and set aside.

Place the marinade in a saucepan and on medium heat reduce to about 3/4 cup. Whisk in the remaining 2 tbsp. olive oil, season to taste, strain and set aside.

Heat a separate saucepan on medium. Rinse the capers and pat dry.

Add 3 tbsp. oil to the pan and add the capers. Shaking the pan all the while, cook the capers until they open and begin to crisp.

Remove the capers and set to drain on a clean cloth.

Heat a grill or heavy-bottomed frying pan on medium high.

Place the prawns on the grill and cook 2-3 minutes on each side or until opaque.

To serve

Place a mound of beet and orange slaw on the plate and top with 2 orange sections.

Place a small mound of the pickled red onions on the plate and top with a few fried capers.

Spoon a pool of the reduced marinade on the plate, top with 3 prawn tails and serve.

Oyster Turnover with Fennel and Mascarpone Cream

For the turnover

Heat a medium-sized sauté pan and add the olive oil, then the onion, garlic and mushrooms. Cook stirring for 3 to 4 minutes. Transfer to a plate to cool.

Into the same pan add the oysters and fennel liqueur. Cook until the oysters begin to firm up and the liquid has evaporated. Transfer to a plate to cool.

Again into the same pan, add the spinach in batches and sauté until all the spinach is wilted. Transfer spinach to a plate to cool.

Lay the prosciutto on a work surface.

On the end nearest to you, place a portion of spinach and top it with a portion of the mushrooms and one oyster.

Roll up the prosciutto tightly and repeat with the rest.

Divide the puff pastry into 8 pieces and roll out each piece into a 4 x 6-inch rectangle. Brush each piece with eggwash.

With the long side closest to you, place an oyster prosciutto roll along the edge.

Roll the pastry to enclose the turnover and tuck under the ends, making sure the seam is on the bottom.

Repeat with the rest and place the rolls on a parchment paper-lined baking sheet. Brush with eggwash and bake in a preheated 400°F oven for 16-18 minutes until golden.

For the turnover
4 tbsp. extra virgin olive oil
1 medium-sized onion, halved
4 large garlic cloves, thinly sliced
2 c. thinly sliced mushrooms
8 medium-sized fresh oysters
2 tbsp. fennel- or anise-flavoured liqueur
10 oz. washed and dried fresh spinach
8 slices prosciutto
1 lb. puff pastry
1 well-beaten egg for eggwash

For the mascarpone cream

Place the cream and oyster liquor in a saucepan and heat. Reduce by half and add the fennel liqueur and lemon juice.

Reduce again by half and add the mascarpone cheese and whisk smooth. Remove from the heat and stir in the fennel leaves.

To serve, remove the turnovers from the oven. Slice into two pieces and serve with the mascarpone cream.

For the mascarpone cream
1/2 c. heavy cream
1/2 c. oyster liquor
2 tbsp. fennel- or anise-flavoured liqueur
2 tbsp. fresh lemon juice
1/2 c. mascarpone cheese
4 tbsp. minced fresh fennel leaves

Spiced Scallops in a Smoked Salmon Broth

For the broth
1 1/2 c. fish stock (page 256)
2 oz. hot-smoked salmon, cut into small cubes, and the skin from the salmon (skin optional)
1/3 c. each carrot, zucchini and turnip, cut into small dice or scooped with a small melon baller
2 tbsp. finely minced fresh chives
1/3 c. finely diced skinned, seeded tomato

For the scallops
16 large sea scallops
2 tsp. ground paprika
2 tsp. ground cumin
1 tbsp. fennel seeds
pinch of cayenne pepper or chili flakes
1/2 tsp. freshly ground black pepper
2 tsp. granulated sugar
1/2 tsp. salt
4 tbsp. extra virgin olive oil

For the broth

Heat the fish stock and add the smoked salmon skin if using.

Simmer for 15-20 minutes, add the carrots and turnip and simmer 2-3 minutes.

Add the zucchini, simmer 2-3 minutes more, then add the diced smoked salmon, tomato and chives to warm through.

For the scallops

Heat a pan large enough to hold all the scallops without crowding.

Combine all the ingredients for the scallops and 1 tbsp. of the olive oil.

Coat the bottom of the pan with 2-3 tbsp. olive oil and sear the scallops 1 1/2 minutes on each side. They should be slightly resistant when pressed. Be careful not to overcook or they will be tough.*

Remove the salmon skin from the pot if you have added it, and ladle some of the broth and vegetables into warm soup bowls.

Place two scallops in each bowl and garnish as desired.

* To ensure the scallops remain tender, cook only to medium or medium-rare.

The garnish in photo is pâte à choux (page 201) piped using a paper cone.

Smoked Salmon Crêpe

For the crêpes

Combine the eggs, salt, pepper, minced fennel and fennel seeds in
a bowl and whisk together.

Add the flour and whisk to combine, then add the milk and whisk
smooth.

Whisk in the olive oil and set the batter aside to rest 20-30 minutes.

Heat an 8-inch nonstick pan on medium. Brush lightly with olive oil
before making the first crêpe. You should not need to oil the pan for
the rest of the crêpes.

Ladle in about 1/4 cup of batter and swirl the pan to coat the bottom.

Cook until the edges brown, then with a heatproof spatula carefully turn
the crêpe over and cook the other side another 10-15 seconds. Remove
to a plate and repeat with the rest of the batter.

For the crêpes
2 eggs
1/4 tsp. salt
1/4 tsp. freshly ground black pepper
1 tbsp. minced fresh fennel leaves
1 tsp. toasted fennel seeds*
2/3 c. all-purpose flour
3/4 c. milk
2 tbsp. extra virgin olive oil

For the filling

Lay out the crêpes on a flat work surface. Spread each with 1 tbsp.
Basil Garlic Mayonnaise.

On one half, place 1 oz. of the salmon, and top with 2 tbsp. of the
cucumber, 1 tbsp. of tomato, and a pinch of mint and lemon zest.
Season with salt and ground black pepper.

Roll into a tight cylinder.

Repeat with the rest of the ingredients, cover and refrigerate.

Serve on a bed of Sea Asparagus Salad (recipe below) with a little extra
Basil Garlic Mayonnaise.

* To toast seeds, place them in a dry pan and heat on medium for
2-3 minutes while continuously stirring. The seeds are done when
they begin to colour slightly and give off a nutty, intensified aroma.

For the filling
8 tbsp. Basil Garlic Mayonnaise (page 251)
8 oz. smoked salmon
1 c. julienned peeled cucumber
1/2 c. seeded and diced Roma tomato
4 tbsp. freshly chopped mint
4 tbsp. minced lemon zest
salt and freshly ground black pepper

Sea Asparagus Salad

*Also known as sea beans, sea asparagus is a salt water plant that grows at the high tide line. It resembles tiny asparagus heads.
You may substitute thin-cut regular asparagus.*

In a large pot bring to a boil 3 quarts of water.

Prepare a bowl of ice water large enough to hold all the sea asparagus
and have it ready before placing the asparagus in the boiling water.

When the water has come to a rapid boil add all the sea asparagus at
once, making sure to submerge it. Remove immediately and immerse it in
the ice water. Allow to cool completely, drain, then place on a clean towel
and gently pat dry.

Combine in a bowl with the rest of the ingredients, cover and refrigerate.

3 c. sea asparagus
1 tbsp. minced garlic
2 tbsp. minced fresh chives
2 tbsp. fresh lemon juice
1 tbsp. fresh lemon zest
3 tbsp. finely sliced red onion
6 tbsp. extra virgin olive oil
salt and freshly ground pepper to taste

Salmon Cakes with Dungeness Crab Salad

This is my version of crab cakes. No matter how often I have had crab cakes I often go away wondering where the crab went. By making a salad from the fresh Dungeness crab and placing it on top of the crispy fried salmon cakes there is no mistaking that delicious west coast flavour.

For the Dungeness crab salad

12 oz. fresh Dungeness crab meat, picked through to remove any pieces of shell

1/4 c. fresh chopped basil

1 tbsp. minced fresh lemon zest

2 tbsp. fresh lemon juice

1/4 c. extra virgin olive oil

1 tsp. salt

1 tsp. freshly ground black pepper

For the salmon cakes

16 oz. minced fresh salmon

4 tbsp. finely minced green onion

1 tbsp. minced garlic

1/2 c. fresh basil leaves coarsely chopped

2 tbsp. minced fresh lemon zest

1 egg, whisked

1 c. fresh white bread crumbs

1/2 tsp. salt

1/2 tsp. freshly ground black pepper

3 tbsp. extra virgin olive oil for frying

Basil Garlic Mayonnaise (page 251) for the plate

For the Dungeness crab salad

Combine all the ingredients and refrigerate until ready to serve.

For the salmon cakes

Place all the ingredients for the salmon cakes in a bowl, using only half of the bread crumbs.

Using a fork, mix lightly until the mixture is uniform.

Form into 16 round, flattened cakes and press the top and bottom into the remaining bread crumbs.

Refrigerate until ready to serve.

To finish the salmon cakes

Heat a sauté pan, large enough to hold all the cakes, on medium heat.

Add the extra virgin olive oil and fry the cakes 2 minutes on each side until golden.

To plate the salmon cakes, place two pools of Basil Garlic Mayonnaise of about 1 tbsp. each on a plate.

Place a salmon cake on each pool of mayonnaise and top each cake with a spoon of the Dungeness crab salad.

TIP

An average-sized Dungeness crab will weigh between 2 and 3 lbs.

To ensure quality and freshness, crab should always be cooked live. Begin with a large pot of boiling, salted water. Allow 2 tsp. salt for each quart of water.

Place the crab directly into the boiling water. Bring the water back to a boil and cook 15 minutes for a 2 1/2 lb. crab.

When the crab is cooked, remove it from the pot and immediately immerse it a large bowl of ice water. Allow the crab to cool completely before draining.

To clean the crab, hold it with the front facing you and grasp the edge of the top shell with one hand. Using your thumbs, pull the top shell away from the bottom and set aside. Remove the apron (the v-shaped piece of shell in the centre of the body). Discard the internal parts, saving the shell for stock, and rinse the crab clean.

To pick the meat from the shell, break off the individual legs and crack them with the back of a heavy knife or mallet. Pull apart the individual sections of leg and remove the large pieces of meat. Use a nut pick or the tip of one of the legs to get at the body meat, making sure not to leave any behind. This should yield approximately 12-14 oz. of crab meat.

Tuna Carpaccio with Fennel and Black Olive Salad

Season the tuna with salt and pepper and rub with the olive oil.

Heat a nonstick pan and sear the tuna approximately 45 seconds on each side, about 3 minutes total.

Remove from heat and place the tuna on a clean dish to cool slightly.

Combine the mustard, garlic and fresh lemon juice and spread evenly over the tuna.

Combine the parsley and fennel and press onto the tuna, making sure to coat evenly.

Wrap tightly in plastic wrap and refrigerate or freeze until firm enough to slice thinly.

Slice with the wrap still on (this makes it easier to handle) about 1/8-inch thick. Remove the wrap carefully and serve three slices per person on a mound of Fennel and Black Olive Salad (recipe below).

> 1 piece of tuna loin, approx. 2 inches thick, 8 inches long, skin removed
> salt and freshly ground black pepper
> 2 tbsp. extra virgin olive oil
> 2 tsp. Dijon style mustard
> 2 tsp. fresh garlic purée
> 2 tsp. fresh lemon juice
> 4 tbsp. fresh Italian parsley, finely chopped
> 4 tbsp. fennel tops, fine part only, finely chopped

Fennel and Black Olive Salad

Combine all the ingredients except the salt.*

Toss well, cover and refrigerate until ready to serve.

* Salt in the olives will be drawn out as the salad chills, therefore, wait until just before serving to taste and add more salt if necessary.

> 1 medium head Florence or bulb fennel, trimmed, quartered and thinly sliced across the grain
> 1 small red onion, peeled, quartered and thinly sliced across the grain
> 1/2 c. pitted sun-dried black olives
> 2 tsp. minced fresh garlic
> 2 tbsp. chopped Italian parsley
> 1 tbsp. capers, rinsed and drained
> 1 medium Roma tomato, seeded and diced
> 3 tbsp. extra virgin olive oil
> minced or grated zest of half a lemon
> 2 tbsp. fresh lemon juice
> salt and ground black pepper to taste

> **TIP**
> To pit olives, just place them on a cutting board and with the flat of a knife or the bottom of a glass press firmly on the olives; the pits will be loosened and easy to remove.

Seared Tuna Medallions with Pickled Summer Squash, Cucumber and Sea Asparagus

For the pickled salad
1 medium zucchini
1 medium yellow summer squash
1 medium cucumber, peeled
1 c. sea asparagus, washed and patted dry
    (or thinly cut regular asparagus)
1/4 c. salt
1/4 c. white wine vinegar
1/4 c. sugar
2 large garlic cloves, peeled and very
    thinly sliced

For the sorrel vinaigrette
1/2 c. fresh sorrel leaves, stems removed
1 large garlic clove roughly chopped
1 tbsp. honey, or to taste
1/4 c. canola oil
1 tbsp. white wine vinegar
2 tbsp. minced chives
2 tbsp. finely minced skinless, seedless
    Roma tomato
salt and freshly ground black pepper
    to taste

For the tuna
16 fresh tuna medallions, 2 inches in
    diameter and 1/2 inch thick, about
    1 oz. each
2 tbsp. honey
1 tbsp. fresh lemon juice
freshly ground black pepper
1-2 tbsp. vegetable oil

For the pickled salad

Trim the ends off the zucchini and slice on a slight bias 1/4 inch thick, then cut the slices into 1/4-inch strips.

Repeat with the summer squash and cucumber, and combine both with the salt, tossing to coat well.

Place the mixture in a colander, set over a bowl and then set another bowl on top.

Place a 2 lb. weight (a couple of cans or a full wine bottle will do) in the top bowl and refrigerate at least 4 hours to allow the water to be extracted.

Combine the white wine vinegar, sugar and sliced garlic in a saucepan and bring to a simmer. Stir to dissolve the sugar and remove from the heat. Pour the mixture into a bowl and place in the refrigerator.

Remove the squash and cucumber mixture from the refrigerator, rinse and pat dry. Combine with the vinegar mixture and the sea asparagus and chill for 1 hour.

For the sorrel vinaigrette

Place the sorrel leaves, garlic, honey, vegetable oil and white wine vinegar in a blender and coarsely blend.

Remove from the blender, add the minced chives and the tomato and season to taste with the salt and ground black pepper. Set aside.

For the tuna

Place the tuna medallions on a tray, cover and keep chilled. Combine the lemon juice and honey and set aside.

On medium to high heat, heat a nonstick pan large enough to hold all the tuna medallions (or use two pans).

Brush the tops of the tuna medallions with the honey and lemon and season with the ground black pepper.

Add the oil to the hot pan and sear the tuna 10-15 seconds, then turn them over and sear just a few seconds more. Remove to a clean tray.

To serve

Place about 2 tbsp. of the pickled salad in the centre of each plate, top with one tuna medallion, then place more pickle on top followed by another medallion.

Drizzle the sorrel vinaigrette around each dish.

Smoked Sablefish and Mascarpone Pâté with Warm Potato Arugula Salad

Sablefish, also known as black cod, is a rich oily fleshed fish that produces a wonderfully moist smoked product. The pâté itself is very quick to make, requiring no cooking. Mascarpone is a sweet rich Northern Italian cream cheese used mainly in cooking, and is the essential ingredient in Tiramisu. For the Potato Arugula Salad substitute red-skinned potatoes if the purple are not available.

If smoked sablefish or black cod is not available substitute smoked salmon, halibut or any fresh smoked fish product. To smoke your own fish follow the recipe for Quick Smoked Trout (page 257).

For the pâté

Cut the smoked fish into 1/2-inch cubes and place in a bowl.

Add the mascarpone, chives, lemon juice and salt and pepper.

With a wooden spoon or rubber spatula combine the ingredients, trying not to break up the fish too much.

Adjust the seasoning if necessary, cover and refrigerate until firm.

For the warm potato arugula salad

Wash and lightly scrub the potatoes.

Bring a pot of lightly salted water to a boil and add the potatoes. Cook until tender but still slightly firm. Drain and set aside to cool slightly.

In a bowl combine the olive oil, lemon juice, lemon zest and a little salt and pepper.

Chop the arugula and parsley slightly if the leaves are large and add to the bowl.

Cut the potatoes into quarters or halves depending on the size and add to the bowl while still warm. Toss gently to combine.

To serve

Portion potato salad onto 8 plates and top each with a Parmesan Crisp.

Remove the pâté from the refrigerator and portion a spoonful on top of each crisp.

Serve while the potatoes are still warm.

For the pâté

6 oz. skinless, boneless, smoked sablefish

4 oz. room temperature mascarpone cheese

1 tbsp. minced garlic chives

1 tsp. fresh lemon juice

salt and ground black pepper to taste

For the warm potato arugula salad

1 lb. small purple potatoes

3 tbsp. extra virgin olive oil

2 c. arugula, washed and spun dry

1/2 c. Italian parsley leaves

juice and zest of 1 lemon

salt and freshly ground black pepper to taste

Parmesan Crisps (page 255) to garnish

Codfish Cakes with Fresh Coriander and Mint

Dried salted cod, which is used in this recipe, is common in Italy, Spain and Portugal. The preparation takes a bit of planning because the fish has to be soaked in several changes of cold water before cooking to remove the excess salt. In one version or another, dried salted cod was always a part of the Christmas Eve dinner at my family's table.

Dried cod comes two ways, either salted and dried, called baccala, or plain dried, in which case it is called stoccafisso.

1 lb. bone-in salt cod (baccala)

2 c. coarsely ground day old bread, crust removed

1-2 egg yolks

1/2 c. extra virgin olive oil

1/4 c. chopped fresh coriander (cilantro)

1 tbsp. chopped Italian parsley

1/4 c. chopped fresh mint

1 tbsp. paprika

1/2 tsp. salt

1/2 tsp. freshly ground black pepper

4 garlic cloves, peeled and halved

8 poached quail eggs (optional)

lemon wedges

Cut the cod into 4- to 5-inch pieces and place in a large bowl. Soak in several changes of cold water for 12-24 hours until soft.

Drain and rinse the cod and place in a pot. Add enough cold water to cover by 1 inch.

Bring to a simmer and cook about 20 minutes until flaky.

Drain the cod, reserving 1/4 cup of the cooking water. Cool the cod, remove and discard all skin and bones and set the meat aside.

Place the bread and egg yolk(s) in a bowl and with a fork slowly work in 1/4 cup of the olive oil. Add the coriander, parsley, mint, paprika, salt and ground black pepper and stir in.

With your finger or a fork, flake the cod and add to the rest of the ingredients, stirring gently with a fork to combine. If the mixture seems dry, add some of the reserved cooking liquid 1 tbsp. at a time.

To form the cakes, moisten hands with cold water and shape into 8 patties. The water will help keep the mixture from sticking.

Cover the cakes and refrigerate until ready to fry.

Heat 1/4 cup olive oil and the garlic together in a large pan that will leave enough room to turn the cakes over.

Turn the garlic once or twice and remove when it becomes golden. Fry the cakes 3-4 minutes on each side until crisp on the outside.

Serve one per person topped with a poached quail egg as a hearty breakfast, or the cakes can also be served with fresh greens and aioli sauce as a first course.

Aioli

Aioli comes from the Latin word for garlic and this spread is definitely for garlic lovers. It is basically a mayonnaise with a punch and can be used in the same way as any mayonnaise. Serve as an accompaniment to grilled meats, fish, or vegetables. It is also a traditional accompaniment for Mediterranean-style fish soups. For variety, add fresh herbs, spices, anchovies or capers.

For a smoother, less pungent version try using roasted garlic. For a quick version, stir finely minced garlic into 1 1/4 cups prepared mayonnaise.

4 large garlic cloves, peeled

2 egg yolks

1 tsp. fresh lemon juice

1/4 tsp. salt

1 c. extra virgin olive oil

Place the garlic, egg yolks, lemon juice and salt into the bowl of a food processor or blender. Process until smooth.

With the machine running, drizzle in the olive oil, very slowly at first, then faster as the mixture begins to thicken and absorb the oil.

When finished the aioli should look like a thick mayonnaise.

White Beans with Prosciutto and Roasted Pepper Salad

Other than the time it takes to cook the beans, this is a relatively simple dish to prepare. If pressed for time, canned beans can be used; just be sure to rinse them before adding dressing.

Be generous with good quality oil and balsamic vinegar and serve with plenty of crusty bread.

For the beans

Drain the beans, reserving about 1/4 cup of the cooking liquid.

Add the basil, oil, vinegar, salt and pepper and toss.

Cover and keep at room temperature until ready to serve.

To serve

Place a mound of Roasted Pepper Salad (recipe below) in the centre of a plate.

Take a slice of prosciutto, fold it in half to make a long narrow strip and wrap it around the pepper salad to form a ring.

Drizzle some of the bean mixture around the ring.

With a sharp vegetable peeler or paring knife cut paper-thin slices of cheese and scatter over the salad.

2 c. cooked white kidney or navy beans
2 tbsp. chopped fresh basil
2 tbsp. extra virgin olive oil
2 tsp. balsamic vinegar
salt and freshly ground pepper to taste
8 slices prosciutto
shaved Parmigiano Reggiano or Pecorino Romano cheese

TIP
To cook dry white beans, soak overnight in cold water and drain. Place in a pot and cover with cold water. Bring to a simmer and cook until tender, 1-2 hours, depending on the variety of bean. One cup of dried beans will yield approximately 2 cups of cooked beans.

Roasted Pepper Salad

This salad can also be served on its own or as part of an antipasto platter. Crimini mushrooms are the common brown cultivated variety.

Rub the peppers with 1 tbsp. oil, place on a roasting pan and place under a 500°F broiler.

Broil until the skins begin to turn black and blister, rotating the peppers to roast each side.

Place in a bowl and cover with plastic until cool enough to handle.

Peel off the skins.

Quarter the peppers lengthwise and discard the seeds. Cut each quarter into 1/2-inch wide strips. Place in a bowl and set aside.

On medium heat, sauté the onions in 2 tbsp. oil until soft.

Add the mushrooms and sauté 2 minutes.

Add the garlic and cook 2 minutes more, then add the mixture to the bowl of peppers.

Add the remaining oil, the vinegar, herbs, salt and pepper, toss well and keep at room temperature until ready to serve.

4 large bell peppers, any colour
1 tbsp. extra virgin olive oil
1 medium onion, halved and thinly sliced
6 oz. Crimini mushrooms, thinly sliced
3 garlic cloves, thinly sliced
4 tbsp. extra virgin olive oil
1 tbsp. balsamic vinegar
2 tbsp. chopped fresh oregano
2 tbsp. chopped fresh Italian parsley
1/2 tsp. salt
1/2 tsp. freshly ground black pepper

TIP
Roasted peppers can also be cooled in a closed paper bag. Enclosing them helps the skins loosen and makes them easier to peel.

Roasted Eggplant and Fennel Tart with Fresh Goat Cheese and Thyme-Scented Honey

For the filling

1 medium-sized eggplant, approximately 1 lb.

1 medium-sized bulb fennel, approximately 1 lb.

1 medium onion

6 large cloves garlic, peeled and thinly sliced

salt and ground black pepper to taste

eight 3-4 inch sprigs fresh thyme

1/3 c. extra virgin olive oil

2 Roma tomatoes, cored, quartered and diced

For the pastry

2 oz. (1/4 c.) cold unsalted butter

2 oz. (1/4 c.) cold shortening (preferably lard)

8 oz. (2 c.) all-purpose flour

1/4 tsp. salt

1/2 tsp. sugar

1 egg

ice water

For the vinaigrette

2 Roma tomatoes, halved and roasted in a 400°F oven 15 mins.

1/4 c. white wine vinegar

1 small garlic clove, minced

1 tsp. honey

3/4 c. extra virgin olive oil

1/4 c. minced Italian parsley

salt and freshly ground black pepper to taste

For the tarts

4 oz. fresh goat cheese, room temperature

1/4 c. honey

three 3-inch sprigs fresh thyme

coarse sea salt

For the filling

Peel the eggplant, dice into 3/4-inch cubes and place in a roasting pan.

Trim the fennel of any tough outer layers, cut off the root end and quarter the remaining bulb. Remove the core and dice remainder into 3/4-inch pieces. Add to the roasting pan containing the eggplant.

Peel and dice the onion into 1/2-inch cubes and add to the roasting pan along with the sliced garlic, salt and pepper, thyme and olive oil. Toss to coat.

Roast in a 400°F oven for 20-30 minutes, turning occasionally.

Add the diced tomato and continue to roast another 5-10 minutes or until the eggplant is tender and the tomato is still firm. Remove from the oven and set aside to cool.

For the pastry

Place the butter, lard, flour, salt and sugar in the bowl of a food processor and pulse until the fats are evenly distributed but still in pieces about 1/4-1/2 inch in size.

Whisk the egg and add to the bowl, pulsing a few times to distribute. Add just enough ice water to moisten the dough enough to come together. This may take only 1-2 tbsp.

Remove the dough from the bowl and on a lightly floured board, knead very briefly and flatten into a disk. Wrap in plastic and refrigerate for 30 minutes.

For the vinaigrette

Combine all ingredients except the parsley in a blender or food processor and blend to desired consistency. Stir in the parsley, season if necessary and set aside.

For the tarts

Remove the pastry dough from the refrigerator and divide into 8 pieces.

Grease and flour eight individual 2 x 2 x 2-inch square or 2-inch round metal forms (or spray with a nonstick vegetable spray). Place on a parchment paper-lined baking tray.

Press a piece of dough into each of the forms to line the bottom and sides. Press evenly to ensure a uniform thickness of about 1/8 inch. Trim the tops flush.

Divide the filling among the forms with the filling heaped slightly over the top.

Bake in a 400°F oven for 20 minutes or until the pastry is lightly browned. Remove from the oven, cool slightly and remove the forms.

Warm the honey in a small pan with the thyme sprigs and set aside.

To serve, place tarts on individual plates and drizzle the vinaigrette around. Place a soup spoon full of the goat cheese on top of each tart, drizzle with the warm honey and garnish with fresh thyme sprigs.

Smoked Pork Hock, Rabbit and Chervil Terrine

Although it does not contain the same ingredients, this terrine is reminiscent of the head cheese or coppa that my parents would make in the winter when they processed pork or veal. Every part of the animal would be utilized. The head was simmered with herbs and spices until extremely tender, then picked clean. The meat was chopped and packed into molds, then topped with the concentrated broth and allowed to set firm before slicing. If rabbit is not available chicken thighs would make a good substitute.

1 whole smoked pork hock, approximately 1 1/2 lbs.

2 rabbit hind legs

cold water

10-12 peeled garlic cloves, halved lengthwise

2 medium carrots, peeled and cut into 1/4-inch dice

1 celery stick, cut into 1/4-inch dice

10-12 small white mushrooms

1 small red onion, peeled and cut into 1/4-inch dice

2 tbsp. small capers, rinsed and drained

1/2 c. loosely packed fresh chervil or parsley leaves

2 tsp. powdered gelatin dissolved in 1/4 c. water

Rinse the pork hock, place in a pot and cover with cold water. Bring to a simmer and cook gently for one hour. Add the rabbit legs to the pot and cook 1 1/2-2 hours more or until the meat falls easily from the bones.

Remove the meats from the pot, strain the liquid and return the liquid to the pot. Bring back to a simmer and reduce to about 1 1/2 cups.

When the meat cools enough to handle, remove it from the bones. Discard any fat but keep the skin from the pork hock. Cut the meats into 1/2-inch strips, cut the pork skin into 1/4-inch strips and set all aside to cool.

When the liquid in the pot has reduced, add the vegetables and garlic and cook until they are soft but still slightly firm. You should have about 1 cup of liquid.

Strain out the vegetables, combine with the meats and the rest of the ingredients and toss gently to combine.

Line a 16 x 2 1/2-inch terrine mold with plastic wrap, leaving enough overhang to cover the top. (Any mold will do; for example, a bread loaf pan.) Spread the mixture into the mold, pressing it in firmly.

Taste the reduced liquid and season with salt if necessary. (The smoked pork should already have enough salt to season the whole mixture.) Stir in the dissolved gelatin.

Pour the liquid over the meat mixture, making sure it is covered evenly. Press gently to make sure the liquid penetrates to the bottom and also covers the exposed filling.

Fold the excess plastic wrap over the top and chill until set and firm enough to slice, preferably overnight.

Remove from the mold and serve slices as part of an antipasto platter or as a first course with Apple Frisée Salad (recipe below).

1/2 c. peeled, cored and cubed crisp apple

2 c. loosely packed small frisée leaves

1/4 c. fresh whole chervil, fennel or Italian parsley leaves

1/2 c. thinly sliced sweet red bell pepper

3 tbsp. apple cider vinegar

1 tbsp. honey

1/4 c. extra virgin olive oil

salt and freshly ground black pepper to taste

Apple Frisée Salad

Frisée is a variety of curly leafed endive. The dark green leaves are serrated and curled with a slight bitterness while the cream or yellow inner leaves are sweeter. The inner leaves are best for this salad. A crisp, tart apple will match well with the greens and the honey in the dressing. This salad makes a light starter on its own or use it as a base paired with pâtés, terrines or grilled seafood.

Place the first four ingredients in a bowl and toss gently to combine.

In a separate bowl combine the cider vinegar, honey and a little salt and pepper. Whisk in the olive oil and add just enough of the dressing to the salad ingredients to coat.

Season the salad if necessary with salt and freshly ground black pepper and serve.

Grilled Summer Vegetable Terrine

A terrine is a meat, fish or vegetable mixture that has been baked or otherwise prepared and allowed to cool or set in its container, traditionally an oblong or rectangular dish. The ingredients for this terrine can be varied. What is important is the method of preparation. Several types of greens can be used following the method described here. I prefer those that have a robust flavour and are a little coarse in texture, such as dandelion greens, arugula or young kale.

For the terrine

Heat a grill to medium high. If you do not have a grill the vegetables can be broiled in the oven.

Lay all the sliced vegetables and the mushroom on a baking sheet or cutting board and season with salt and ground black pepper. Drizzle with oil and place on the hot grill, beginning with the firm vegetables that take the longest to cook.

Grill the vegetables on both sides until soft and remove to a tray to cool. Slice the mushroom into 6-8 strips.

Combine the roasted garlic, goat cheese and herbs. Season with a little salt and ground black pepper.

Line a 4-cup terrine mold or a bread loaf pan with plastic wrap, leaving enough overhang to cover the top once the mold is filled.

Place a layer of grilled eggplant on the bottom, cutting to fit if necessary.

The order in which the vegetables go into the mold is not important but it is important to spread a thin layer of the goat cheese in between each layer to hold it all together.

Fill the mold with layers of the grilled vegetables alternating with thin layers of the goat cheese and ending with a layer of vegetables. Press down firmly as you fill the mold to compact the terrine.

Once all the vegetables and goat cheese have been used, fold the extra plastic wrap over the top to cover. To ensure the terrine will be firm you may lay a board or thick cardboard inside the mold with a weight placed on top.

Refrigerate for several hours or preferably overnight.

For the greens

Place the 3 tbsp. olive oil and peeled garlic in a large sauté pan and heat to medium. Cook stirring occasionally until the garlic is golden in colour. Remove the garlic and reserve.

Add the greens and vinegar, toss until greens are barely wilted, then drizzle with the honey if using.

Season with salt and ground black pepper and add the cooked garlic.

To serve

Remove the terrine from the mold and slice.

Serve with the wilted greens.

For the terrine
1 large portobello mushroom, stems removed
1 medium eggplant, peeled and cut into 1/2-inch slices
1 medium zucchini, cut into 1/2-inch slices
1 each red and yellow bell pepper, seeded and quartered
2 Roma tomatoes, cored, halved and seeded
1 red onion, peeled and cut into 1/2-inch slices*
1/2 c. extra virgin olive oil
salt and freshly ground black pepper
3 tbsp. roasted garlic cloves (page 62)
6 oz. soft goat cheese at room temperature
1/4 c. chopped fresh basil
1 tbsp. chopped fresh oregano

*To keep the onion slices from coming apart push a wooden skewer through them before cooking. Remove the skewer before assembling the terrine.

For the greens
3 tbsp. extra virgin olive oil
3-4 garlic cloves, peeled and sliced
1 lb. fresh dandelion or other fresh greens
2 tbsp. red wine vinegar
1-2 tbsp. honey (optional)
salt and ground black pepper to taste

Tip
Use a long thin-bladed knife dipped in warm water to make slicing terrines or pâtés easier.

Preparing Vegetables

Vegetables are often overlooked when it comes to completing a meal. Vegetables needn't be time consuming to be flavourful and interesting. Whether from your own backyard, the local market or nearby farm, vegetables are at the peak of their flavour at the time they are harvested. When treated simply with just a few additions, the flavours can be more appreciated.

For easy mixed vegetables as a side dish, heat some extra virgin olive oil in a large sauté pan. Add a few peeled garlic cloves and cook on medium heat for a few minutes, turning the cloves in the oil to brown lightly and to flavour the oil. Remove the garlic to prevent burning and set it aside to be added later if desired.

Add prepared vegetables every few minutes, turning them occasionally to brown lightly. Begin with the larger, firmer pieces. You could start with sliced new potatoes and onions followed by small squash, beans, and peas, and ending with the more tender vegetables and fresh chopped or whole tomatoes. Just before serving, toss in a few chopped fresh herbs, such as basil and Italian parsley, and drizzle with good quality extra virgin olive oil.

It is important to season lightly with salt and freshly ground pepper after each addition, then again at the end so that every part of the dish is seasoned.

side dishes

Chanterelle Mushrooms with
Roasted Chestnuts and Garlic   116
Corn Cake   116
Braised Curly Endive   117
Gratin of Fresh Greens   117
Fennel Polenta Cake   118
Potato, Cauliflower and Roasted Garlic Purée   118
Whole Grain Pilaf   119
Rhubarb with Red Wine and Rosemary   119

Photo: Chanterelle Mushrooms with Roasted Chestnuts and Garlic

side dishes

Chanterelle Mushrooms with Roasted Chestnuts and Garlic

Serve this dish as an accompaniment to your favourite roast.

A cast iron or other heavy-bottomed pan works well for roasting the chestnuts. With a sharp paring knife score an X in one side of each nut, making sure to cut through the shell and into the flesh itself. Place the nuts in a roasting pan and bake in a preheated 375-400°F oven for 25-30 minutes. Set aside to cool slightly, then peel off the shells and inner skin.

1 lb. fresh chanterelle mushrooms
2 tbsp. unsalted butter
2 tbsp. extra virgin olive oil
2 whole heads fresh garlic, sectioned, peeled and the cloves left whole
6-8 small onions, peeled and cut into 8 wedges each
1 lb. fresh chestnuts
1 c. chicken stock (page 256)
2 tbsp. fresh thyme leaves, coarsely chopped
1 tbsp. fresh chopped rosemary
1/4 c. chopped Italian parsley
salt and ground black pepper to taste

TIP
When buying fresh chestnuts look for unblemished nuts that feel hard when pressed. Any give in the shell indicates age or infestation.

Heat a heavy-bottomed sauté pan on medium high heat and add the butter and olive oil.

Add the mushrooms and cook for 2-3 minutes, turning them over to sear both sides.

Remove the mushrooms from the pan and set aside.

Add a little more butter or oil to the pan if necessary and toss in the garlic cloves and sectioned onions. Stir to prevent burning and cook a few minutes until the garlic begins to brown slightly.

Add the roasted peeled chestnuts, the chicken stock, thyme, rosemary and salt and pepper to taste.

Cover, reduce heat and simmer 10-15 minutes, adding more stock or water if the pan becomes too dry.

Remove the lid and add the mushrooms to the pan.

Heat the mushrooms through, stir in the parsley and season if necessary.

Corn Cake

Serve these tasty cakes as a substitute for the usual rice or potato side. The ingredients can be varied to your own taste. Add crispy fried bacon or pancetta when serving the cakes with a meat dish or some minced jalapeño pepper to add a little spice. Blanched broccoli or cauliflower or any favourite vegetable combination would also work well.

1/3 c. all-purpose flour
2/3 c. yellow cornmeal
1 tsp. baking powder
1/4 tsp. salt
1/4 tsp. freshly ground black pepper
1 c. milk
2 tbsp. extra virgin olive oil
1 egg
3/4 c. fresh or frozen corn kernels
2 tbsp. minced red onion
2 tbsp. minced green onion

In a bowl large enough to hold all the ingredients, combine all the dry ingredients including the salt and pepper.

In a smaller bowl combine the wet ingredients.

Add the wet mixture to the dry and combine with a few strokes using a wooden spoon or rubber spatula.

Grease 8 portions of a regular-sized muffin pan and divide the mixture into them.

Bake at 350°F for 10 minutes. This will produce a soft moist cake. For a firmer texture bake 2-3 minutes longer.

Remove from the pan and serve hot.

Braised Curly Endive

Curly endive is a slightly bitter long-leafed lettuce with distinctive curly green leaves. The pale yellow leaves closer to the centre are a little sweeter than the outside leaves. Endive is a great addition to mixed salads to add variety in taste and texture. It is also very good cooked as a side dish. Cooking removes some of the bitterness.

Heat a medium saucepan. Cut the pancetta into 3/4-inch pieces and add to the pan.

Cook on medium heat until it begins to brown, then add the garlic cloves.

Cook until the pancetta is crisp, remove along with the garlic and set aside.

Remove any large dark green leaves from the outside of the endive, trim the ends and reserve for another use.

Add 1 tbsp. of olive oil to the pan and add the endives cut sides down.

Allow the endives to brown slightly, then turn them. Add the stock or water, a little salt and pepper to taste and cover with a lid. Cook for 10 minutes or until the bases of the endives are tender.

Sliver the anchovies and add to the pan along with the sun-dried tomatoes and honey (if using). Cook 1-2 minutes more, drizzle with balsamic vinegar, top with the grated cheese and serve.

> 2 heads of curly endive, rinsed well, quartered and set aside to drain
> 4 thick slices pancetta or bacon (about 3 oz.)
> 8 large garlic cloves, peeled and halved
> 2 tbsp. extra virgin olive oil
> 1/2 c. chicken or vegetable stock (page 256) or water
> salt and ground black pepper to taste
> 4 salted anchovy fillets, rinsed
> 1/4 c. slivered sun-dried tomatoes
> 1 tbsp. honey (optional)
> 2-3 tbsp. balsamic vinegar
> 2 tbsp. grated Parmigiano Reggiano or Pecorino Romano cheese

Gratin of Fresh Greens

Although any fresh garden greens would be fine cooked in this method, I prefer the hardier types like kale, chard or beet tops. They take a little more time to cook but have much more flavour.

Wash and drain the greens. Trim off the tough ends of the stems and place all the greens in a large pot of boiling salted water.

Stir occasionally and cook until greens are tender, approximately 10-15 minutes. Drain into a colander and set aside until cool enough to handle.

Meanwhile, heat a large sauté pan on medium heat and add the olive oil.

Add the onion and cook a few minutes until soft.

Add the garlic and chili and cook stirring until the garlic begins to soften.

Place the cooked greens on a cutting board and cut roughly into 1- to 2- inch lengths.

Add to the pan and cook 5-10 minutes, stirring until soft and well combined. Stir in grated nutmeg and tomatoes.

Place the greens into an oiled casserole or baking dish.

Combine the bread crumbs and cheese, season with salt and pepper and spread evenly on top of the greens.

Drizzle extra olive oil over the crumbs and bake in a 400°F oven until the crumbs are browned and crispy.

Remove from the oven and serve.

> 2 1/2 lbs. mixed greens (e.g., kale, Swiss chard, spinach)
> 1/3 c. extra virgin olive oil
> 1 medium onion diced
> 6-8 large garlic cloves, peeled and thinly sliced
> 1 small red chili, minced, or 1 dry chili, crumbled
> salt and freshly ground black pepper
> 1 tsp. freshly ground nutmeg
> 2 Roma tomatoes, diced
> 1 c. coarsely chopped fresh white bread crumbs
> 1/4 c. grated Parmigiano Reggiano or Pecorino Romano cheese
> extra olive oil for topping

Fennel Polenta Cake

1 medium-sized fresh fennel bulb
1 small onion
1/4 c. finely diced red bell pepper
2 large garlic cloves
5 tbsp. extra virgin olive oil
2 eggs, separated
1/4 tsp. cream of tartar
1 c. milk
1/4 c. finely ground white cornmeal
1/2 c. sifted all-purpose flour
1/4 tsp. freshly ground nutmeg
1/2 tsp. salt
1/2 tsp. freshly ground black pepper
1/4 c. minced fresh fennel tops
eight 3- to 4-oz. ramekin molds plus
    extra olive oil and cornmeal to coat the
    insides (if you don't have the ramekins
    you can use a muffin pan)

Trim off the top and bottom of the fennel bulb, then cut into quarters lengthwise and lay each piece on the flat. Slice across the grain as thinly as possible. You should have about 1 1/2-2 cups.

Slice the onion in half and slice very thin across the grain.

Peel the garlic and slice very thin.

Heat 2 tbsp. olive oil on medium and add the fennel, pepper and onion.

Cook 1-2 minutes, then add the garlic, 1/4 tsp. salt and 1/4 tsp. pepper.

Cook until all the vegetables are soft, remove from the pan and cool.

Coat the insides of the ramekins with olive oil, then dust with cornmeal and set aside.

Whisk the egg yolks and remaining olive oil to combine, add the milk and set aside.

In a separate bowl combine the cornmeal, sifted flour, nutmeg, remaining salt and pepper and the minced fennel tops and set aside.

In another bowl whisk the egg whites with the cream of tartar until stiff.

Combine the vegetables with the milk mixture, then add it to the flour.

Mix gently with a spoon, then fold in the whipped egg whites, being careful not to overmix. A few lumps and streaks of egg white are fine.

Spoon the mixture into the prepared ramekins or muffin pan.

Place the ramekins in a roasting pan and pour in enough hot water to rise halfway up the sides of the ramekins. Bake at 350°F for 20-25 minutes.

Cool slightly, then lift out and serve as an accompaniment to meat or fish.

Potato, Cauliflower and Roasted Garlic Purée

16 oz. peeled and diced red-skinned
    potatoes
8 oz. cauliflower, roughly chopped
1 tsp. salt
1 tsp. freshly ground black pepper
1 medium head of roasted garlic (page 62)
    removed from its skin and pressed
    into a paste
1/4 tsp. ground saffron threads dissolved
    in 1/4 c. hot water
1/4 c. minced fresh chives
2 tbsp. extra virgin olive oil

Place the potatoes, cauliflower and salt into a pot with just enough water to cover the mixture.

Bring to a boil and cook covered on medium to low heat until tender.

Drain any remaining water and press the mixture through a potato ricer or use a potato masher to purée the mixture. Do not use an electric mixer or food processor, as this will make the mixture gummy.

Return the mixture to the pot and on low heat stir in the ground black pepper, garlic paste, dissolved saffron, chives and olive oil.

Season if necessary and keep warm until ready to serve.

Whole Grain Pilaf

This is a tasty healthy alternative to potatoes or rice that combines well with grilled or roasted meats. The whole grains are available at most health food stores. I've chosen this combination because they all cook in relatively the same time.

Heat a 2-quart sauce pot on medium heat and add the grains.

Stirring frequently to avoid burning, cook the grains until slightly toasted. They will give off a nutty aroma as they toast and will pop slightly.

Remove the grains from the pot and return the pot to the heat.

Add the oil, then the onion, carrot and celery.

Cook stirring for about 30 seconds, then add the garlic and continue to cook 3-4 minutes longer.

Add the toasted grains and stir to coat the grains evenly with oil. Then add the water or stock.

Bring to a low simmer and cook for approximately 45 minutes until the grains begin to get soft.

Season with the salt and pepper and cook 15-20 minutes more until the grains have reached the desired doneness. They will still be slightly firm and chewy when done. If you prefer the grains to have a softer bite continue to cook a few more minutes, adding a little more water or stock to prevent burning.

When done, stir in the butter and chopped herbs, season to taste if necessary and serve.

1/3 c. wheat kernels
1/3 c. rye kernels
1/3 c. kamut kernels
1/3 c. oat kernels
1/3 c. spelt kernels
2 tbsp. vegetable oil
1/2 c. finely minced red onion
1/4 c. diced carrot
1/4 c. diced celery
1 tbsp. minced garlic
4 c. water or stock (meat or vegetable) (page 256)
2 tsp. salt
1-2 tsp. freshly ground black pepper
3 tbsp. unsalted butter (optional)
1/2 c. freshly chopped herbs of choice

Rhubarb with Red Wine and Rosemary

Rhubarb cooks quickly. It can go from firm to soft in a matter of 1-2 minutes. Therefore, a large sauté pan is best for this so that the pieces cook evenly without becoming too soft. Serve this as an accompaniment to grilled or roasted meats, game meats or fowl.

Heat a 12-inch sauté pan on medium and add the oil to coat the bottom.

Add the red onion and garlic and cook stirring for 1-2 minutes until they begin to soften.

Stir in the sugar and stir frequently for 3-4 minutes until the sugar begins to take on a golden colour.

Add the red wine and reduce by half, then add the rhubarb pieces and the rosemary.

Cook at medium to low heat until the rhubarb is tender but still has a little firmness to it.

With a slotted spoon remove the rhubarb to a warm plate and reduce the liquid in the pan until it is syrupy.

Remove the pan from the heat, whisk the cold butter into the pan, season with salt and pepper and pour the sauce over the rhubarb.

1 1/2 lbs. fresh rhubarb cut into 2-inch pieces
2 tbsp. extra virgin olive oil
1 small red onion cut into 1/2-inch dice
4 large garlic cloves, thinly sliced
1/2 c. granulated sugar
1/3 c. medium to full-bodied red wine
six to eight 3-inch long sprigs of fresh rosemary
2 tbsp. cold unsalted butter
salt and freshly ground black pepper to taste

Pasta

An extraordinary variety of shapes are made from this simple dough. There are two basic types of pasta. Fresh pasta is made with eggs and cooks in a few minutes. Dried pasta, usually made without eggs, takes 8-12 minutes to cook, depending on the brand. Both are made with hard (high gluten or protein) wheat flour, or in the case of fresh homemade, can also be made with all-purpose flour.

Northern Italian dishes usually call for fresh flat ribbon-like pasta, which is easy to make at home.

Dishes from the south call for the dried tubular pastas, which are commercially manufactured. Of course there are many exceptions.

Both types are often coloured and flavoured with a variety of herbs, vegetable purées and other concentrated flavours.

Risotto

Risotto is Italy's most famous rice dish. The type of rice used is crucial to a good finished product. Italy grows the best rice for risotto, the three main varieties being Arborio, Carnaroli and Vialoni Nano. All of these are short-grain, high-starch rices, the starch contributing to the creamy texture of the finished risotto. Arborio is usually the easiest to find, but you can use any of these three in risotto recipes. Always look for fine or superfine on the label when buying rice for risotto.

All risotto is basically made in the same manner. In a pot or pan, the rice is coated with butter or oil, then simmering stock is added to cover and the rice is stirred until the stock has been absorbed. More stock is added a ladle at a time until the rice is cooked, 18-20 minutes from start.

Risotto can be flavoured with an endless variety of ingredients and can be served as a light starter course or, with the addition of meats or fish, can also be a substantial meal.

The final risotto is always finished with butter or oil for its unique creamy texture.

pasta & risotto

Ricotta Lemon Ravioli with Mascarpone Lemon Cream 122

Penne with Sausage and Roasted Eggplant 123

Squash and Sage Agnolotti with Brown Butter Walnut Sauce 125

Squash and Sage Filling 125

Smoked Chicken Ravioli with Cilantro Pumpkin Seed Pesto 126

Molded Chicken Cannelloni "Stack" 129

Egg Noodles with Tomato and Fresh Herbs 130

Fresh Egg Pasta 130

Apple, Rosemary and Sage Risotto 131

Swiss Chard Risotto 131

Wild Mushroom Risotto 133

Mussel Risotto 133

Polenta with Parmesan and Fresh Herbs 135

Couscous with Roasted Garlic and Pine Nuts 135

Gnocchi 136

Using a Home-Style Pasta Rolling Machine

Homemade fresh pasta is traditionally rolled by hand with a rolling pin, which can be a challenge. Home-style pasta rolling machines that either clamp to the edge of your counter or come as attachments to electric mixers make things go much quicker.

After making the dough, let it rest. Cut the dough and work with one piece at a time.

Begin at the widest setting for the machine. Flatten the piece of dough enough to fit between the rollers. Crank the dough through, fold in half and crank through again.

Repeat the folding and rolling one more time.

Adjust the machine to the next setting and roll the dough through. Continue rolling the dough through, adjusting the setting each time until you have reached the desired thickness for the particular pasta noodles you are making.

Photo: Ricotta Lemon Ravioli with Mascarpone Lemon Cream

pasta & risotto

Ricotta Lemon Ravioli with Mascarpone Lemon Cream

The preserved lemon adds an intense lemon flavour to the otherwise traditional flavours combined in this tasty first course.

For the ravioli

half recipe Fresh Egg Pasta (page 130)
2 egg yolks
1 c. ricotta cheese
1/4 c. grated Parmigiano Reggiano cheese
1/2 c. minced Preserved Lemons (page 250)
1/4 c. minced Italian parsley
salt and freshly ground black pepper
1 egg white, whisked with 1 tbsp. water
2 garlic cloves, peeled and thinly sliced
10 oz. fresh tender greens such as
    spinach, Swiss chard or arugula
2 tbsp. extra virgin olive oil
1/2 c. toasted pine nuts
1/4 c. dark raisins
1/4 c. sun-dried tomatoes, slivered
Parmesan Crisps (page 255) to garnish

For the mascarpone lemon cream

1/2 c. mascarpone cheese
3/4 c. heavy cream
1/3 c. dry white wine
salt and freshly ground black pepper
    to taste

For the ravioli

Make the Fresh Egg Pasta and set aside, covered.

Combine the egg yolks, ricotta, Parmigiano Reggiano, 1/4 cup Preserved Lemon, parsley and salt and pepper to taste.

Divide the dough into four pieces.

Working with one sheet at a time, roll the dough to 1/16-inch thick (usually the third smallest setting on a pasta machine). On a well-floured board, cut out sixteen 21/4-inch circles with a round cutter.

Moisten half the circles with some of the whisked egg white and place 1 tbsp. filling in the centre.

Top with one of the remaining circles and press to seal, making sure to push out as much air as possible.

Using the top of a 11/2-inch cutter gently press around the filling to create an even mound, then with a fork dipped in flour press gently all around to ensure a good seal. Place on a well-floured board or clean towel while finishing the rest.

Repeat with the rest of the dough and filling, re-rolling any trims of dough.

Cook in plenty of salted boiling water 2-3 minutes.

For the mascarpone lemon cream

Combine all ingredients plus remaining Preserved Lemons in a saucepan and whisk smooth. Heat to a simmer and set aside, keeping warm.

To serve

Heat the 2 tbsp. olive oil with the sliced garlic on medium heat until the garlic begins to colour. Add the greens and cook until wilted.

Season with salt and pepper and add the raisins and pine nuts.

Place a small mound of greens in the centre of each serving plate and top with a cooked ravioli.

Spoon sauce over and around the ravioli and top with a Parmesan Crisp. Scatter a few slivers of sun-dried tomatoes in the sauce and serve.

Penne with Sausage and Roasted Eggplant

Penne is a tubular pasta named after the Italian word for feathers due to its pointed ends. It comes either smooth or "rigate," with lines on it. Either will work in this recipe.

Slice the eggplant, salt it quite liberally and arrange it in layers in a colander. Cover the eggplant with a plate and weigh it down with a heavy can or bottle. Leave it for several hours to drain the juices, then rinse well and dry.

Place on a baking sheet and coat with 1/4 cup of the oil. Roast in a 375-400°F oven until tender. Cool slightly, cut into 1/2-inch strips and set aside.

Heat 1/4 cup olive oil in a 10- to 12-inch skillet and add the sausage. Cook until the sausage begins to brown and add the chili, onion and garlic. Stir and cook 1-2 minutes until the onion has softened.

Add the tomatoes, tomato paste and wine. Stir together and simmer for 10-15 minutes.

Add the reserved eggplant, basil and oregano and heat through. Season to taste.

In a large warmed serving bowl combine the sauce with the cooked hot noodles and the grated cheese and serve.

1 medium eggplant
plenty of salt
1/2 c. extra virgin olive oil
10-12 oz. Italian sausage cut into
  1/2-inch slices
1 tbsp. chili flakes
1 small onion, diced
4 garlic cloves sliced thin
2 c. whole peeled plum tomatoes
2 tbsp. tomato paste
1/2 c. dry red wine
1/2 c. torn fresh basil
2 tbsp. chopped fresh oregano
salt and ground black pepper to taste
1/2 c. grated Parmigiano Reggiano cheese
1 lb. penne noodles, cooked

Squash and Sage Agnolotti with Brown Butter Walnut Sauce

Agnolotti is a northern Italian name for ravioli and it is usually a half-moon shape. The finished agnolotti can be frozen and bagged for a later use.

Divide the pasta dough into six pieces. Working with one piece at a time roll out the dough to desired thickness.

On a well-floured board cut out circles using a 2-inch round cutter.

Brush a little egg onto half the circle and place a teaspoon of filling in the centre.

Fold in half and press firmly between two fingers to seal, making sure to press out as much air as possible. To ensure a good seal press the edges with a fork dipped in flour.

Place the finished agnolotti on a well-floured board or kitchen cloth. Repeat with the rest of the dough and filling, gathering up and re-rolling the trims.

To cook the agnolotti bring a large pot of water to a boil. Add salt to taste and cook the agnolotti for 3-4 minutes or until they float and are tender. Drain well and toss gently in Brown Butter Walnut Sauce.

1 recipe basic Fresh Egg Pasta (page 130)
1 recipe Squash and Sage Filling (below)
1 egg beaten with 1 tbsp. water

For the Brown Butter Walnut Sauce

In a large saucepan melt 6 oz. of the butter on medium heat. As the butter begins to brown slightly, swirl the pan to colour evenly.

When the butter has browned more and gives off a nutty aroma, add the walnuts and toast slightly. Remove from the heat and allow to cool slightly, then slowly add the wine and lemon juice.

Increase heat and reduce the sauce by about 1/4, then add the chopped sage. Cook 30 seconds, then swirl in the remaining cold butter only until melted through and the sauce has thickened slightly.

Add the cooked agnolotti and toss gently. Serve with extra grated cheese.

For the Brown Butter Walnut Sauce
6 oz. (3/4 c.) cold unsalted butter, plus 4 tbsp.
1 c. coarsely chopped walnuts
1/3 c. dry white wine
1 tbsp. fresh lemon juice or to taste
1/4 c. chopped fresh sage

Squash and Sage Filling

For this pasta filling choose a firm textured winter squash with a low moisture content. This will produce a firmer filling with a more pronounced flavour and will be easier to work with.

Heat the olive oil in a wide sauté pan on medium to high heat and add the squash and onion.

Cook stirring until the squash begins to soften, then add the garlic and a little salt and ground pepper. Continue to cook until the squash is tender, stirring frequently to prevent sticking.

Add the sage and cook 3-4 minutes more. Remove from the heat and stir in the nutmeg, cheese and bread crumbs.

Mash the mixture with a fork until well combined. If the mixture seems a little wet, add more bread crumbs and/or cheese to firm it. Season to taste and set aside to cool.

Use this filling for a variety of filled pastas.

2 tbsp. extra virgin olive oil
4 c. peeled, diced winter squash, e.g., acorn, hubbard, butternut
1/2 c. minced onion
1 tbsp. minced fresh garlic
1 tsp. salt
1 tsp. freshly ground black pepper
3 tbsp. chopped fresh sage
3 tbsp. grated Asiago or Parmigiano Reggiano cheese
1/4 tsp. grated nutmeg
approximately 1/3 c. dry white bread crumbs

Smoked Chicken Ravioli with Cilantro Pumpkin Seed Pesto

Pesto is the Italian word for sauce or paste. Most of us are familiar with the famous basil and garlic version from Liguria, but almost any ingredient can be used to make your own version of this sauce.

1 tbsp. extra virgin olive oil

1/4 c. minced onion

6 oz. fresh spinach, rinsed and dried

1 tbsp. minced fresh garlic

1/2 tsp. salt

1/2 tsp. freshly ground black pepper

4 oz. finely minced smoked chicken (page 257)

1/3 c. ricotta cheese

1/4 c. freshly grated Pecorino Romano

1/4 c. freshly grated Parmigiano Reggiano

half recipe Fresh Egg Pasta using two eggs and 1 1/2 c. flour (page 130)

1 recipe Cilantro Pumpkin Seed Pesto (page 252)

2 c. well-flavoured chicken broth (page 256)

1/4 c. peeled, seeded and finely diced tomato

cilantro leaves for garnish

For the filling

Heat a sauté pan on medium and add the olive oil and minced onion.

Cook 1-2 minutes until the onion begins to soften then add the spinach leaves, garlic, salt and pepper. Turn the mixture over in the pan until the spinach is completely wilted and any moisture has evaporated.

Turn the mixture out onto a clean cutting board, cool slightly and chop fine.

Place the mixture in a bowl, add the chicken and the three cheeses and chill.

For the ravioli

Make the pasta.

Divide it into four pieces. Roll two pieces into sheets and keep the other two covered while you work.

Lay one sheet on a work surface.

Space two rows of teaspoon-sized mounds of filling 2 inches apart, the full length of the pasta sheet.

Brush lightly with water in between the mounds and along both edges.

Place the second sheet on top and working quickly, press down between the mounds to seal, forcing out as much air as possible.

With a sharp knife or ravioli cutter separate the individual ravioli, seal the edges with a floured fork and place onto a floured tray. Re-roll any pasta trims to make more ravioli until all the filling has been used.

To finish

Bring a large pot of well-salted water to a boil. Add the ravioli and stir gently to avoid sticking. Cook 3-4 minutes or until the ravioli float.

Meanwhile heat the chicken broth and add the diced tomato. Season to taste.

Serve 3-4 ravioli in a bowl with some of the broth and 1-2 tbsp. of the pesto. Garnish with cilantro leaves and extra grated cheese if desired.

Molded Chicken Cannelloni "Stack"

This filling calls for the dark meat from the chicken. I find it to be more moist and flavourful than the breast. If ground dark meat is not available, it can be easily made by grinding deboned chicken thighs in a food processor at home. You can also substitute turkey, veal or pork. The filling and pasta are traditional with a slightly different presentation.

For the filling

Heat the olive oil in a medium sauté pan and add the minced onion. Cook until soft but not browned, then add the minced garlic and chili flakes. Cook stirring for 30 seconds. Add the ground chicken and cook until the meat is no longer pink.

Add the chopped spinach, stir to combine and cook 3-4 minutes until the excess moisture has cooked out. Remove from the heat, place the mixture in a bowl and cool to room temperature. Stir in 1/4 cup Parmigiano Reggiano, 1/4 cup Pecorino Romano, the ricotta cheese, the nutmeg and salt and pepper.

Taste for seasoning and adjust if necessary. Add the eggs and set aside to cool in the refrigerator.

For the pasta

Divide the pasta dough into 3 pieces and roll each one into a sheet of medium thickness. Cut 2 sheets into 8 pieces and blanch 3-4 at a time in plenty of boiling salted water for 15 seconds. Rinse in cold water and cool on a clean kitchen towel. Cut the remaining sheet into 3 pieces and blanch as above.

To assemble

Line the mold with parchment paper cut large enough to fold over and cover the top once it is filled. Ladle enough tomato sauce in to just cover the bottom of the mold.

Lay the 3 longer pieces of blanched pasta inside the mold, leaving the excess for overhang. These pieces will eventually encase the filled cannelloni. Ladle a little more sauce in and spread to coat the pasta.

Lay one of the shorter pieces on a flat work surface. Place 1 soup spoon full of the cooled filling on the edge closest to you and roll the pasta into a cylinder. Make sure you get filling in the entire length of the cannelloni. Place the cannelloni at one end of the mold on the sauce layer.

Repeat and continue to place the rolled cannelloni end to end in the mold until you have a complete layer, with no spaces. Ladle a little more of the tomato sauce on top of the first layer, then repeat with the rest of the ingredients until the mold is full.

Top with a layer of tomato sauce, then the remaining Parmigiano Reggiano and Pecorino Romano cheeses. Fold the overhanging pasta over the top to enclose the cannelloni. Fold the extra parchment paper over the top. Cover with aluminum foil and bake the mold in a preheated 375°F oven for 45 minutes.

Remove from the oven and cool 5-10 minutes before unmolding. While the mold is cooling pass the remaining tomato sauce through a sieve or food mill and heat.

To serve the cannelloni, turn the mold over onto a cutting board. Remove the parchment paper and slice into 8 portions. Ladle the remaining tomato sauce onto 8 plates. Place a portion of cannelloni on top of the sauce and sprinkle with extra grated cheese. Garnish with Parmesan Crisps.

For the filling
2 tbsp. extra virgin olive oil
1/4 c. minced onion
1 tbsp. minced garlic
1/4 tsp. red chili flakes
10 oz. ground chicken, preferably dark meat
10 oz. fresh spinach, blanched, cooled in ice water, squeezed dry and chopped
1/3 c. freshly grated Parmigiano Reggiano cheese
1/3 c. freshly grated Pecorino Romano cheese
3/4 c. ricotta cheese
1/4 tsp. grated nutmeg
salt and ground black pepper to taste
2 eggs

For the cannelloni
half recipe Fresh Egg Pasta (page 130)
1 recipe Basic Tomato Sauce (page 251)

For the assembly
15 x 2 1/2 inch half-round ovenproof mold
parchment paper to line the mold
Parmesan Crisps (page 255) to garnish

Egg Noodles with Tomato and Fresh Herbs

A simple accompaniment to grilled prawns, fish or poultry.

half recipe of Fresh Egg Pasta (recipe
   below), cut into thin spaghetti
1/4 c. extra virgin olive oil
3 large garlic cloves, sliced very thin
1 c. diced fresh ripe tomatoes
3 tbsp. freshly chopped Italian parsley
2 tbsp. freshly chopped mint
4 tbsp. butter
salt and freshly ground black pepper
   to taste
freshly grated parmesan cheese (optional)

Have ready a large pot of well-salted water at a low boil.

In a sauté pan large enough to toss the cooked pasta heat the olive oil and garlic on medium heat until the garlic begins to take on a faint golden colour.

Bring the water to a rolling boil and add the fresh egg noodles.

Add the tomatoes and herbs to the garlic oil and toss to heat the tomatoes through.

Strain the pasta (the fresh pasta cooks in 1-2 minutes) and add it to the pan along with the butter and toss to combine.

Season with salt and black pepper and serve immediately.

Fresh Egg Pasta

See tips on using a home-style pasta rolling machine on page 120.

2 1/2 c. all-purpose flour
3 large eggs
1 tbsp. extra virgin olive oil

Place the flour on a work surface and make a well in the centre.

Break the eggs into the well and add the olive oil.

With a fork, beat the eggs and oil, then incorporate the flour a little at a time, being careful not to let the egg run out of the well.

When a rough dough has formed, knead it until you have a smooth firm dough. You may not need all the flour.

Form the dough into a ball. Rub the top with a little extra olive oil and cover. Let it rest for about 10 minutes.

Prepare the pasta machine by dusting the rollers with flour and setting them at their widest setting (see page 120).

Divide the dough into 6 pieces. Working with one piece at a time, flatten the dough and begin running it through the machine, folding in half each time, three times in total. After the third time run the pasta through successively smaller openings one time each until you have the desired thickness.

Use right away for lasagna, ravioli or cannelloni or allow to dry about 10 minutes before cutting into noodles.

Apple, Rosemary and Sage Risotto

A good accompaniment to roasted meats, especially pork and pork sausage.

Heat a 10- to 12-inch sauté pan on medium low and add the diced bacon.

Cook stirring until the bacon pieces begin to get crispy, then remove with a slotted spoon and set aside.

Pour off all but 2 tbsp. of the bacon fat and add the butter, then the onion, celery and the apple. Cook stirring for 1 minute.

Add the rice and continue to stir 1-2 minutes.

Add the wine and brandy and cook stirring until the liquid has evaporated.

Add the hot stock ½ cup at a time to just cover the rice.

Season with salt and ground black pepper.

Continue to stir and add more stock as it reduces.

After about 15 minutes add the roasted garlic paste, herbs and cream and continue to cook for 2-3 minutes.

Stir in the rest of the butter and parmesan cheese, season if necessary and turn off the heat.

Cover and allow to rest 2-3 minutes before serving.

Note: Apples vary in flavour and tartness throughout the season. If you are using early season apples that may be a little too tart, try adding 1-2 tsp. honey near the end of the cooking. This will help balance the flavour.

3 oz. smoked bacon, diced

6 tbsp. unsalted butter

1 small onion, finely diced

1 celery stick, finely diced

2 firm tart apples, peeled, cored, diced and tossed with 2 tbsp. fresh lemon juice (about 1½ c.)

2 c. arborio rice

¾ c. dry white wine

¼ c. Calvados (apple brandy) (optional)

5-6 c. hot chicken or vegetable stock (page 256)

2 heads roasted garlic, pressed into a paste (page 62)

3 tbsp. fresh chopped rosemary leaves

3 tbsp. slivered fresh sage leaves

¼ c. heavy cream

½ c. grated parmesan cheese

salt and freshly ground black pepper to taste

Swiss Chard Risotto

In a saucepan, bring the stock to a simmer and keep hot.

In a 12-inch sauté pan warm the oil and add the onions, garlic and anchovies. Fry gently for 2-3 minutes, stirring to dissolve the anchovy.

Add the rice and stir to combine, coating the rice with the oil and toasting it slightly, then stir in enough stock to cover the rice, stirring continuously.

As the liquid is absorbed by the rice, keep adding more stock a ladle at a time to keep the rice moist.

When the rice is almost cooked, add the chopped Swiss chard and cook 5 minutes longer.

Remove the pan from the heat, stir in the parmesan cheese, 2 tbsp. unsalted butter and the parsley.

Season to taste with salt and pepper and serve with extra grated cheese on the side.

6 c. chicken stock (page 256)

4 tbsp. extra virgin olive oil

1 small onion, finely diced

1 tbsp. minced garlic

2 anchovy fillets

2 c. arborio rice

1 lb. Swiss chard, washed, blanched and roughly chopped

¾ c. freshly grated Parmigiano Reggiano

2 tbsp. unsalted butter

¼ c. chopped parsley

salt and freshly ground black pepper

Wild Mushroom Risotto

photo, left

Heat a 10- to 12-inch heavy-bottomed skillet on medium heat and add 2 tbsp. of the olive oil.

Add the mushrooms, cook approximately 1 minute or until just cooked through then remove from the pan and set aside.

Add the remaining 2 tbsp. olive oil and then the vegetables and cook stirring 1 minute.

Add the rice and stir to coat with the oil. Cook stirring until slightly toasted. Add the white wine, stirring until it has been absorbed.

Add enough stock to cover the rice and simmer on low heat until the stock is almost absorbed, stirring frequently.

Continue to add stock 1/2 cup at a time until all the stock is absorbed and the rice is tender, but still a little firm in the centre.

Stir in the roasted garlic paste, butter, cheese and parsley.

Taste for seasoning and serve with extra grated cheese on the side.

1/4 c. extra virgin olive oil

4 oz. dried wild mushrooms, reconstituted and thinly sliced or 12 oz. fresh mushrooms, sliced

1 small onion, finely diced

1 celery stick, finely diced

1 medium carrot, finely diced

3/4 c. dry white wine

2 c. arborio rice

5 c. hot chicken stock (page 256)

1 head of roasted garlic, pressed into a paste (page 62)

2 tbsp. unsalted butter

1/2 c. grated Pecorino Romano, Asiago or Parmigiano Reggiano cheese

2 tbsp. chopped Italian parsley

salt and freshly ground black pepper to taste

Mussel Risotto

Due to the natural salt content in mussels and clams, I recommend tasting the risotto before adding any extra salt.

Wash and debeard the mussels. Place in a large pot, add 1/2 cup of the white wine, cover and steam on high heat approximately 4-5 minutes, tossing once or twice, until the shells open.

Remove from heat, cool slightly and remove the meat from the shells, discarding any that did not open. Strain and reserve the liquid.

Heat the olive oil in a large sauté pan and add the vegetables.

Cook for 1 minute and add the garlic and anchovies, cooking for 1 minute more.

Add the rice and stir to coat with the oil; cook until slightly toasted.

Add the rest of the wine and allow it to almost cook away, then add hot stock and the reserved liquid to cover the rice. Add salt and pepper.

Simmer on low, stirring frequently, and adding more stock a ladle at a time as it evaporates and is absorbed.

After 16-18 minutes, when the rice is almost tender, add the mussels, lemon zest and orange zest.

Cook 1 minute and stir in the butter, parsley and cream (if using).

Re-season if necessary and serve.

2 1/2 lbs. fresh mussels

1 c. dry white wine

1/4 c. extra virgin olive oil

1 small onion, finely diced

1 stick celery, finely diced

1 medium carrot, finely diced

2 large garlic cloves, thinly sliced

2 anchovy fillets, rinsed and minced

2 c. arborio rice (Italian short grain)

5 c. hot fish stock (page 256)

1/2 tsp. salt

1/2 tsp. freshly ground pepper

1 tbsp. fresh lemon zest

1 tbsp. fresh orange zest

2 tbsp. butter

1/4 c. fresh chopped parsley

2-4 tbsp. heavy cream (optional)

Polenta with Parmesan and Fresh Herbs

Traditionally polenta is served plain with a tomato/meat sauce and grated cheese on the side for diners to help themselves. The herbs give it extra flavour. Diced vegetables also make a nice addition.

The consistency of polenta varies from cook to cook. This is a firm version. For a soft polenta, add up to 2 cups more water.

Bring the water to a boil in a large pot and add the salt and pepper.

While whisking, pour the cornmeal into the boiling water in a steady fine stream.

Lower the heat and continue to whisk the mixture smooth.

Switch to a wooden spoon if the mixture becomes too thick. Stir occasionally for 15-20 minutes more until the mixture begins to pull away from the sides of the pot.

Stir in the chopped herbs, cheese and butter and cook a few more minutes.

Portion the polenta onto individual plates, or as my mother would do, spread the polenta out on a serving board using a wet knife or spatula.

Place the board in the centre of the table and when the polenta has cooled slightly and firmed up, let individuals cut the portion they would like. Serve with a tomato/meat sauce on the side with extra grated cheese.

To bake or grill the polenta

When it is finished cooking, spread the polenta on a baking tray or other flat surface and allow to cool.

When it is firm, cut into desired shapes. Oil a heated pan and sear the polenta on both sides, or oil the polenta and place on a well-oiled grill for 2-3 minutes each side. Place in a hot oven to finish heating through.

Ingredients
12 oz. (2 c.) yellow cornmeal
5^1/$_2$ c. water
2 tsp. salt
1 tsp. freshly ground black pepper
^{1}/$_2$ c. grated parmesan cheese
2 tbsp. chopped Italian parsley
2 tbsp. chopped fresh oregano
2 tbsp. chopped fresh basil
3 tbsp. unsalted butter

Couscous with Roasted Garlic and Pine Nuts

A quick side dish when in a pinch or if you are looking for something a little different. Couscous is made from semolina wheat and it looks like a grain. Traditionally, it is soaked in cold water, then steamed in stages for up to 1 hour. Instant couscous, which has already been steamed and dried, takes just 5 minutes to cook.

Bring the water or stock and salt to a boil in a 3- to 4-quart saucepan.

Add the rest of the ingredients and stir to combine.

Cover with a tight-fitting lid and remove from the heat.

Set aside for 5 minutes.

Remove the lid, fluff the couscous with a fork and drizzle with a little more olive oil.

Re-season if necessary and serve.

Ingredients
1^1/$_4$ c. water or stock (page 256)
1 c. instant couscous
1 tsp. salt
^{1}/$_2$ tsp. freshly ground black pepper
^{1}/$_2$ c. toasted pine nuts
6-8 roasted garlic cloves, peeled and pressed into a paste (page 62)
2-3 tbsp. capers, rinsed and drained
^{1}/$_3$ c. chopped fresh tomatoes
^{1}/$_2$ c. fresh chopped Italian parsley
2 tbsp. extra virgin olive oil

Gnocchi

Gnocchi are little pillow-shaped potato dumplings. They require an experienced hand to get them just right so you may have to experiment with them a few times. If too much flour is added they will be tough, and if too much potato is used they will fall apart. They should be tender but keep their shape.

The gnocchi are shaped in a number of different ways depending on the cook. All the methods are designed to hold more sauce. One way is to make an indentation in the gnocchi with a floured thumb. Another is to press and roll the individual gnocchi off the back of a fork to create lines that will hold sauce. Yet another way is to roll the gnocchi off a specially made wooden paddle that has a series of lines cut into it.

2 lb. potatoes
1 egg
12 oz. (2-2 1/4 c.) all-purpose flour

Boil the potatoes with the skin on. Peel and purée them while still hot. (Do not use a food processor for this; it will make them pasty.) A potato ricer or a good old-fashioned masher both work well.

Gently knead the potatoes with the egg and flour on a lightly floured board until the dough is well mixed and smooth.

Roll pieces of the dough into ropes about 3/4 inch in diameter.

Cut these ropes into 3/4- to 1-inch segments.

Dust the segments with flour and roll each one on the concave side of a fork, pressing with your thumb in a quick flicking motion. They should have an indentation on one side and the imprint of the fork on the other.

Keep the gnocchi separate from each other on a floured tray or board.

In a large pot of boiling salted water, add the gnocchi a few at a time and cook only until they float, about 2-3 minutes.

Lift out the gnocchi with a slotted spoon and place in a serving bowl.

Toss with the sauce of your choice* and serve immediately.

*Recommended sauces include Basic Tomato Sauce (page 251), Gorgonzola Walnut Cream (page 251) and Basil or Arugula Pesto (page 252).

Sorbetti and Graniti

These flavoured ices are intended to be served as an intermezzo or middle course. The purpose is to provide a refreshing, cleansing break before the main course.

The basic difference between sorbetto and granita is the proportion of sugar with sorbetto having up to 2-3 times the amount as the granita. This difference gives the sorbetto a much smoother, softer consistency while the granita is more coarse or granular with larger ice crystals.

All the recipes are a balance of sweet and acid, the acid being from citrus juice and/or dry white wine.

Both the sorbetto and granita should be slightly tart to the palate, leaving a clean crisp finish without any lingering sweetness.

Some can be used as part or all of a dessert, especially when accompanied by fresh fruit or berries.

For a sweeter finish, the sugar and acid balance can be adjusted to personal taste.

Many flavours can be used to substitute the ingredients called for. Slightly tart fruits and berries work best, but for a dessert sorbetto or granita try experimenting with sweeter, less acidic flavourings.

sorbetti & graniti

Making Sorbetti and Graniti	140
Fresh Fig Sorbetto	140
Lemon Sorbetto	141
Kiwi Sorbetto	141
Sparkling Wine Sorbetto	141
Vermouth and Cucumber Sorbetto	143
Green Apple and Honey Sorbetto	143
Quince and Pineapple Sage Granita	143
Rhubarb Lemon-Thyme Granita	144
Tomato Rosemary Granita	144
Gummi Berry Sorbetto	144

Photo: Fresh Fig Sorbetto

sorbetti & graniti

Making Sorbetti and Graniti

Sorbetti and graniti can be frozen in an ice cream maker following the manufacturer's instructions. They can also be made in a shallow tray or bowl.

Pour the mixture into the container and place in the freezer.

When the edges freeze (after 20-30 minutes depending on the freezer), scrape the sides and stir the ice crystals into the liquid portion.

Repeat every 20 minutes or so until you have a uniform semi-frozen mixture. This will take approximately 2-4 hours, depending on your freezer.

Allow to freeze completely, then transfer to a container and cover. Keep frozen until needed.

If the sorbetto or granita is too hard to scoop, let it sit in the refrigerator for 30-45 minutes before serving.

Fresh Fig Sorbetto

photo, page 139

2¹/4 c. water
10 oz. (1²/3 c.) granulated sugar
16 oz. fresh or frozen figs (substitute
    cherries, raspberries or a combination)
juice and finely minced zest of
    1¹/2 lemons* (about ¹/4 c. plus 1 tbsp.)
zest of 1 orange, finely minced

Place the water, sugar and figs in a pot and bring to a simmer.

Cook until the figs are soft and the sugar has dissolved.

Purée the fruit and if necessary pass it through a fine sieve. Place in a bowl.

Add the lemon juice, zest and orange zest.

Freeze according to the directions above.

* You may use more or less lemon juice depending on your preference and the sweetness of the fruit.

Lemon Sorbetto

Combine the sugar, water and minced lemon zest and bring to a simmer.

Simmer until the sugar has dissolved, then pour the mixture into a bowl and chill thoroughly.

Add the lemon juice and fold in the whipped egg whites.

Freeze according to the directions above.

Variation

To make Lemon Mint Sorbetto add 3 cups coarsely chopped fresh mint to the sugar and water. Simmer for 5 minutes, remove from heat and steep 5 minutes. Strain the mixture into a bowl and chill thoroughly.

Add the lemon juice and lemon zest, and fold in the whipped egg whites.

Freeze according to the directions on page 140.

14 oz. (2^1/$_3$ c.) sugar
2 c. water
finely minced zest of 3 lemons
3/4 c. fresh lemon juice
2 egg whites, whipped stiff but not dry

Kiwi Sorbetto

Kiwi fruit, also known as a Chinese gooseberry, is rich in vitamin C. This fruit keeps well stored at a cool temperature but matures quickly at room temperature. When kiwis become a little too soft for eating, I just freeze them until I have enough to make this sorbetto.

Place the sugar and water in a pot and bring to a simmer, stirring to dissolve the sugar.

Pour into a bowl and cool.

Purée the fruit and if necessary pass it through a fine sieve into a bowl.

Add the lemon juice, the zest and cooled sugar syrup.

Freeze according to the directions on page 140.

10 oz. (1^2/$_3$ c.) granulated sugar
2 c. water
16 oz. peeled kiwi (8-10 kiwi)
juice and finely minced zest of 2 lemons*
    (about 1/4 c. plus 1 tbsp.)

* You may use more or less lemon juice depending on your preference and the sweetness of the fruit.

Sparkling Wine Sorbetto

Combine the sugar and water and bring to a low simmer.

Simmer until the sugar has dissolved, pour the mixture into a bowl and chill thoroughly.

Add the lemon juice and sparkling wine, then fold in the whipped egg whites.

Freeze according to the directions on page 140.

8 oz. (1^1/$_3$ c.) granulated sugar
1 c. water
2 tbsp. fresh lemon juice
1^1/$_2$ c. sparkling wine
2 egg whites, whipped stiff but not dry

Vermouth and Cucumber Sorbet

photo, top left

Place the water, sugar, cucumber and lemon zest in a pot and bring to a simmer.

Cook until the cucumber has softened and the sugar has dissolved.

Strain the mixture through a fine sieve and set aside approximately half of it.

Place the remaining cucumber mixture in a blender or food processor, purée with approximately half of the liquid, then combine with the reserved cucumber mixture and the rest of the liquid.

Add the lemon juice, rice vinegar and vermouth. You can adjust the flavour to individual taste by adding more lemon, vinegar or vermouth.

Cool completely and freeze according to the directions on page 140.

1 c. water

1 oz. (2 tbsp.) granulated sugar

8 oz. cucumber, peeled, seeded and diced (about 1/2 long English cucumber)

juice and grated zest of 1 lemon

1 tbsp. rice vinegar

2 tbsp. dry white vermouth

Green Apple and Honey Sorbetto

photo, top right

The first honey crop of the season just happens to coincide with the earliest apples of the season. If you cannot get underripe apples, a Granny Smith would be a good substitute.

Place the sugar, honey and apples in a pan with 2 cups water.

Bring to a boil and simmer 5 minutes, or until the apples are tender, then remove from the heat, pour into a bowl and cool slightly.

Purée the mixture and if necessary pass it through a fine sieve.

Stir in the lemon juice and zest.

Cool completely and freeze according to the directions on page 140.

8 oz. (1 1/3 c.) granulated sugar

8 oz. honey

2 c. water

10 oz. peeled, cored and diced tart, slightly underripe apples (2-3 medium-sized apples)

juice and finely minced zest of 1 1/2 lemons (about 1/4 c. plus 1 tbsp.)

Quince and Pineapple Sage Granita

photo, bottom

Over medium heat, combine the water, sugar and diced quince.

Bring to a simmer and cook until the quince is completely soft.

Purée the mixture in a blender or food processor and strain through a fine sieve.

Pour into a shallow pan or wide bowl and cool slightly.

Add the ginger juice, lemon juice, white wine and then the chopped pineapple sage.

Stir to combine and freeze according to the directions on page 140.

2 1/2 c. water

5 oz. (2/3 c. plus 2 tbsp.) granulated sugar

2 1/2-3 c. diced fresh quince (2-3 medium quince)

1 tbsp. ginger juice*

3 tbsp. fresh lemon juice

1/4 c. dry white wine

3 tbsp. chopped fresh pineapple sage

* To make ginger juice

Process approximately 4 oz. of fresh ginger with 2-3 tbsp. water in a food processor until very fine.

Line a fine sieve with cheesecloth and squeeze the juice through it into a small bowl.

Rhubarb Lemon-Thyme Granita

photo, top left

2 c. water

5 oz. (2/3 c. plus 2 tbsp.) granulated
    sugar

1 tbsp. ginger juice*

8 oz. diced rhubarb, cooked and puréed

2 tbsp. chopped fresh lemon thyme

2 tbsp. fresh lemon juice

1/4 c. dry white wine

Over medium heat, dissolve sugar in water. Pour into a mixing bowl and cool.

Add the ginger juice, rhubarb purée, thyme, lemon juice and wine.

Cool the mixture completely and freeze according to the directions on page 140.

* To make ginger juice, see page 143.

Tomato Rosemary Granita

photo, top right

Try this one with a variety of tomatoes. I like to include different colours, especially in summer when there is an abundance of tomatoes. Tomatoes can also be frozen to be used at a later time. Also experiment with different herbs.

5 oz. (2/3 c. plus 2 tbsp.) granulated
    sugar

2 tbsp. finely minced fresh rosemary

1 3/4 c. water

juice of 2 large lemons (approximately
    1/3 c. of juice)

1/4 c. dry vermouth

1/4 c. white wine

6 fresh ripe tomatoes, halved, seeded
    and puréed

Combine the sugar, rosemary and water in a saucepan, heat until sugar dissolves.

Pour into a stainless bowl or shallow baking pan and cool.

Stir in the rest of the ingredients and cool completely.

Freeze according to the directions on page 140.

Gummi Berry Sorbetto

photo, bottom

Gummi berries, pronounced "goomee" and called crugnali in Italian, are another hand-me-down fruit from my father's garden. Gummi berries are native to Asia and China, and also grow wild in Italy. They grow on a large bush that if given space can grow into a medium-sized tree.

The fruit grows on a stem like a cherry and is oblong in shape, very similar to a jelly bean. The flavour is unique in its tartness, being quite astringent even when fully ripe, with hints of cherry and raspberry.

2 1/4 c. water

14 oz. (2 1/3 c.) granulated sugar

14 oz. gummi berries (substitute cherries,
    raspberries or a combination)

juice and finely minced zest of
    1 1/2 lemons (about 1/4 c. plus 1 tbsp.)

zest of 1 orange, finely minced

Place the water, sugar and berries in a pot and bring to a simmer.

Cook until the berries are soft and the sugar has dissolved.

Purée the fruit and if necessary pass it through a fine sieve into a bowl.

Add the lemon juice, zest and orange zest.

Cool completely and freeze according to the directions on page 140.

Crab and Shellfish

We are truly blessed here on the west coast of North America. We have access to some of the best quality and most flavourful seafood available anywhere.

I have had the opportunity to taste many types of crab in the course of my travels and my two favourites are from our local waters. The first, which unfortunately is rarely available, is the red rock crab, and the second is the better known Dungeness crab, which thrives up and down the west coast. Both crabs have a delicious, sweet, savoury flesh. It is best appreciated simply cooked in plenty of salted water and cracked at the table (with plenty of napkins at hand).

I take the same approach to sourcing my shellfish as I do the rest of my ingredients – the closer to home the better. We have pink swimming scallops, which are so named because of their ability to propel themselves through the water when escaping predators. They are tender, sweet and are eaten much like a clam where the entire flesh is eaten, not only the muscle. We also have weathervane scallops, which are much larger and similar to sea scallops.

Oysters; honey mussels; small Manila, savory, and Cherrystone clams; spot prawns; and pink and side stripe shrimp, caught in the waters off Sooke, BC, are some of the varieties available from our coastal waters. This abundance of seafood is reflected in the wide range of seafood and shellfish recipes found in this book.

Fresh caught shellfish is always the best, but if you do not live on or near the coast, frozen shellfish can be substituted in most of the recipes. It is well worth the effort, however, to seek out the best and freshest.

fish & shellfish

Braised Ling Cod in White Wine Tomato Broth   148

Braised Sablefish with Leeks and Poached Oysters   149

Poached Trout Fillet with Cilantro Citrus Sauce   150

Halibut Fillet with Spiced Scallops and Tomato Olive Sauce   151

Salmon, Prawn and Scallop Timbale   152

Baked Halibut Fillet with Fresh Herb and Lemon Salad and Yukon Gold Potatoes   155

Red Snapper Fillet in Phyllo Pastry   156

Salmon Fillet with Pear Cider Sauce and Asian Pear Salad   159

Whole Seed-Crusted Fish Fillet with Basil Lemon Butter Sauce   160

Trout Fillet with Roasted Mediterranean Salad   163

poultry

Roasted Breast of Game Hen with Mushroom and Walnut Stuffing   165

Pan Roasted Game Hen with Honey Brandy Glaze   166

Braised Duck Leg   169

Pheasant Breast with Garlic Potato Crust and Salal Berry Sauce   170

Stuffed Turkey Cutlet with Quince and Cranberries   173

Roast Turkey Breast with Dried Fruit Stuffing   174

meats

Mushroom Crusted Beef Tenderloin with Gorgonzola Onion Stuffing   177

Wild Mushroom Crusted Lamb Loin   178

Braised Lamb Shanks with Winter Vegetables   181

Crusted Pork Loin Chop with Caramel Honey and Orange Sauce   182

Espresso Pork Tenderloin   185

Pork Medallions with Wild Mushrooms   185

Pork Tenderloin Medallions with Merlot and Sun-dried Cranberry Sauce   187

Venison Medallions with Pork and Venison Sausage   189

Homemade Sausages   190

Roast Rabbit with Italian Sausage and Bacon   191

Beer Braised Oxtail with White Beans and Chick Peas   194

Braised Veal Shank (Osso Buco)   196

Gremolata   196

Photo: Braised Ling Cod in White Wine Tomato Broth

main course

Braised Ling Cod in White Wine Tomato Broth

If possible, purchase a 3-4 lb. dressed ling cod for this recipe*. The steaks from a fish this size will be thick enough to hold up to the longer cooking. The bones and trim can be used to make a stock that will enhance the flavour of the finished dish. The flavours I have used here are reminiscent of the way my mother would make this dish. I've added the vegetables to make it a more complete meal and boned out the steaks for presentation.

eight 5-6 oz. boneless ling cod steaks, about 2-2¹/₂ inches thick

salt and freshly ground black pepper

¹/₄ c. extra virgin olive oil

¹/₂ c. flour for dredging

¹/₄ c. minced onion

4 large garlic cloves, peeled and thinly sliced

1 c. peeled, seeded, ripe plum tomatoes, coarsely chopped

1 tbsp. tomato paste

1 c. dry white wine

1 c. fish stock (page 256) or water

2 medium carrots, cut into 2-inch by ¹/₄-inch strips

1 medium parsnip, cut into 2-inch by ¹/₄-inch strips

2 sticks celery, cut into 2-inch by ¹/₄-inch strips

¹/₄ c. fresh oregano leaves, coarsely chopped

¹/₂ c. fresh basil leaves, coarsely chopped

³/₄ c. diced fresh Roma tomato

butcher's twine

Tie each cod steak with a length of butcher's twine to hold its shape while it cooks.

Season with salt and ground black pepper. Set aside.

In a stock pot or sauté pan large enough to hold all the steaks in one layer, heat the olive oil over medium-high heat.

Dredge the cod steaks in the flour, shake off the excess and fry in the oil about 1 minute on each side or until lightly browned.

Remove from the pan. Add the minced onion to the pan, adding more oil if necessary.

Cook stirring for 1-2 minutes, then add the sliced garlic. Cook 1-2 minutes more, then add the tomatoes, tomato paste and wine.

Stir to dissolve the tomato paste, then add half the fresh herbs, the fish stock or water and the chopped tomatoes.

Bring to a simmer and cook for 8-10 minutes. Add the carrot, parsnip and celery and then lay the cod steaks on top. Cover and cook until the flesh flakes easily.

Take the steaks out of the broth, remove the strings and keep warm.

Add the rest of the herbs and the diced tomato to the broth, and season with salt and pepper if necessary.

Serve in warm soup bowls with the cod steak on top of crusty bread or large croutons (recipe below).

* Dressed fish has been eviscerated and the head removed.

Braised Sablefish with Leeks and Poached Oysters

In a small food processor, combine 1/2 cup olive oil and the chervil and process until fine. Remove from the processor and set aside.

Season the sablefish fillets with salt and ground black pepper, dredge in the cornstarch and set aside.

In a sauté pan combine the leeks, sliced garlic, 2 tbsp. olive oil, 1/4 c. dry vermouth, nutmeg and a little salt and ground pepper. Bring to a simmer and reduce to very low, stirring occasionally. Simmer until tender but still bright green and keep warm.

Place a nonstick sauté pan on medium heat and add 2 tbsp. olive oil. Sear the fillets 1 minute on each side, then remove to a plate.

Add the remaining vermouth, the water or fish stock and the oyster liquor to the pan and bring to a simmer. Add the fillets back to the pan, reduce to low and cover. Cook 2-3 minutes, then remove the lid and add the oysters. Cook 2-3 minutes or until the edges of the oysters just begin to curl.

To serve, place a small mound of the braised leeks on each serving plate and top with 1 fillet, then two oysters.

Increase the heat and reduce the liquid in the pan to 1/2 cup. Whisk in the butter, lemon juice and zest, then spoon the sauce over the oysters and fillet.

Drizzle each of the plates with the chervil oil.

For the chervil oil
1/2 c. extra virgin olive oil
1 c. fresh chervil or Italian parsley

For the fish
eight 4-5 oz. skinless, boneless sablefish fillets
salt and freshly ground black pepper
1/4 c. cornstarch
2 c. thinly sliced leeks, white and light green parts only
5-6 large garlic cloves, thinly sliced
4 tbsp. extra virgin olive oil
3/4 c. dry white vermouth
1/2 tsp. fresh grated nutmeg
1/2 c. water or fish stock (page 256)
16 small to medium freshly shucked oysters and their liquor
1/3 c. cold unsalted butter cut in small pieces
1 tbsp. fresh lemon juice
2 tbsp. minced fresh lemon zest

Poached Trout Fillet with Cilantro Citrus Sauce

This quick one-pan dish accents the freshness of the trout very well. A good accompaniment could be fresh spinach or other leafy green vegetable quickly wilted in garlic oil with a few drops of toasted sesame oil.

2 boneless, skinless 6-8 oz. trout fillets
1/2 c. water
1/2 c. dry white wine
zest of 1 orange
2 tbsp. fresh orange juice
1 tbsp. fresh lemon juice
1 tbsp. fresh lime juice
2 tbsp. finely minced red onion
2 tbsp. finely minced celery
2 tbsp. finely minced carrot
2-3 tbsp. extra virgin olive oil
1/2 c. chopped fresh cilantro (fresh coriander)
salt and freshly ground pepper to taste

Combine the water, wine, zest, juices, minced vegetables and a pinch of salt in a saucepan just large enough to hold the trout fillets.

Simmer on low heat for 10-15 minutes to combine the flavours.

Place the trout fillets in the poaching liquid and cook at a low simmer 5-6 minutes or until opaque.

With a spatula carefully lift the fillets onto a warm plate and keep warm while you finish the sauce.

Increase the heat and reduce the liquid to 1/3-1/2 cup.

Remove from the heat and quickly whisk in the extra virgin olive oil and then the chopped cilantro.

Season to taste with salt and pepper and pour over the trout fillets.

Halibut Fillet with Spiced Scallops and Tomato Olive Sauce

eight 4 oz. boneless, skinless halibut fillets
16 large scallops
salt and freshly ground black pepper
3/4 c. chopped parsley
1/2 c. flour, seasoned with salt and pepper
1/4 c. extra virgin olive oil
2 tbsp. thinly sliced garlic
1 tbsp. fennel seeds
1/2 c. minced onion
1 tsp. chili flakes
1 c. dry vermouth
1 c. fish or chicken stock (page 256)
1 1/2 c. skinned and coarsely chopped
    canned plum tomatoes
1/2 c. each sun-dried black olives and
    green Sicilian olives, pitted and halved
1/2 c. chopped fresh oregano

Season the halibut and scallops with salt and pepper and 1/4 cup of the parsley, then dredge the halibut in the seasoned flour.

In a large skillet, heat the olive oil until it starts to smoke slightly and sear the halibut 2 minutes on each side. Remove and keep warm.

Add the scallops to the pan and cook 30 seconds on each side. Remove and keep warm.

Add more oil to the pan if necessary and add the onions, garlic, chili and fennel seeds. Stir until the onions are soft, making sure not to brown the garlic.

Carefully add the vermouth and reduce by half, scraping any residue from the bottom of the pan. Then add the fish stock and reduce by half again.

Add the tomatoes and olives and cook 5-10 minutes. Place the halibut and scallops back in the pan and cook at a low simmer, covered, for 2-3 minutes until the halibut is firm.

Portion the halibut and scallops onto 8 serving plates and stir the chopped oregano and the remaining parsley into the sauce, season if necessary and spoon over the fish.

Salmon, Prawn and Scallop Timbale

1¹/₂ lb. fresh boneless, skinless salmon fillet

12 jumbo scallops (10-12 oz.)

12 medium-sized prawns

2 eggs, separated

¹/₄ c. heavy cream

salt and freshly ground black pepper

3 tbsp. minced fresh tarragon

3 tbsp. minced fresh chives

2 tsp. minced garlic

2-3 tbsp. extra virgin olive oil

1 c. small diced fresh fennel bulb

¹/₂ c. dry white wine

1¹/₂ c. fresh Roma tomato, peeled, seeded and diced

pinch of dry chili flakes

2 tbsp. cold unsalted butter

eight 2 x 2-inch round metal rings (page 248)

Line the sides of the metal rings with parchment paper cut to fit. Place on an oiled ovenproof tray and set aside.

Use a long, sharp slicing knife and cut thin slices on a bias off the salmon fillet. You will need approximately 32-40 slices, or enough to line the inside of each metal ring.

As the salmon is sliced lay each piece on a tray, keeping the pieces separate. If the slices are to be stacked, place a sheet of plastic wrap or parchment paper between the layers.

Using 4-5 slices per ring, carefully lay one slice at a time against the inside of each ring, leaving a little on the bottom to cover and hanging the remainder over the outside of the ring. Refrigerate after all the rings are lined.

Set aside 8 each of the best looking scallops and prawns. Coarsely mince the rest, along with any remaining trims of the salmon fillet.

In a bowl whisk together the egg yolks and cream. Stir in 2 tbsp. each of the minced herbs, 1 tsp. garlic and a little salt and pepper.

Stir in the shellfish mixture and set aside.

Place the egg whites in a bowl and beat with a whisk or electric mixer until airy but still slightly runny.

Fold into the shellfish mixture and fill the lined rings, dividing the filling equally.

Fold the overhanging salmon ends over the tops of the filled rings to seal. Drizzle each with a little olive oil to prevent them from drying out in the oven.

Bake in a preheated 350°F oven for 15-18 minutes.

To finish, heat a medium pan and add 1-2 tbsp. olive oil. Add the reserved scallops and prawns and cook 30 seconds. Add the garlic and diced fennel and cook 1 minute, then add the wine.

Cook 1 minute and stir in the tomatoes and a little salt and black pepper. Add the remaining diced herbs and chili flakes.

Swirl in the butter until melted, remove from heat and set aside in a warm spot.

Remove the salmon and shellfish mixture from the oven. Remove the rings and place one portion on each plate.

Garnish with one scallop, one prawn and the sauce.

Baked Halibut Fillet with Fresh Herb and Lemon Salad and Yukon Gold Potatoes

Cook the potato slices in boiling salted water until slightly tender when pierced with a fork. Drain and set aside to cool.

Pat the fillets dry with a clean dish towel. Season with salt and pepper and set aside.

Coat the bottom of a baking dish large enough to hold all the fillets with 1 tbsp. of the oil.

Lay the cooked potato slices in the baking dish in eight rows of three to form beds for the fillets.

Place the fillets on top.

Combine the remaining ingredients in a small bowl, season to taste and cover each fillet with a portion of the mixture.

Bake in a preheated 375°F oven for 20-25 minutes.

Remove and place one serving on each plate.

Pour the excess juices into a small saucepan and bring to a boil.

Remove from heat and whisk in the remaining 2 tbsp. of olive oil. Spoon a little over the top of the fillets and serve.

4 medium Yukon Gold or other yellow-fleshed potatoes, peeled and sliced 1/4-inch thick

eight 5 oz. boneless, skinless halibut fillets

4 tbsp. extra virgin olive oil plus 2 tbsp. to finish the sauce

1 c. thinly sliced celery

1/2 c. thinly sliced red onion

4 large garlic cloves, peeled and thinly sliced

2 Roma tomatoes, diced

1 tbsp. capers, rinsed and drained

1/2 c. fresh parsley, coarsely chopped

1/2 c. fresh oregano leaves

1/2 c. fresh fennel leaves, coarsely chopped

sections from 2 large lemons

2 tsp. balsamic vinegar

1/2 c. dry white wine

salt and freshly ground pepper to taste

TIP

To section a lemon, cut 1/2 inch off each end. Stand the lemon on one end and following the contour of the lemon, slice off the skin, including the white pith. Working over a bowl, take the lemon in one hand and cut between the membranes to remove the individual sections.

Red Snapper Fillet in Phyllo Pastry

For the snapper
8 sheets phyllo pastry
1/2 c. extra virgin olive oil
1/2 c. chopped fresh oregano
1/2 c. chopped fresh basil
eight 3-4 oz. skinless, boneless red
    snapper fillets
8 oz. fresh spinach, blanched and
    squeezed dry
1 recipe Oven-dried Tomatoes (page 250)
salt and freshly ground black pepper

For the white wine reduction
1 c. fish stock, preferably from white fish
    bones (do not use very fat or oily fish)
    (page 256)
1/2 c. dry white wine
1/4 c. cold unsalted butter, cut in
    1/2-inch cubes
salt and freshly ground black pepper

To prepare the snapper

Lay one sheet of phyllo pastry on a work surface so that the long side is closest to you.

Brush lightly with extra virgin olive oil, season with a little salt and pepper and sprinkle some of the chopped oregano and basil over the sheet.

Fold the pastry in half crosswise so that it is now half as long.

Brush lightly with more olive oil and place a fillet at the end nearest you.

Top with some of the spinach, then 3 slices of the oven-dried tomatoes.

Fold the pastry over top of the fillet, then fold the two sides over top to enclose the package.

Brush lightly with more oil and completely roll the package into a cylinder. Brush the top with oil and place on a nonstick baking sheet.

Repeat with the rest of the fillets and bake at 400°F for 12-15 minutes until the pastry is lightly browned.

To prepare the white wine reduction

In a medium-sized saucepan, heat the fish stock over medium heat and reduce by half.

Add the wine and reduce by half again.

With the heat on low, whisk in the cold butter a few pieces at a time until it is all incorporated. Season to taste and remove from the heat.

To serve

Spoon some of the reduction onto each plate.

With a serrated knife trim the ends of each phyllo-wrapped snapper fillet to create a straight edge.

Slice in half on a bias and stand one half in the sauce with the other half laid down in front to expose the filling.

TIP
To store fresh fish or shellfish for more than one day, place in a colander inside a bowl. Cover with ice cubes and a clean wet kitchen towel. Place in the coolest part of the refrigerator. This will keep the fish very cold and at the same time allow the melting ice to drain from the fish. Use within 2-3 days.

Salmon Fillet with Pear Cider Sauce and Asian Pear Salad

This is a delicious, crisply flavoured dish that is a combination of hot and cold ingredients. It is equally as good if the salmon is cold. If serving the salmon cold, slightly undercook the fillet to retain its moisture and to ensure that it is tender.

For the salmon

Season the salmon pieces with salt and pepper and set aside.

In a steamer large enough to hold all the salmon pieces, add 1 inch of water and bring to a simmer.

Heat the fish stock in a wide saucepan, reduce to 1/2 cup and keep warm.

Heat a separate saucepan on medium and add 1-2 tbsp. butter.

Add the diced onion, garlic and ginger and cook briefly to combine without colouring.

Add the pear cider and increase the heat. Reduce to about 1/2 cup.

Add the reduced fish stock and reduce to about 3/4 cup. Strain and set aside to keep warm.

Place the salmon in the prepared steamer and steam for approximately 5-8 minutes.

For the salad

While the salmon is steaming, combine the pear strips, lemon juice, celery, pumpkin seeds and poppy seeds in a bowl.

In a separate small bowl, whisk together the rice wine vinegar, honey, mustard and walnut oil and combine with the pear and celery combination. Season to taste and set aside.

To serve

Finish the sauce by adding the diced pear and heating through.

Whisk in the remaining cold butter, season to taste and remove from the heat.

Place a small mound of the pear salad in the centre of each plate and top with a piece of steamed salmon.

Spoon the cider sauce on top and garnish with extra seeds.

For the salmon
eight 5 oz. skinless, boneless salmon fillets
salt and freshly ground black pepper
2 c. fish stock (page 256)
5-6 tbsp. cold unsalted butter, cut into cubes
1/2 c. finely minced red onion
1 tbsp. finely minced garlic
1 tbsp. finely minced fresh ginger
1 bottle dry pear cider
1 c. peeled, cored and diced Asian pear

For the salad
2 c. peeled, cored Asian pear, cut into thin 2-inch long strips
1 tbsp. fresh lemon juice
2 sticks celery, preferably the lighter-coloured tender pieces from the centre, cut on a bias into thin 2-inch strips
1/2 c. toasted pumpkin seeds
1 tbsp. poppy seeds
1 tbsp. rice wine vinegar
1 tbsp. honey
2 tsp. Dijon mustard
2 tbsp. walnut oil

Whole Seed-Crusted Fish Fillet with Basil Lemon Butter Sauce

Use this technique for any firm-fleshed fish or scallops.

For the fillets

eight 5 oz. skinless fish fillets (salmon, halibut, snapper or other firm-fleshed fish)

salt and freshly ground black pepper

1/3 c. all-purpose flour

1 egg white, lightly beaten

2 tbsp. each of whole flax, sunflower, poppy, pumpkin and sesame seeds (The variety of seeds can vary depending on what is available. You will need about 3/4 c. in total.)

3-4 tbsp. extra virgin olive oil

For the sauce

3/4 c. dry white wine

1 c. fish stock (page 256)

juice and zest of 1 large lemon

1-2 tbsp. honey

3 oz. cold unsalted butter, cut into small pieces

1 bunch of fresh basil, stems removed, coarsely chopped

For the fillets

Season the fillets on both sides with salt and pepper.

Dredge both sides lightly with the flour, then dip the flesh side only in the egg white. Press the egg white side into the mixed seeds to coat. Set aside.

Heat a large skillet big enough to hold all the fillets or use a smaller skillet and cook the fish in two batches.

When the pan is hot, add 3-4 tbsp. olive oil and add the fillets seed-side down. Sear about 1 minute to get a well-toasted crust, adding more oil if necessary.

Turn over and cook about 2 minutes more.

Remove from the skillet and place in a warm oven (275-300°F) while making the sauce.

For the sauce

Drain excess oil from the pan.

Return the pan to the heat, add the white wine and reduce by approximately half.

Add the fish stock and reduce by two-thirds.

Add the lemon juice, lemon zest and honey to taste.

Reduce slightly, then add the butter and quickly whisk or swirl to incorporate.

Add the chopped basil and cook for 30 seconds more.

Season if necessary and portion onto serving plates, placing the fillets on top of the sauce.

Trout Fillet with Roasted Mediterranean Salad

For 2

This is an easy, quick way to prepare trout or any small fish fillets. The presentation is simple and rustic.

Rinse and pat dry the trout fillets.

Season with salt and pepper and set aside.

Coat the bottom of a baking dish large enough to hold both fillets with 1 tbsp. of the oil.

Lay the cooked potato slices in the baking dish in two rows to form a bed for the fillets. Place the fillets on top.

Combine the rest of the ingredients and season to taste. Cover each fillet with half the mixture.

Bake in a preheated 375°F oven for 20-25 minutes until the trout is tender.

Remove from the oven and place on two serving plates.

Whisk 2 tbsp. of olive oil into the liquid remaining in the baking dish. Season to taste and spoon over the top of the fillets.

two 5-6 oz. boneless trout fillets

2 medium yellow-fleshed potatoes, peeled, sliced 1/4-inch thick and cooked in boiling, salted water until tender but still firm

1/2 small fennel bulb, trimmed, quartered and sliced thinly (about 1/2 c.)

1/4 c. thinly sliced red onion

1 large garlic clove, peeled and thinly sliced

1/2 of one Roma tomato, diced

1 tbsp. capers, rinsed and drained

1/4 c. pitted good quality black olives, halved

3 tbsp. coarsely chopped fresh parsley

3 tbsp. fresh oregano leaves

3 tbsp. torn fresh basil leaves

1 tbsp. fresh lemon juice

4 tbsp. extra virgin olive oil

1/2 c. dry white wine

salt and freshly ground pepper to taste

Roasted Breast of Game Hen with Mushroom and Walnut Stuffing

It is important to debone the birds with the skin intact. The skin will be used to wrap the breast with the stuffing made from the dark meat.

For the breasts

Place one hen on a cutting board and with a sharp boning knife make a cut through the skin from the top of the breast down to the bottom, cutting through to the bone. Working with one side of the hen at a time, cut the breast away, being careful to stay close to the bone and leaving the breast still attached to the skin.

Repeat the procedure with the thigh and leg, keeping them attached to the skin. Turn over the hen, make a cut down the middle of the back and remove the breast with the leg attached.

Pull the skin back from the leg and cut the leg away. Trim the meat off the leg and thigh and separate from the bones. Set the meat aside.

Trim the breast of any excess fat and sinew. Set aside with the skin still attached. Repeat with the other half and the rest of the hens.

For the sauce

In a roasting pan, roast the bones in a 450°F oven, approximately 30 minutes.

Add the vegetables, stir in the tomato paste and sprinkle the flour on top. Roast approximately 15-20 minutes more, stirring halfway through.

Place the contents of the roasting pan in a stock pot, add the wine and water to cover and simmer 3-4 hours.

Strain the broth into a clean pot, discarding the bones and vegetables. Add the sherry and simmer approximately 1/2 hour until it reaches sauce consistency.

Season and keep warm until ready to serve.

For the stuffing

Sauté the onion, mushrooms, garlic and walnuts in the 2 tbsp. oil. Add the salt and pepper.

Remove from heat, add the rosemary and sherry, then cool completely.

Combine the mushroom and nut mixture with the dark meat and refrigerate.

To prepare the breasts

Loosen the skin from the breast meat, leaving it intact on the wing bone. Repeat with the rest of the breasts.

Season with salt and ground black pepper. With all the breasts laid out on a board, divide the cooled stuffing onto the tops and fold the skin over to wrap each portion with the ends of the skin underneath.

Lay them on a baking sheet, rub the tops with a little oil and season with salt and pepper.

Roast in a 400°F oven for approximately 20-25 minutes. Allow to rest 10 minutes before slicing. Ladle sauce to cover the bottom of serving plate and place a sliced breast on top.

For the breasts
4 whole game hens weighing about 1 lb. each

For the sauce
reserved bones and trim
1/2 c. chopped celery
1 c. chopped onion
1/2 c. chopped carrots
2 tbsp. tomato paste
1/4 c. flour
2 c. red wine
1/4 c. sherry
1 tsp. salt
1 tsp. freshly ground black pepper

For the stuffing
2 tbsp. extra virgin olive oil
1/2 c. onion, diced
1 tbsp. garlic, minced
3 c. sliced mushrooms
1/2 c. walnut pieces
1 tbsp. fresh rosemary, chopped
dark meat from the hens, coarsely chopped
2 tbsp. sherry
1 tsp. salt
1 tsp. freshly ground black pepper

Pan Roasted Game Hen with Honey Brandy Glaze

Deboning the hens makes them much easier to slice once they are cooked. The technique of wrapping the meat back into the skin helps to keep the meat moist.

4 whole game hens about 1 lb. each

salt and freshly ground black pepper

4 tbsp. chopped fresh rosemary

4 tbsp. chopped fresh sage

3-4 large garlic cloves, peeled and thinly sliced

juice of 1 lemon

4 tbsp. extra virgin olive oil

1/4 c. honey

3 tbsp. brandy

1/2 c. dry white wine

4 tbsp. cold unsalted butter

1/4 c. chopped Italian parsley

16 lengths of butcher's twine about 8 inches long

To debone the hens place a hen back side down on a cutting board and with a sharp boning knife make a cut through the skin along one side of the breast bone, cutting all the way through to the bone. It is important to keep the skin intact.

Being careful to stay close to the bone, cut the breast and wing away from the carcass, then move down to the thigh and leg and cut that away from the carcass also. Cut around to the back, then cut away the breast and leg completely. Repeat with the other side and the rest of the hens.

Carefully cut the meat away from the thigh bone, then remove the thigh bone leaving the drumstick intact. Trim off the wing from the breast and set the boned-out halves aside while you finish the rest. Reserve the bones for another use.

Spread each half onto a cutting board with the meat side up. Season with the salt, pepper, rosemary, sage and garlic slices, then wrap the meat into the skin.

Tie each half with two lengths of the twine to help keep its shape while it cooks.

Lay the hens on a flat dish, sprinkle with the fresh lemon juice and refrigerate until needed.

Remove the hens from the refrigerator 20 to 30 minutes before cooking.

Season the outside with salt and ground black pepper.

Heat the oil in a heavy-bottomed sauté pan. In two batches sear the hens breast side down for 2 minutes, then turn and sear the other side 2 minutes. Remove the pan from the heat.

Combine the honey and 2 tbsp. of the brandy. Brush half the mixture onto the tops of the hens and place in a 425°F oven for 10 minutes.

Brush again with the honey brandy glaze and place back in the oven another 10 minutes.

Remove the hens from the pan and keep warm.

Place the pan on medium heat and add the remaining brandy. Cook slightly, then add the wine.

Reduce by half, then turn off the heat and whisk or swirl in the butter. Stir in the parsley and serve with hens.

Braised Duck Leg

Trim the duck legs of excess fat and skin and remove the thigh bone.

For the marinade

In a non-reactive bowl combine the ingredients for the marinade, saving 4 tbsp. of the olive oil for later.

Add the duck legs to the mixture, turning to coat well. Cover and refrigerate for several hours or overnight.

For the braise

Heat a large heavy-bottomed frying pan on medium heat.

Remove the duck legs from the marinade. Remove any herb or garlic pieces and dry the legs with a clean kitchen cloth. Dredge the legs in the flour, shaking off the excess.

Add 2 tbsp. of olive oil to the pan and place the legs in the oil, skin side down. (If your pan is not large enough, fry the legs in two batches so as not to crowd them.)

Brown well on both sides, then remove and place in a roasting pan.

Add the remaining 2 tbsp. olive oil to the pan and add the diced vegetables.

Stir and cook for 2-3 minutes, then stir in the tomato paste, allowing it to brown slightly. Add the stock and wine.

Increase heat to high and cook for 10-15 minutes until reduced slightly.

Pour the contents over the duck legs and cover with a lid or foil. Place in a 325°F oven for 2 1/2-3 hours or until the meat is tender.

To finish

Remove the roasting pan from the oven. Take out the legs and place them in a heatproof container. Cover and keep warm.

Bring the braising liquid and vegetables to a boil and skim off excess fat.

Cook until the liquid begins to thicken, then add the minced herbs.

Cook 10 more minutes and remove from heat. Whisk or stir in the butter and season to taste if necessary.

Serve the legs with the braising liquid over top.

For the marinade
8 duck legs (drumstick and thigh)
1 c. dry red or white wine
6-8 large garlic cloves, crushed
6 sprigs of fresh rosemary
6 sprigs fresh sage
6 sprigs fresh oregano
6 tbsp. extra virgin olive oil
1/2 tsp. salt
1 tsp. freshly ground black pepper

For the braise
1/2 c. all-purpose flour
2 medium carrots, peeled and cut into 1/4-inch dice
2 celery sticks, cut into 1/4-inch dice
1 medium parsnip, peeled and cut into 1/4-inch dice
1 small onion, peeled and cut into 1/4-inch dice
1/4 c. tomato paste
2 c. duck stock (or substitute chicken) (page 256)
2 c. dry red or white wine

To finish
2 tbsp. minced fresh sage
2 tbsp. minced fresh rosemary
2 tbsp. minced fresh oregano
3 tbsp. cold unsalted butter

Pheasant Breast with Garlic Potato Crust and Salal Berry Sauce

Pheasant and other game birds or meats are enhanced by the use of wild berries in marinades or sauces. Here I use juniper berries in the marinade, enhanced by a little gin, which is also flavoured by the berries. Pheasant is a lean meat that requires extra care to prevent overcooking and drying out.

For the pheasant
4 boneless, skinless pheasant breasts
4 garlic cloves, peeled and sliced
12 fresh or dried juniper berries, crushed
1 tbsp. black peppercorns, crushed
1/2 c. sliced onion
2 bay leaves, crumbled
2 tbsp. gin
1/4 c. extra virgin olive oil plus 2 tbsp.
3 tbsp. honey
1/2 c. dry white wine

For the crust
12 oz. yellow-fleshed potatoes
    (2-3 medium-sized potatoes)
8-10 (or more to taste) garlic cloves,
    peeled and chopped
2 tbsp. cream or milk
3 egg yolks
salt and freshly ground black pepper

For the sauce
strained reserved marinade
2 c. brown chicken stock (page 256)
1 c. salal berries or blueberries
2 tbsp. cold unsalted butter, cubed
salt and freshly ground black pepper
    to taste

For the pheasant

Combine all ingredients for the pheasant, reserving 2 tbsp. olive oil, and refrigerate overnight.

Remove the pheasant breast from the marinade and pat dry on a clean kitchen cloth. Reserve the marinade.

Heat a heavy-bottomed pan on medium heat and add the 2 tbsp. oil.

Season the breast with salt and pepper and sear, skin side down, 1-2 minutes. Remove from the pan and set aside.

For the crust

Scrub the potatoes and place in a pot with the garlic. Cover with cold water, 1/2 tsp. salt and bring to a boil. Cook until the potatoes are tender.

Drain the potatoes, peel while still warm and press through a potato ricer or mash by hand.

Cool slightly and whisk in the cream or milk, the egg yolks and a little salt and ground pepper.

Cool the mixture and place in a pastry bag fitted with a 3/8-inch plain tip.

Pipe the potato mixture decoratively onto each breast to cover and set aside in the refrigerator until ready to cook. (The potatoes can also be spread with a metal spatula.)

To finish, place the breasts on a baking tray and roast in a 400°F oven for 15 minutes or until the potato crust has browned and the pheasant is slightly firm to the touch.

For the sauce

Heat the reserved marinade in a small saucepan to a simmer and remove from heat. Strain through several layers of cheesecloth and place back in the pan with the brown chicken stock. Bring to a low boil and reduce to about 1 cup.

Add the salal berries and cook 4-5 minutes. When the sauce has reduced to desired consistency, whisk in the cold butter, season to taste and portion onto serving plates.

Remove pheasant breasts from oven and place on top of the sauce.

Stuffed Turkey Cutlet with Quince and Cranberries

This recipe was inspired by a wine called Rotberger, which I tasted on an Okanagan wine tour. It is a true rosé that goes very well with the tart cranberries and the turkey. The quince seemed a natural addition as it is also ready to harvest at Thanksgiving time.

Place a heavy-bottomed pan over medium heat and add the diced bacon and 1/4 cup olive oil.

Cook until the bacon begins to crisp, stirring occasionally.

Add the diced onion, quince and 1/3 cup honey. Stir frequently until the honey begins to caramelize, then add 1 1/2 cups of the cranberries and 1 cup of wine.

Cook over medium to low heat until the quince and cranberries are tender and the liquid has thickened to a syrup.

Add the sage and parsley and cook 1 minute. Season and set aside to cool completely.

One at a time, place the turkey cutlets between two pieces of plastic wrap or waxed paper and pound with a meat mallet to about 1/4-inch thick.

Lay the flattened cutlets in a row and divide the filling among all eight.

Starting at one end, roll each cutlet to enclose the filling and set aside.

Cut the remaining four slices of bacon in half. Run the back of a knife along each slice to stretch it. Wrap each cutlet with a piece of bacon and secure with a toothpick.

Heat a heavy-bottomed pan on medium to high heat. Add 1/4 cup olive oil and sear the cutlets 1-2 minutes on each side.

Remove to an ovenproof dish and bake at 325°F for 10-15 minutes.

On high heat, deglaze the pan with the remaining wine.

Add the stock, remaining 3 tbsp. honey and 3/4 cup cranberries, and cook until the cranberries are soft.

Press through a fine strainer into a smaller saucepan and add the mustard.

Reduce until slightly thickened, season to taste and keep warm.

Remove the turkey cutlets from the oven and remove the toothpicks.

Strain any liquid into the sauce. Season if necessary.

Slice the cutlets on a bias into two and serve with the sauce.

---

8 slices smoked bacon, with 4 cut into 1/2-inch dice
1/2 c. extra virgin olive oil
3/4 c. minced red onion
2-3 medium-sized fresh quince, quartered, cored and cut into 1/2-inch dice (about 3 c.)
1/3 c. plus 3 tbsp. honey
2 1/4 c. whole fresh cranberries
2 c. dry white wine
1/4 c. thinly sliced fresh sage
3/4 c. chopped fresh Italian parsley
salt and freshly ground black pepper
eight 3-4 oz. turkey breast cutlets
2 c. turkey or chicken stock (page 256)
1 tbsp. Dijon mustard

TIP
Deglazing is a process of dissolving the particles remaining in the bottom of the roasting pan using wine, fruit juice, stock or water.

Roast Turkey Breast with Dried Fruit Stuffing

2¹/2-3 lb. boneless, skinless turkey breast
2 tbsp. extra virgin olive oil
4 tbsp. unsalted butter
1/4 c. minced onion
1 tbsp. sliced garlic
1/2 c. dry white wine
2 tbsp. apple cider vinegar
1/2 c. peeled and diced tart apple
3 tbsp. minced dried apricots
3 tbsp. sun-dried cranberries
3 tbsp. dried pears
3 tbsp. dried cherries
1/4 c. minced sun-dried tomatoes
3 tbsp. honey
3 tsp. flour plus 3 tbsp. for dredging
salt and freshly ground black pepper
1 tbsp. fresh minced sage
2 tbsp. fresh thyme leaves
2 c. apple cider or apple juice
butcher's twine for tying the roast

Lay the turkey breast on a cutting board with the side that had the skin facing down.

With a sharp boning knife or slicer butterfly the breast by making a horizontal cut through the side to open it up like a book. Starting from the middle repeat the process with the left and right side to open each side again so that you have four parts, all still intact. Refrigerate while you make the stuffing.

Heat a medium sauté pan and add 1 tbsp. olive oil and 1 tbsp. unsalted butter.

Add the onion and garlic and cook 1-2 minutes. Add 1/4 cup white wine, the cider vinegar, dried fruit, diced apples, sun-dried tomatoes and 1 tbsp. honey. Cook a few minutes to reduce the liquid.

Sprinkle with 3 tsp. flour and stir to combine. Season with salt and pepper to taste and remove from heat. Stir in the herbs and set aside to cool completely.

Lay the breast on a work surface and season with salt and pepper.

Spread the stuffing over three quarters of the breast leaving one quarter bare.

Fold the bare portion over to enclose part of the stuffing, then roll the whole breast into the shape of a roast with the skin side on top. Season with salt and pepper and dredge on all sides with flour.

Tie with lengths of butcher's twine in about 5-6 places to help keep the shape while cooking.

Heat a heavy-bottomed pan on medium heat and add 1 tbsp. oil and 1 tbsp. butter.

Sear the roast lightly on all sides and remove from the pan.

Drain the excess oil from the pan and add the apple cider and remaining honey. Bring to a boil.

Add the roast back to the pan and place in a 375°F oven for 30 minutes, basting with the liquid in the pan 4-5 times during the cooking time.

Remove the roast from the oven, take it out of the pan and keep in a warm spot loosely covered with aluminum foil.

Bring the remaining pan juices to a boil, reduce to about 1 cup and stir in the 2 tbsp. of butter. If the sauce is on the sweet side adjust with a little lemon juice or extra cider vinegar.

Season to taste and serve with slices of the roast.

Mushroom Crusted Beef Tenderloin with Gorgonzola Onion Stuffing

Combine the sliced shallots, minced garlic, 2 tbsp. olive oil and 1/2 tsp. each salt and pepper in a pan and cook on low heat until soft and slightly coloured, about 20 minutes.

Add half the rosemary and thyme and cook another minute. Remove from the pan and cool completely, then combine with the bread crumbs and cheese.

In an electric coffee grinder or small food chopper, mince the dried mushrooms, leaving some pieces larger for texture. Set aside.

With a sharp paring knife cut a pocket in each tenderloin by first pushing the point into the side, then working it from side to side. Push in about 1 tbsp. of the mixture, making sure to press it in all the way.

Cut 8 lengths of twine and tie around each tenderloin to help maintain the shape when cooked.

Season each tenderloin with salt and pepper and rub a little of the Dijon mustard on the top and bottom.

Press the tops and bottoms of the tenderloins into the minced mushrooms and refrigerate for 1-2 hours.

Sear in a medium hot pan with 2 tbsp. olive oil for 1-2 minutes on each side. Remove and place in a roasting pan. Roast in a 400°F oven for approximately 10-12 minutes for medium rare.

eight 4-5 oz. beef tenderloin steaks
2 c. thinly sliced shallots
2 tbsp. minced garlic
4 tbsp. extra virgin olive oil
1 tsp. each salt and freshly ground
    black pepper
2 tbsp. minced fresh rosemary
2 tbsp. minced fresh thyme
3 oz. Gorgonzola cheese
1/2 c. fresh bread crumbs
3 oz. assorted dried mushrooms
3 tbsp. Dijon mustard
butcher's twine

For the sauce

Into the same pan add the 2 tbsp. olive oil, shallots, mushrooms and garlic cloves. Allow to colour slightly, then add the wine. Reduce by half and add the beef stock.

Reduce by half again and add the rest of the rosemary and thyme and the cream if using.

Reduce slightly, whisk in butter, season to taste and serve.

For the sauce
2 tbsp. extra virgin olive oil
8 small peeled shallots, quartered
1 c. assorted fresh mushrooms
8 large peeled garlic cloves, quartered
1 c. full-bodied red wine
1 1/2 c. beef stock (page 256)
1/4 c. heavy cream (optional)
3-4 tbsp. cold butter

Wild Mushroom Crusted Lamb Loin

The loin or short loin is the section of a lamb that would come from behind the rack. It is equally as flavourful as the rack and a little more economical. If you are not comfortable taking the meat from the bone, ask your butcher to do it for you. Be sure to take the bones to make the brown sauce for the recipe. The trims can be used to make a delicious lamb sausage. Use the procedure described on page 190, and flavour with rosemary and sage.

4 lamb loin roasts on the bone

salt and freshly ground black pepper

3-4 tbsp. extra virgin olive oil

1 c. assorted dried mushrooms

1 c. fresh white bread crumbs

1 tbsp. minced garlic

3-4 tbsp. whole grain mustard

1 c. dry red wine such as a Merlot or Cabernet

3 tbsp. Salal Berry Honey Vinegar (page 253) (substitute 1 tbsp. berry syrup, 1 tbsp. honey and 2 tbsp. red wine vinegar)

2-3 tbsp. cold butter, cut into small pieces

2 c. brown meat stock using lamb bones from the loin roasts (page 256)

With a sharp boning knife carefully remove the meat from each bone in one neat piece.

With a heavy knife or cleaver, cut each bone into 5-6 smaller pieces, and follow the recipe for Brown Meat Stock (page 256), substituting the lamb bones for the beef bones.

While the stock is simmering, trim the loin of any sinew and excess fat and season with salt and freshly ground black pepper.

Heat a large heavy-bottomed skillet to medium and add 2 tbsp. olive oil.

Carefully place the loins in the pan and sear 30 seconds on each side.

Remove the loins from the pan and set aside to cool along with the pan to use for finishing the sauce.

Place the mushrooms into the bowl of a food processor or a blender and pulse several times to a consistency that still shows small pieces of mushroom.

Combine mushroom pieces with the bread crumbs, minced garlic, salt and ground black pepper on a tray.

Pat the loins dry to remove excess oil and spread each one with the mustard to form a thin coat. This will help to make the mushroom mixture stick.

Press each lamb loin into the mushroom mixture to coat all sides.

Place the coated loins on a nonstick baking sheet and drizzle with extra virgin olive oil.

At this point the lamb can be refrigerated until needed. Remove from the refrigerator 30 minutes before roasting.

Roast in a 400°F oven to desired doneness – approximately 12 minutes for medium rare.

Remove from the oven, cover loosely and allow the meat to rest in a warm spot for 10 minutes before slicing.

To make the sauce

Reheat the pan used for searing the loins and add the wine. Bring to a boil and reduce to approximately 1/2 cup, then add the Salal Berry Honey Vinegar and reduce again.

Add 2 cups of the stock and reduce to about 1 cup. Keep warm.

To finish, heat the sauce and whisk in the cold butter until thoroughly incorporated.

Season to taste, strain if desired and serve with slices of the lamb loin.

Braised Lamb Shanks with Winter Vegetables

Season the lamb shanks with salt and pepper and dredge in the flour.

Heat two sauté pans large enough to hold four shanks each and add 1/4 cup oil to each.

Brown the shanks well on both sides and remove to a roasting pan large enough to hold all eight along with the vegetables and stock.

Divide the vegetables into the two pans and sauté until they start to colour.

Add the mushrooms and garlic to both pans and sauté until the mushrooms soften.

Add the tomato paste and cook until slightly brown, then add the red wine and chicken or beef stock along with the thyme.

Bring to a boil and pour the contents of both pans over the shanks. Season with a little more salt and pepper, cover and place in a 300°F oven for 2 1/2 hours.

After 2 1/2 hours, uncover and add the tomatoes and half of the chopped parsley to the pan.

Cover again and place back in the oven for 30 to 60 minutes more, or until the meat is tender.

Remove from the oven, skim excess fat from the braising liquid and season if necessary. Serve the shanks with the vegetables, braising liquid and the remaining fresh parsley.

8 lamb shanks
1 tbsp. salt
2 tsp. freshly ground black pepper
1/2 c. flour
1/2 c. extra virgin olive oil
2 c. diced onions
2 c. diced carrots
2 c. diced celery
2 c. diced parsnips
1 c. diced rutabaga or turnips
12 oz. fresh Crimini mushrooms, quartered
2 medium heads fresh garlic, sliced
3 tbsp. tomato paste
2 c. dry red wine
3 c. rich chicken or beef stock (page 256)
1 small bunch fresh thyme
1 1/2 c. diced fresh tomato
1 c. chopped fresh Italian parsley

Crusted Pork Loin Chop with Caramel Honey and Orange Sauce

For the pork loin

eight 6 oz. pork loin chops with rib bone attached
1/4 c. all-purpose flour
3 tbsp. paprika
1 tsp. ground cumin
2 tsp. whole cumin seeds
1 1/2 tsp. freshly ground black pepper
1/4 c. honey
1/4 c. whole grain mustard
3 tbsp. finely minced garlic
1/2 c. mustard seeds
3 tbsp. extra virgin olive oil
butcher's twine

For the sauce

1 tsp. lemon juice
1/2 c. honey
3/4 c. orange juice
1/3 c. dry white wine
1 1/2 c. chicken stock (page 256)
8 tbsp. cold butter

For the pork loin

With butcher's twine, tie each chop to help keep its shape.

Dredge both sides of each chop with flour and set aside.

Combine the rest of the ingredients except the olive oil and coat both sides of the chops with some of the mixture, leaving the sides bare.

Heat two nonstick pans on medium and add half the olive oil to each (or do in two batches).

Sear the chops 1-2 minutes on each side, being careful not to have the pan too hot or the honey in the topping will burn.

Remove the chops and place on an ovenproof tray and bake at 400°F for 10-12 minutes.

When the chops are still a little soft to the touch when pressed with a finger, remove them from the oven. They will continue to cook slightly while resting.

Allow the chops to rest at least five minutes while you finish the sauce.

For the sauce

In the same pan that the chops were seared in, heat the honey and lemon juice.

Bring to a boil and cook until the honey begins to caramelize, stirring a little to let it colour evenly. Continue until the honey is a light brown colour.

Carefully add the orange juice, then the wine and chicken stock and reduce to an almost syrupy consistency.

On low heat, swirl in the cold butter, then remove the pan from the heat.

Season with salt and pepper and serve immediately with the pork chops.

Espresso Pork Tenderloin

Serves 8 generously

This recipe is for coffee lovers. The espresso gives the meat a beautiful dark colour and makes for a rich, flavourful sauce.

Place all ingredients for the marinade in a bowl and whisk to combine.

Trim the pork tenderloins of any fat and sinew if necessary and place in a heavy plastic freezer bag large enough to hold the meat and marinade.

Pour the marinade into the bag. Squeeze out as much air as possible, then seal the bag.

Turn over the bag to coat the tenderloins and place on a plate or tray. Refrigerate for at least 6 hours or overnight.

Remove the tenderloins from the marinade and pat dry with paper towels or a clean kitchen cloth and set aside.

Heat a heavy-bottomed frying pan large enough to hold all four tenderloins or use a smaller pan and sear the tenderloins in two batches.

When the pan is hot add the vegetable oil and sear the tenderloins 1 1/2-2 minutes on each side.

Remove to an ovenproof tray and place in a preheated 400°F oven. Roast for 8 minutes until medium (still slightly pink in the centre).

Remove from the oven, cover lightly and set aside, allowing the tenderloins to rest before slicing.

While the tenderloins are in the oven, strain the marinade into the frying pan, bring to a boil and reduce by half.

Add the stock and reduce by approximately 2/3 or until it looks syrupy.

Lower the heat and whisk in the cold butter.

Season to taste with salt and pepper and remove from the heat.

Slice the tenderloins on a bias into 1/2-inch medallions and serve with the sauce.

For the marinade
1 c. cold espresso or strong regular coffee
6 large garlic cloves, peeled and sliced
1/4 c. coarsely chopped onion
2 tbsp. honey
1/4 c. dark rum
1/2 tsp. freshly ground black pepper
2-3 whole cloves
1/4 tsp. fresh grated nutmeg

For the pork tenderloin
4 whole pork tenderloins, approximately 12 oz. each
3-4 tbsp. vegetable oil
2 c. chicken stock (page 256)
2-3 tbsp. cold unsalted butter
salt and freshly ground black pepper to taste

Pork Tenderloin Medallions with Merlot and Sun-dried Cranberry Sauce

Trim the tenderloins of any fat or sinew and portion each into 8 medallions.

Flatten the medallions with a meat mallet to about 1/2-inch thick to tenderize and assure even thickness.

Combine the rest of the ingredients except the salt and pour into a non-reactive dish or casserole.

Add the pork and coat evenly with mixture. Cover and refrigerate 4-6 hours or overnight.

Remove from refrigerator a half hour before cooking. Scrape off the marinade and discard.

Season both sides of the medallions with salt.

Heat a large sauté pan on medium to high heat and scar the medallions approximately 3 minutes on each side. Remove from the pan and keep warm.

In the same pan, make the Merlot and Sun-dried Cranberry Sauce (recipe below), then place the seared medallions back in the sauce.

Cook on low heat until heated through, turning them over once to coat.

Variation:

For an alternative sauce, sauté 1/2 c. minced onion and 2 minced garlic cloves in 3-4 tbsp. extra virgin olive oil. Add 1 c. red wine and reduce by half. Add 2 c. Brown Meat Stock and reduce by half again. Whisk in 2 tbsp. mustard and reduce until slightly thickened. Season to taste and serve.

For variety, add mushrooms, cream and fresh herbs.

2 whole pork tenderloins, approximately 16 oz. each
6-8 rosemary sprigs
6-8 fresh thyme sprigs
4 garlic cloves, thinly sliced
1/3 c. extra virgin olive oil
1/4 c. Merlot wine
1 tbsp. freshly ground black pepper
zest of 1 large orange, in large strips
1 tsp. salt

Merlot and Sun-dried Cranberry Sauce

In a 10-inch saucepan heat the oil over medium heat.

Add the onion and cook until soft, about 1 minute.

Add the garlic and sauté about 15 seconds, until it becomes aromatic.

Add the Merlot, increase the heat and reduce by half.

Add the stock, cranberries and honey and reduce by half again.

Set aside and keep warm until ready to serve.

Before serving, on very low heat, whisk in the cold butter until incorporated. Season with salt and freshly ground black pepper to taste.

1 tbsp. extra virgin olive oil
1/2 c. finely minced onion
1 tbsp. minced garlic
2 c. Merlot wine
1 c. brown beef or chicken stock (page 256)
1/2 c. dried cranberries
2 tbsp. honey
3 tbsp. cold butter
salt and freshly ground pepper to taste

Venison Medallions with Pork and Venison Sausage   *Serves 4 generously*

Venison is available in many of the same cuts as for beef. One of the most economical cuts is from the hind leg. It is referred to as Denvered Leg, where the meat is trimmed from the bone and the tough sinew is removed. The meat is then cut along the natural seams in the muscle into manageable pieces. Venison, like other game meats, is very lean, so it must not be overcooked or it will be dry and tough. It is best cooked no more than medium rare.

For the venison
1¹/2 lb. boneless trimmed venison leg
4 garlic cloves, peeled and sliced
12 juniper berries, crushed
2 star anise, crushed
1 tsp. whole black peppercorns crushed
4-5 whole cloves
¹/4 c. sliced onion
1 tbsp. honey
2 tbsp. extra virgin olive oil

For the sausage
6 oz. venison trim
6 oz. boneless pork shoulder
2 oz. smoked bacon
1 garlic clove, peeled and crushed
¹/2 tsp. salt
¹/2 tsp. freshly ground black pepper
2 tsp. minced fresh rosemary
2 tbsp. red wine
sausage casing (about 30 inches)

For the sauce
2 c. brown beef or chicken stock (page 256)
2 c. red wine
strained reserved marinade
¹/2 oz. grated bittersweet or unsweetened
    chocolate
1 tbsp. cold unsalted butter, cubed
salt and ground black pepper to taste

For the garnish
12 large garlic cloves roasted in their
    skins (page 62)

For the venison

Combine all ingredients for the marinade and set aside.

Cut the venison into 2-inch-wide strips in the direction of the fibers. Then cut into eight 1¹/2- to 1³/4-inch thick medallions.

Tie the medallions with a piece of butcher's twine to help maintain the shape.

Turn medallions in the marinade to coat and refrigerate covered 4-6 hours or overnight.

For the sausage

Combine the trims of venison with the pork shoulder, bacon and garlic and grind in a meat grinder using the small die. (The mixture can also be ground by pulsing in the bowl of a food processor.)

Add the salt and pepper, minced herbs, and red wine. Mix well and refrigerate 4-6 hours or overnight.

Stuff the mixture into the sausage casing following one of the methods on page 190 and carefully twist into 8 sausages.

To finish

Remove the venison from the marinade, pat dry on a clean kitchen towel and set aside, covered.

Combine the marinade, brown stock and red wine and bring to a simmer. Reduce on low heat until you have about 1¹/2 cups. Strain through a fine meshed sieve or cheesecloth and set aside.

Heat a heavy-bottomed pan on medium to high heat and sear the sausages well on all sides.

Remove and place in a 300°F oven while finishing the medallions.

Wipe the pan clean and heat on medium high. Sear the medallions approximately 2 minutes on each side, remove strings and place in a warm oven while you finish the sauce.

Bring the sauce to a boil and reduce slightly. Reduce heat to low, add the grated chocolate and whisk in the cold butter. Season to taste and place a pool of sauce on four serving plates.

Place 2 medallions and 2 sausages on each plate and serve garnished with the roasted garlic cloves.

Homemade Sausages

Sausages can easily be made at home using meat trims and your favourite herbs and spices. Natural or collagen sausage casings can be found at most butcher shops. They are available in large or small size, with the small size usually used for breakfast sausages.

Grind the meat in a meat grinder using the small die, or by pulsing in a food processor. Add salt and pepper, minced herbs, and a little wine, stock or juice to flavour.

Mix well and refrigerate 4-6 hours or overnight.

Stuff the sausages using the attachment on your food grinder. Carefully twist into sausages.

With a sharp skewer or needle gently poke holes in several places all over the sausages to allow the fat to drip out and prevent the sausages from bursting while cooking.

Variation: In the absence of a sausage stuffer the sausages can also be stuffed using a regular pastry bag and a $^1/_2$-inch round tip. Just fit the bag with the tip and fill with the meat mixture. Slide the casing over the end of the tip and squeeze the mixture out into the casing, carefully twisting into links.

Roast Rabbit with Italian Sausage and Bacon

This recipe requires a little more patience. You may want to save this one for a special occasion. Mastering the job of de-boning the rabbit takes time and practice but the results are well worth the effort. The procedure may sound a bit daunting but is not as difficult as it sounds. The rabbit when ready to roast is stuffed and tied into a roll, making the finished product easy to serve. If you cannot get Italian sausage with fennel use a good fresh pure pork sausage and add 2 tsp. of fennel seeds.

For the rabbit

Place the rabbit on its back and spread open.

Using a sharp boning knife or paring knife, start at the neck end and make a cut down the length of the backbone.

Working on one side at a time, work the blade of the knife along the backbone to begin to release the flesh, being careful not to puncture the exterior of the meat.

When working around the rib section release the individual bones by first scraping along the inside of the bone with the sharp edge of the knife and then carefully cutting away.

Continue to work along the length of the rabbit, staying as close to the bone as possible, until you have released all the flesh from one side, including the legs.

Repeat for the other side, reserving the bones for the sauce.

Trim away any loose ends on the rabbit and reserve for the stuffing.

Refrigerate the rabbit while you prepare the rest of the ingredients.

In a food processor combine the trims and one slice of bacon.

With the casing removed, add the sausage to the bowl and pulse to combine, being careful not to overprocess. Set aside.

Heat a small sauté pan and add 1 tbsp. of the olive oil, then the onions and garlic, and cook until soft.

Add the chopped herbs, cook briefly to release the flavours, cool, then combine with the bacon and sausage mixture.

In the same pan sauté the mushrooms in 1 tbsp. olive oil 1-2 minutes on each side and cool.

Season the greens with salt, ground black pepper and the nutmeg.

To assemble the roast lay the boned-out rabbit on its back on a work surface.

Season the inside and spread the greens mixture down the middle, leaving about 2 inches of space on either side.

Next take the sausage mixture and spread it in a row down the middle of the greens.

Place the mushrooms in an overlapping row on top of the sausage and press in.

For the rabbit
one whole 2$\frac{1}{2}$- 3 lb. rabbit
6 oz. fresh Italian sausage with fennel
2 tbsp. extra virgin olive oil
$\frac{1}{4}$ c. minced white onion
1 tbsp. minced garlic
1 tbsp. chopped rosemary
1 tbsp. chopped sage
8-10 medium-sized fresh shiitake
   mushrooms
8-10 oz. Swiss chard, beet tops or
   spinach leaves, blanched, cooled,
   squeezed dry and coarsely chopped
$\frac{1}{4}$ tsp. freshly grated nutmeg
10 strips smoked bacon
salt and freshly ground black pepper
about 4 feet of butcher's twine

continued on page 193

Roast Rabbit with Italian Sausage and Bacon
continued from page 191

Pick up one edge of the rabbit and fold it over the stuffing. Repeat with the other edge to seal the roast, wrapping it tightly. Set aside.

Take the remaining bacon slices and working with one at a time stretch them by holding one end in one hand and pushing along the length of the slice with the back of a knife.

Lay the slices of bacon on a sheet of plastic wrap or wax paper slightly overlapping one another to form a rough square wide enough to wrap the whole rabbit.

Place the rabbit on top of the bacon slices and using the plastic wrap lift the slices over the rabbit and roll to enclose.

Carefully remove the plastic wrap and tie the roast with the butcher's twine, knotting it at 6-8 intervals the length of the roast.

To roast, heat a heavy-bottomed sauté pan and add 2 tbsp. olive oil. Sear the roast well on all sides, then place in a 375°F oven for 20 minutes or until the internal temperature is 160°F.

Allow to rest at least 10 minutes before slicing.

For the sauce

Heat the olive oil in a heavy-bottomed saucepan. Add the reserved bones and brown well.

Add the onion, carrot and celery and brown lightly, then add the tomato paste. Cook to brown the tomato paste, then add the garlic, wine, bay leaves, peppercorns and water.

Reduce heat and simmer 3-4 hours, skimming off any fat. Remove the bones, then set aside sauce until needed.

To serve

Once the roast has been removed from the roasting pan, cover with aluminum foil and keep warm. Drain any excess fat from the pan.

Place the pan on the heat and add the reserved sauce, stirring in any residue off the bottom.

Reduce if necessary to about 1 cup. Strain and whisk in the cold butter and season to taste.

Serve with slices of the rabbit roast.

For the sauce
reserved rabbit bones
2 tbsp. extra virgin olive oil
1/2 c. chopped onion
1/2 c. chopped carrot
1/2 c. chopped celery
1 tbsp. tomato paste
2 garlic cloves, crushed
2 c. dry red or white wine
2 bay leaves
1 tbsp. black peppercorns
2 c. water
2 tbsp. cold unsalted butter

Beer Braised Oxtail with White Beans and Chick Peas

Serves 4

3 lbs. oxtail cut into approximately
   2-inch pieces
salt and freshly ground black pepper
1/4 c. all-purpose flour
1/4 c. extra virgin olive oil
4 slices thick-cut smoked bacon, slivered
1 tbsp. minced fresh garlic
1/4 c. diced red onion
1/4 c. diced carrot
1/4 c. diced celery
1 tsp. chili flakes
2 bottles honey lager or ale
1/2 c. puréed yellow or red tomatoes
3/4 c. cooked small white beans
3/4 c. cooked chick peas
1/3 c. chopped fresh mint

Heat a heavy-bottomed pan on medium.

Season the oxtail with salt and ground black pepper, then dredge with flour.

Add the olive oil to the pan and sear the oxtail well on all sides.

Remove from the pan and add the bacon.

Cook the bacon, stirring occasionally until beginning to crisp.

Drain off the oil and add the garlic and diced vegetables and chili flakes.

Cook 2-3 minutes, then add the beer. Stir to release any residue from the bottom of the pan and bring to a boil.

Place the oxtail back in the pan and reduce the heat to a simmer.

Add the tomato purée and a little more salt and ground black pepper to taste. Cover the pot.

Simmer on low heat on top of the stove or in a 325°F oven for 2 1/2-3 hours or until the meat is tender.

Add the cooked beans and simmer another 15-20 minutes.

To thicken the sauce remove about 1/2 cup of the beans with some of the liquid, purée in a blender and add the purée back to the pot.

Stir in the chopped mint, and cook a few more minutes.

Portion onto individual plates or serve family-style.

Drizzle with extra virgin olive oil and serve with lots of crusty bread.

Braised Veal Shank (Osso Buco) with Gremolata

Serves 4

Directly translated osso buco means bone with a hole, referring to the tender marrow inside the bone. The marrow is an acquired taste but is delicious spread on crusty bread or eaten with the tender meat. Serve this dish the traditional way with saffron risotto or soft polenta.

4 pieces veal shank, approximately
　6-8 oz. each
salt and freshly ground black pepper
flour for dredging
1/4 c. extra virgin olive oil
4 large garlic cloves, peeled
1 carrot, peeled and chopped
1 stick celery, chopped
1 medium onion, peeled and chopped
1 1/2 c. chopped ripe Italian plum
　tomatoes
3/4 c. dry white wine
water or chicken or beef stock (page 256)
1 recipe Gremolata (below)
1/2 c. minced sun-dried tomatoes

TIP

To make saffron risotto, follow the recipe for Swiss chard risotto (page 131), substituting approximately 1 tsp. saffron threads for the anchovy fillets, and omitting the Swiss chard.

Season the veal with salt and pepper and dredge in the flour.

Heat a heavy-bottomed pan on medium. Add the olive oil to the pan and sear the veal shanks well on all sides. Remove from the pan.

Chop the garlic cloves and add to the pan along with the rest of the chopped vegetables.

Cook stirring for a few minutes until the vegetables begin to brown slightly.

Add the tomatoes, wine, a little salt and pepper and bring to a simmer.

Add the veal shanks back to the pan along with enough water or meat stock to come halfway up the sides of the veal and cover with a lid.

Simmer on low heat on top of the stove or place in a 325°F oven for 2 hours or until the meat is tender.

Carefully remove the veal from the pan and keep warm.

Strain the liquid through a fine sieve into a separate saucepan, pressing gently on the vegetables to get as much liquid out as possible.

Bring to a boil and add half the Gremolata and the sun-dried tomatoes. Reduce the liquid to a sauce consistency.

Portion the veal onto 4 plates and spoon on some of the reduced sauce. Sprinkle with the rest of the Gremolata and serve.

Gremolata

A versatile mixture for adding a fresh zip to finished dishes. Traditionally Gremolata is used to top off Osso Buco, or braised veal shank. It is also useful for adding flavour to a variety of seafood dishes.

3 tbsp. Italian parsley leaves
1 tbsp. peeled garlic
1 tbsp. each lemon and orange zest

Pile the ingredients on a cutting board and with a sharp, heavy knife mince them all together to a fine and uniform consistency.

Store covered in the refrigerator.

Chocolate

When buying chocolate, whether to be eaten as is or to use in recipes, it is important to read the label to know exactly what you are buying.

Good quality chocolate consists of very few ingredients: cocoa solids, cocoa butter, sugar, vanilla and lecithin.

Cocoa beans are found in the large pod of the cacao tree. Each pod may contain up to 50 beans. After they are removed from the pod, the beans are fermented in the sun, roasted and crushed to produce cocoa paste, or mass. The mass is then pressed to remove the cocoa butter. The remaining cakes are crushed and ground into a fine powder, producing cocoa powder.

To make chocolate, cocoa butter, sugar and vanilla are added to the crushed cocoa mass, along with lecithin, derived from soybeans, to help bring out the cocoa flavour.

The type of chocolate – sweet, semi-sweet, bitter-sweet, dark or bitter – is determined by the ratio of cocoa solids to sugar. Semi-sweet or bitter-sweet must have a minimum 50% cocoa mass. The higher the ratio of cocoa to sugar, the darker and more flavourful the chocolate will be.

Milk chocolate has at least 25% cocoa solids, 14% dry milk solids, milk fat and a maximum 55% sugar. White chocolate, which is not really chocolate at all because it does not contain any cocoa solids, is made from cocoa butter, sugar, milk solids and fats.

For eating or for use in recipes where the flavour of the chocolate is crucial, always use good-quality chocolate. For the recipes in this book, semi-sweet or dark chocolate both work well. Although the flavour of bitter or extra-bitter chocolate would be more pronounced, the ratio of sugar and cocoa butter in the chocolate could possibly affect the outcome of the finished product.

desserts

Lemon-Lime and White Chocolate Éclairs with Mint and Citrus Salad	200
Pâte à Choux (Cream Puff Paste)	201
Almond Plum Cake with Spiced Merlot Plum Sauce	203
Avocado Hazelnut Semifreddo	204
Plum Cake (Coffee Cake)	204
Fresh Fruit Terrine	207
Gingersnaps	208
Gingersnaps with Mascarpone Filling	208
Chocolate Crème Brûlée	210
Ginger and Vanilla Bean Crème Brûlée	211
Hazelnut, Cherry and Chocolate Pouches on Orange Custard Sauce	212
Lemon, Fig and Raisin Cheese Tart	213
Honey Walnut Tart with Caramel Brandied Oranges	215
Hazelnut Fig Cake	216
Raspberry, Fig and White Chocolate Bread Pudding	219
Salal Berry Rice Pudding with Caramel Pears	220
Tuille Paste	220
Zabaglione with Vanilla Grappa	223
Chocolate Pine Nut Sugar Cookies	223
Chocolate Hazelnut Torte	224
Chocolate for Garnishes	224
Bittersweet Ganache on a Honey Nut Phyllo Nest	227
Sourdough Chocolate Brew Cake	228
Mini Chocolate Cheesecakes	231
Molten Mocha Chocolate Cakes	232
Strawberry Mascarpone Ice Cream	233
Salal Berry Ice Cream	233
Rum and Honey Ice Cream	235
Raspberry Frozen Yogurt	235
Pumpkin Seed Ice Cream	235
Pine Nut Praline and Honey Ice Cream	236
Chocolate Hazelnut Ice Cream	236
Vanilla Spice Ice Cream	236

Photo: Lemon-Lime and White Chocolate Éclairs with Mint and Citrus Salad

desserts

Lemon-Lime and White Chocolate Éclairs with Mint and Citrus Salad

For the éclairs
1/4 recipe Pâte à Choux (Cream Puff
  Paste) (page 201)
1 recipe Lemon-Lime Curd (page 260)
2 oz. melted white chocolate
icing sugar for dusting
Sugared Lemon and Lime Slices (page 262)

For the mint and citrus salad
2 pink grapefruits
1 large orange
1 mandarin orange
3 tbsp. sugar
2 tsp. powdered gelatin
3/4 c. fresh mint
2 tbsp. Lemoncello or other citrus-
  flavoured liqueur

For the éclairs

Follow the recipe for Pâte à Choux.

Place the batter into a pastry bag fitted with a #5 round tip (1/2 inch) and pipe small 2-inch-long éclairs onto a parchment-lined or nonstick baking sheet, leaving 1 1/2 inches between each one. This should give you at least 24 éclairs. With a moistened fingertip, flatten any points that may stick up from the piped éclairs.

Bake in a preheated 400°F oven for 10 minutes. Reduce the heat to 350°F and bake another 20-25 minutes until the éclairs are browned and crisp.

Remove from the oven and cool on a rack.

For the mint and citrus salad

Trim the ends of the grapefruits and oranges.

With a sharp paring knife remove the skin and pith, leaving the separate sections exposed.

Place a sieve or strainer over a bowl. With the knife remove the separate sections by cutting in between the membrane, saving as much juice as possible.

Cut the sections into 1/2- to 3/4-inch pieces and place in a separate bowl.

Combine the sugar and gelatin powder in a heatproof bowl.

Set aside 2 tbsp. of mint leaves. Coarsely chop the rest and add to the bowl with the sugar and gelatin.

Measure the reserved citrus juice and squeeze extra if needed to make 3/4 cup.

Add half to the gelatin mixture and place over a pot of barely simmering water to dissolve.

Remove from the heat and let steep for 5-10 minutes to extract flavour from the mint.

Strain through a fine sieve or cheesecloth, squeezing to extract all the liquid.

Add the rest of the juice, the Lemoncello and the citrus segments.

Stir carefully to combine and place in the refrigerator to set.

To finish

Split the éclairs in half to form a top and a bottom.

Spoon or pipe some Lemon-Lime Curd into the bottom half and replace the top.

Drizzle with melted white chocolate and dust with icing sugar.

Place three éclairs on a plate.

Remove the Citrus Salad from the refrigerator. Dip a soup spoon into hot water, scoop a portion of the salad and place it next to the éclairs.

Garnish with whipped cream and Sugared Lemon and Lime Slices.

Pâte à Choux (Cream Puff Paste)

This is a simple basic batter that can be used to make many varying shapes and sizes of pastries from éclairs to profiteroles, pastry swans, soup garnishes and so on. Omit the sugar if the pastry will be used to hold a savoury filling. The batter can be stored for a day or two in the refrigerator, but is best used right away. This recipe will make 4-5 dozen 2-inch round shells.

Place the water or milk, butter and salt in a heavy-bottomed saucepan and bring to a boil.

Add the flour and sugar all at once and stir with a wooden spoon. It will look rough at first but then will begin to come together.

Stir faster until the mixture no longer sticks to the spoon or the sides of the pan.

Remove from the heat and place the batter in a mixing bowl.

With an electric beater or heavy whisk beat the mixture while adding the eggs one at a time, waiting until each egg is incorporated before adding the next.

Continue to add the eggs until the batter no longer looks greasy.

With a wetted spoon or pastry bag form the desired shapes on a greased baking sheet.

Sprinkle or spray a few drops of water onto the shapes before baking. Bake at 400°F for 10 minutes, then reduce heat to 350°F and bake another 25 minutes. For smaller shapes adjust the time accordingly.

The shells should be firm and light to the touch when done.

Remove and cool in a draft-free spot. Before filling, cut in half with a sharp knife and remove any soft filaments that may be inside.

2 c. water or milk
5 oz. unsalted butter
1/4 tsp. salt
12 oz. (2-2 1/4 c.) all-purpose flour
1 tbsp. sugar
8-10 eggs

To Make a Paper Pastry Bag

Cut a triangle of parchment paper. Grasp the middle of the long side with the thumb and forefinger of your left hand. With the right hand bring the top corner down to the middle, folding under and around to form a cone.

Hold the paper with the left hand beneath the point formed and use the right thumb to push the paper toward the point and roll up the paper cone completely.

The point must be completely tight. Fold the projecting end of the paper over to the inside to hold the cone's shape.

With a spoon, fill the bag about halfway with tempered chocolate (page 224) or icing.

Holding the seam firmly, fold over the top, then fold the ends from the outside in.

Cut off the tip with a sharp knife or scissors. The size of the hole will determine the thickness of the piping.

Almond Plum Cake with Spiced Merlot Plum Sauce

For the sauce

Combine all ingredients except the butter in a medium saucepan and heat to a simmer while continuing to stir.

Simmer 1-2 minutes to cook the cornstarch and adjust consistency with more wine if needed.

Stir in the cold butter until smooth and pour the sauce into a bowl. Set aside, stirring occasionally to prevent a skin from forming.

To make the cake

Combine the flour, ground almonds, salt and sugar in a mixing bowl.

In a measuring cup combine the egg yolk, almond extract and enough yogurt to make 1 1/4 cups.

Stir in the melted butter and lemon zest.

Whip the egg white to soft peaks. With a rubber spatula combine the yogurt mixture with the flour mixture, then fold in the whipped egg white.

Spoon the mixture into 8 parchment paper-lined 2 x 2-inch metal rings or into a 2 x 8-inch round cake pan.

For the topping

Combine all the ingredients for the topping except the butter.

Spread the topping mixture over the tops of the prepared cakes, pressing the plums down slightly.

Dot the tops with the butter.

Bake in a preheated 350°F oven approximately 20 minutes for the rings and 30 minutes for the large cake.

Remove from the oven. Remove from rings or pan while slightly warm and dust with icing sugar.

Serve slightly warm or at room temperature with the sauce.

For the sauce
1 1/2 c. Merlot wine
1/2 c. honey
1 tsp. ground cinnamon
1/2 tsp. ground ginger
1/4 tsp. ground allspice
1 1/2 tbsp. cornstarch
1 tbsp. cold unsalted butter
1/2 c. diced fresh Italian prune plums

For the cake
3 oz. (3/4 c.) sifted all-purpose flour
1/2 c. ground blanched almonds
1/4 tsp. salt
2 tbsp. sugar
1 egg, separated
1/2 tsp. almond extract
plain yogurt
2 oz. (1/4 c.) melted unsalted butter
1 tbsp. grated fresh lemon zest

For the topping
2 c. diced fresh Italian prune plums
3 oz. (1/2 c.) brown sugar
1 tsp. ground cinnamon
1/2 tsp. ground ginger
1/4 tsp. ground allspice
1/4 c. sliced blanched almonds
3-4 tbsp. unsalted butter

Avocado Hazelnut Semifreddo

Semifreddo in Italian means half cold. Here it refers to a frozen dessert; basically a frozen mousse. It is best to remove the semifreddo from the mold 20 minutes or so before serving and allow it to soften a little in the refrigerator for a better texture.

1 firm but ripe avocado, peeled
   and diced to make about 1 c.
2 tsp. fresh lemon juice
4 oz. (2/3 c.) sugar
2 tbsp. Hazelnut Paste (see below)
   or 3 tbsp. skinned hazelnuts,
   toasted and finely ground
1 3/4 c. heavy cream
3 egg yolks

To make the Hazelnut Paste, heat 3 oz.
(1/2 c.) sugar and 3 oz. (2/3 c.) water in a
small pot. Set aside to cool.

Place 4 oz. (about 1 c.) toasted, skinned
hazelnuts in the bowl of a food processor
and add half the syrup. Process until
smooth, adding more syrup as needed.

Place the diced avocado, lemon juice, 1/3 cup sugar and Hazelnut Paste in the bowl of a food processor, purée until smooth and set aside.

Whip the cream until firm but still slightly runny and set aside.

Place the egg yolks and remaining sugar in a heatproof bowl and whisk together over a pot of hot water until thick and pale yellow in colour.

Add the avocado purée and about 1/3 of the whipped cream to the egg yolks and stir to combine.

Carefully fold in the rest of the whipped cream to combine. Divide the mixture into 8 buttered or oiled 4-oz. ramekins and freeze.

To serve, dip the bottoms and sides of the ramekins in hot water to loosen the mixture and turn out onto individual serving plates.

Serve as is or with a fruit sauce, and garnish as desired.

Variation: To add a bottom on the Semifreddo, follow the recipe for Almond Sheet Cake (page 260). When the cake is cool, cut rounds to fit the individual ramekins once they have been filled with the avocado mixture.

Plum Cake (Coffee Cake)

A quick and easy treat for coffee break or any time. This makes a great late summer dessert when there is an abundance of fresh ripe fruit available. Serve warm with Vanilla Spice Ice Cream (page 236) or flavoured whipped cream. Apples, pears, peaches, cherries or any other firm ripe fruit can be used in this recipe. If the fruit is extra juicy, reduce the amount of liquid by 1-2 tbsp.

5 oz. (1 c.) all-purpose flour
2 tsp. baking powder
1/4 tsp. salt
2 tbsp. brown sugar
3 tbsp. chilled unsalted butter
1 egg, plus milk to make 3/4 c.
3/4 tsp. pure vanilla extract
2 tbsp. grated or minced fresh lemon zest
2 c. pitted and quartered fresh plums

For the topping
4 1/2 oz. (3/4 c.) brown sugar
2 tbsp. ground cinnamon
1 tbsp. ground ginger
1/2 tsp. fresh grated nutmeg
3-4 tbsp. melted butter

Sift together the flour, baking powder and salt, then combine with the brown sugar.

Add the chilled butter and work into the mixture as you would a pastry dough.

In a measuring cup beat the egg, add milk to make 3/4 cup, then add the vanilla extract and zest.

Combine with the flour mixture to make a stiff batter. Press into a greased and floured 9-inch round pan.

Scatter the plums evenly on top of the batter and press in. Combine the brown sugar, spices and melted butter and spread evenly over the fruit.

Bake in a 375-400°F oven about 25 minutes.

Fresh Fruit Terrine

Try this with any variety of fruits. It is especially good with an assortment of seasonal berries. For best effect, you will need a half-round terrine mold 15 x 2¹/2 inches long.

Set the strawberries flat and trim the two sides slightly so that they will fit snugly into the mold. Prepare the rest of the fruit and set aside along with the strawberry trims.

Cut a piece of the almond sheet cake 15 x 6 ¹/2 inches, keeping the parchment paper on, and line the inside of the terrine mold with the parchment against the mold.

Cut another piece of sheet cake 15 x 2¹/2 inches and set aside.

Combine the peach preserves, powdered gelatin, brandy and water and set over barely simmering water to dissolve.

Whip the cream to soft peaks and set aside.

Combine the egg yolks and granulated sugar and whisk over barely simmering water until pale yellow and thickened, removing from the heat occasionally if it gets too hot.

Combine the gelatin mixture, strawberry trims and the egg yolks and allow to cool slightly.

Stir in about a quarter of the whipped cream, then add the mixture to the rest of the cream.

Fold gently but thoroughly and then pour about half the mixture into the cake-lined mold.

Working quickly, place a row of kiwi pieces down each side of the lined mold.

Place the strawberries down the middle of the cream so that they are touching each other and the flat end is facing up. Top with a little more cream and smooth with a spatula.

Lay the slices of melon and 1 cup of the berries onto the cream in the same fashion. Save 1 cup of the best berries for the garnish.

Top with remaining cream, smooth and top with the remaining piece of sheet cake, with the parchment paper facing out.

Press firmly, turn over onto a flat tray and refrigerate until firm, about 2 hours.

To serve, remove the paper from the top and turn out the terrine onto a cutting board.

Peel off the remaining parchment. Slice with a serrated knife into 8 portions.

Decorate 8 plates with a fruit purée of choice and additional fresh fruit or berries.

Place one portion on each plate and dust with icing sugar.

---

1 recipe Almond Sheet Cake (page 260)

10-12 large fresh strawberries,* hulled, with the bottoms cut flat

2 fresh kiwi, peeled and cut lengthwise into 8 pieces each

8 strips of fresh firm melon, each approximately ¹/4-inch thick by 4 inches

2 c. fresh berries*

4 tbsp. peach preserves

1 tbsp. powdered unflavoured gelatin

1 tbsp. peach brandy or schnapps

2 tbsp. water

1 c. heavy cream

3 egg yolks

2 tbsp. granulated sugar

icing sugar

* The fruit used can vary with what is available throughout the seasons, e.g., raspberries, blueberries, grapes.

Gingersnaps

Use this recipe to make a variety of shapes and sizes of crisp, spiced treats. They can be formed into tubes or cups or can just be served as a flat cookie along with ice cream, mousse or a variety of desserts.

This recipe will make approximately thirty 3-inch gingersnaps.

5 oz. all-purpose flour
4 oz. unsalted butter, room temperature
5 oz. golden syrup
5 oz. granulated sugar
1/2 tsp. ground ginger
1/4 tsp. allspice
1 tbsp. brandy

Note that the equivalents are not given in this recipe because the correct proportions of the ingredients are necessary for the batter to spread properly.

Combine all ingredients in the bowl of an electric mixer. Beat the mixture until smooth.

Refrigerate for 1 hour or more until firm.

Form mixture into 1-inch balls and place on a parchment-lined or nonstick baking pan. Space the balls 4-5 inches apart to allow for spreading.

Flatten the balls slightly and bake at 350°F for 10-12 minutes until they are uniformly coloured and lacy in texture.

Remove the gingersnaps from the oven and cool slightly.

To form tubes that are to be filled

Using a spatula, carefully lift one edge and roll the gingersnap around a wooden dowel or metal cannoli mold. Allow it to cool, then carefully remove it.

If the gingersnaps cool before they can be shaped, simply place them back in the oven to soften again.

Store unused gingersnaps in an airtight container up to two weeks or freeze.

Gingersnaps with Mascarpone Filling

sixteen 3-inch gingersnaps formed into tubes (recipe above)
1/2 c. heavy cream
3/4 c. mascarpone cheese at room temperature
4 tbsp. granulated sugar
2 tbsp. orange liqueur
1/4 c. finely chopped semi-sweet chocolate or mini-chips
2 tbsp. minced candied ginger
1 tbsp. minced fresh orange zest
icing sugar for dusting

Whip the cream to soft peaks and set aside.

With an electric mixer or a wooden spoon, beat the mascarpone with the sugar until light and fluffy.

Add the liqueur and blend well.

Fold in the whipped cream, chocolate, ginger, and orange zest and refrigerate the mixture approximately 30 minutes, or until slightly firm.

Fill a pastry bag fitted with a 1/2-inch round tip with the mixture and squeeze about a tablespoon of the mixture into each end of the gingersnaps.

Arrange the gingersnaps on a serving tray, or present individual portions, dust with icing sugar and serve immediately. The gingersnaps will begin to soften as they absorb moisture from the filling.

Chocolate Crème Brûlée

Place eight 4-oz. ramekins in a baking pan with at least 2-inch sides.

Mix cream and sugar in a heavy medium-sized pot. Place over medium heat and stir to dissolve the sugar.

Bring to a simmer, reduce heat to low and simmer 5 minutes. Remove from heat and stir in the chocolate. Stir until smooth.

Whisk the yolks in a separate bowl until well blended, then gradually add the chocolate cream mixture, stirring just to blend. Do not overstir or you may incorporate air into the mixture which will result in a less than smooth custard when baked. Stir in the liqueur.

Divide the mixture into the 8 ramekins and pour enough hot water in the pan to come halfway up the sides of the ramekins.

Carefully place in a preheated 325°F oven and bake approximately 30 minutes. The custards should be almost set in the centre. Remove from the pan and cool in the refrigerator for 3 hours or up to 2 days.

2¹/₃ c. heavy cream
¹/₂ c. granulated sugar
3¹/₂ oz. chopped semi-sweet chocolate
6 large egg yolks
¹/₄ c. Irish cream liqueur (such as Baileys™)
16 tsp. granulated sugar for the topping

For the topping
16 tsp. granulated sugar

Follow the method described on page 211 to make the topping.

Ginger and Vanilla Bean Crème Brûlée

A classic creme brulée with a little added flavour. For those who would prefer this without ginger, it can simply be omitted.

For White Chocolate Peach Crème Brûlée stir in 2 oz. chopped white chocolate to the cream after removing from the heat. Cut 2 pitted peaches into thin slices, cook briefly in a mixture of 2 tbsp. unsalted butter, 1 tbsp. sugar and 2 tsp. fresh lemon juice, then place in the bottom of the custard cups before filling.

Place eight 3- to 4-oz. ramekins in a baking pan with at least 2-inch sides.

Mix cream, sugar and ginger in a heavy medium-sized pot. Scrape the seeds from the vanilla bean and add to the pot along with the bean.

Place over medium heat and stir to dissolve the sugar.

Bring to a simmer, reduce heat to low and simmer 5 minutes. Remove from heat and set aside for 15-20 minutes to infuse the flavours. Strain into a bowl.

Whisk the yolks in a separate bowl until well blended, then gradually add the strained cream mixture, stirring just to blend. Do not overstir or you may incorporate air into the mixture, which will result in a less than smooth custard when baked.

Divide the mixture into the 8 ramekins, then pour enough hot water into the pan to come halfway up the sides.

Carefully place in the oven and bake approximately 25 minutes. The custards should be almost set in the centre. Remove from the pan and cool in the refrigerator for 3 hours or up to 2 days.

For the topping

Sprinkle 2 tsp. sugar evenly on the tops of the custards. Working with one custard at a time move a blow torch flame from side to side over the sugar to caramelize it evenly. (If you do not have a blow torch the sugar can be browned under the broiler in your oven.)

Refrigerate at least 1-2 hours to allow the sugar to harden and to set the custards. Do not refrigerate more than a few hours or the sugar will soften again.

Serve with a garnish such as fresh fruit, wafer cookies, or shaved chocolate.

For the custard
2 c. heavy cream
1/2 c. granulated sugar
2 tbsp. peeled, chopped fresh ginger
1 vanilla bean, split lengthwise
5 large egg yolks

For the topping
16 tsp. granulated sugar

Hazelnut, Cherry and Chocolate Pouches on Orange Custard Sauce

For the orange custard sauce
2 c. milk
2 tbsp. sugar
1 tbsp. cornstarch
2 egg yolks
1/4 c. orange marmalade
1 tbsp. orange liqueur
1 tsp. pure vanilla extract
extra milk for thinning the custard

For the filling and pouches
1/2 c. hazelnuts, toasted, skinned and
    chopped
2 c. preserved cherries, pitted and
    drained well
1/2 c. semi-sweet chocolate, chopped,
    or chocolate chips
1 tbsp. icing sugar
1 tbsp. orange-flavoured liqueur
2 tbsp. orange zest, minced
1/3 c. melted unsalted butter
2 tbsp. cocoa powder, sifted
8 sheets phyllo pastry

For the orange custard sauce

Combine 1 1/2 cups milk and 1 tbsp. sugar and bring to a simmer.

In a small bowl, whisk together 1 tbsp. cornstarch and 1 tbsp. sugar. Add 1/2 cup milk and the egg yolks, whisking until smooth.

Stir the cold milk mixture into the simmering milk. Bring back to a simmer and cook stirring for 1 minute.

Remove from the heat and stir in the orange marmalade, orange liqueur and vanilla extract. Pour into a clean bowl and cover with plastic wrap, pressing the wrap onto the surface of the custard, and refrigerate. Thin to desired consistency with extra milk before serving.

For the filling and pouches

Make the filling by combining all ingredients except the phyllo pastry, butter and cocoa.

To make the pouches, lay one sheet of phyllo on a flat work surface. Combine the butter and cocoa powder. Brush pastry lightly with the mixture. Lay another sheet on top and press to remove any air pockets.

Brush again with the butter mixture. Cut the pastry into 4 pieces by first cutting down the middle lengthwise and then cutting across.

Place 1 1/2 tbsp. filling on each piece. Gather up the corners, and pinch them together to form a pouch. Place on a parchment-lined baking sheet.

Repeat with the rest of the pastry and filling and bake at 375°F for 8-10 minutes. Serve warm with the orange custard sauce. Makes 16 pouches.

Lemon, Fig and Raisin Cheese Tart

Makes 8 individual tarts or one 10-inch tart

Quark cheese is a type of cream cheese used mostly in Europe. It is a little more tart than regular cream cheese and much lower in fat, with a milk fat of 4% as opposed to 36%.

You can substitute regular cream cheese for the quark, and sour cream in place of the yogurt.

Coat the tart tins or pan with butter or nonstick spray and set aside.

Roll out the Shortcrust Dough to about 1/8-inch thick and line the tart tins. Refrigerate while you make the filling.

Beat together the cheese and sugar until smooth, then beat in the yogurt, lemon juice and lemon zest.

Add the eggs and beat only to combine. Add the raisins and minced figs.

Fill the tarts 2/3 full and bake in a 325°F oven 20-25 minutes or until the filling is slightly firm in the centre.

Cool before removing from the tins.

Serve with whipped cream and a tart berry sauce.

> 6 oz. (3/4 c.) quark cheese
> 2 oz. (1/3 c.) granulated sugar
> 1/4 c. plain yogurt
> juice and grated zest of one lemon
> 2 eggs
> 1 oz. (1/4 c.) dark raisins
> 11/2 oz. (1/2 c.) minced dried figs
> Shortcrust Dough (page 263)

Honey Walnut Tart with Caramel Brandied Oranges

For a variation, add 2 oz. finely chopped semisweet chocolate to the filling.

For the dough

In the bowl of an electric mixer, beat the unsalted butter and sugar together until just combined, then beat in the egg.

Sift together the all-purpose flour with the baking powder and add to the bowl.

Beat only until the mixture begins to come together, then gather the dough together with your hands.

Knead the dough briefly on a lightly floured board until it is mixed evenly, form into a flat ball, wrap with plastic wrap and refrigerate for 15-30 minutes to firm slightly.

Remove the dough from the refrigerator and divide into 8 pieces.

Place the metal rings on a nonstick baking tray and oil or spray the insides with nonstick spray.

Line the inside of each ring with one slice of dough. It should be an even thickness on the bottom and sides to about 3/4 of the height of the rings. Refrigerate while you make the filling.

For the filling

Beat together the butter and sugar, then beat in the egg.

Stir in the orange brandy, heavy cream and honey, then add the walnuts.

Divide the mixture into the 8 prepared rings and bake in a preheated 350°F oven for 20 minutes.

Remove from the oven and cool on the tray.

For the caramel brandied oranges

In a heavy bottomed pot or saucepan, combine the sugar and water and bring to a boil.

Reduce the heat and cook until all the water has evaporated and the sugar becomes golden, swirling the pan occasionally to make it colour evenly.

Remove from the heat and carefully stir in the honey, then the extract, brandy, zest, the oranges and juice.

To serve place one tart on a plate and spoon some of the orange sections around it. Garnish with whipped cream and toasted walnuts if desired.

See page 261 to make the caramel sugar garnish shown in photo.

For the dough
3 oz. (6 tbsp.) unsalted butter
3 oz. (1/2 c.) granulated sugar
1 egg
8 oz. (2 c.) all-purpose flour
2 tsp. baking powder
eight 2 x 2-inch round metal rings or
    eight 2 1/2-inch fluted brioche molds
oil or nonstick spray

For the filling
3 tbsp. unsalted butter, room temperature
2 tbsp. granulated sugar
1 egg
1 tbsp. orange brandy
2 tbsp. heavy cream
1/4 c. honey
2 c. chopped walnuts

For the caramel brandied oranges
3 oz. (1/2 c.) granulated sugar
1/4 c. water
1/4 c. honey
1/2 tsp. vanilla extract
1 tbsp. orange brandy
zest of 2 oranges
4 medium oranges, sectioned, plus any
    extra juice

Hazelnut Fig Cake

A rich moist cake that keeps very well. Serve small portions of this flavourful cake with ice cream or flavoured whipped cream. The recipe also works with well-ripened plums.

3 oz. (³/4 c.) sifted all-purpose flour
1/4 tsp. baking powder
1/4 tsp. baking soda
1/2 tsp. grated nutmeg
1/3 c. ground toasted hazelnuts
2 oz. (¹/4 c.) unsalted butter, room
    temperature
4 oz. (³/4 c.) sugar
1 egg
1/4 c. yogurt
2/3 c. puréed fresh figs
2-4 tbsp. of a favourite liqueur

Combine the sifted flour, baking powder, baking soda, nutmeg and ground hazelnuts and set aside.

Beat the butter and sugar together until light and fluffy, then beat in the egg.

Stir in the yogurt and fig purée. Combine with dry ingredients.

Butter and flour a 6-inch round cake pan or ring and pour in the batter.

Bake in a preheated 350°F oven for 20 minutes or until the centre springs back when pressed.

Remove from the oven and cool slightly. While the cake is still warm, drizzle with the liqueur. The warm cake will absorb the liqueur quickly to produce a dense, moist cake.

Cool to room temperature and serve with your favourite ice cream.

Raspberry, Fig and White Chocolate Bread Pudding

Coat the insides of eight 4-oz. ramekins with the extra butter or a nonstick spray.

Combine the first 8 ingredients using 1/4 cup of the brown sugar.

In a separate bowl combine the figs, chocolate and raspberries.

Place one round of bread in the bottom of each ramekin and top with the chocolate fruit mixture.

Whisk the egg mixture to combine evenly and pour half of it into the 8 ramekins.

Soak the remaining 8 bread rounds briefly in the remaining egg mixture and place one in each ramekin, press firmly, then top with the remaining egg mixture.

Divide the remaining brown sugar onto the tops of the puddings and dot with the butter.

Set aside for 30 minutes to allow the bread to absorb the liquid and soften.

Place the puddings in a roasting pan and pour in enough hot water to come halfway up the sides of the ramekins.

Bake in a 300°F oven for 30 minutes or until crusty on top.

Remove from the oven and serve warm.

3 eggs
1 1/3 c. milk
1 1/2 oz. (3/4 c.) brown sugar
1 tbsp. orange zest
1 tbsp. lemon zest
1/4 tsp. allspice
1 tsp. ground ginger
1 tsp. cinnamon
4 oz. (1 c.) dried figs, cut into small dice
3 oz. white chocolate, cut into small dice
3 oz. (3/4 c.) raspberries
sixteen 2-inch rounds of day-old white
    bread, 1/2-inch thick
2 oz. (1/4 c.) unsalted butter
extra butter to coat the ramekins

Salal Berry Rice Pudding with Caramel Pears

For the rice pudding
2 c. milk
1/3 c. granulated sugar
half a vanilla bean split or 1/2 tsp. pure
   vanilla extract
1/4 tsp. ground cinnamon
2 tsp. grated lemon zest
1 tbsp. grated fresh ginger
2 tbsp. fresh lemon juice
2 egg yolks
2 c. cooked short grain rice
1 c. salal berries*

* Salal berries are a wild west coast berry.
You can substitute blueberries or other
small berries. If substituting, reduce the
amount of lemon juice by half.

For the pears
2 medium-sized pears, ripe but still firm,
   cut into 12 wedges
1 tbsp. unsalted butter
2 tbsp. sugar
2 tsp. fresh lemon juice

For the rice pudding

Combine the milk, sugar, vanilla bean if using, cinnamon, lemon zest and ginger. Bring to a simmer for 3-4 minutes, then remove from heat and set aside.

Combine the lemon juice and egg yolks and whisk until light in colour and thickened slightly, about 1 minute.

Remove the vanilla bean from the milk mixture, scrape out the seeds and add seeds back to the pot.

Whisk the milk mixture into the egg yolks, then stir in the cooked rice.

Carefully fold in the berries.

Divide into eight 4-oz. ramekins or into one large mold. Place in a roasting pan and fill pan with enough hot water to reach halfway up the sides of the dishes.

Bake in a 300°F oven, loosely covered, for 20-25 minutes.

Serve warm or cold with the grilled pears and a little whipped cream.

For the pears

Heat a nonstick pan on medium to high heat and melt the butter. Add the pear slices and toss carefully.

Sprinkle the sugar over the pear slices and allow the pears to brown a little along with the sugar.

When all the sugar has melted and caramelized, add the lemon juice. Cook a little to reduce the liquid and remove from the heat.

Serve the rice pudding with the pears on top. Garnish, if desired, with a tuille (recipe below).

Tuille Paste

Tuille (pronounced "tweel") paste is similar to a fortune cookie batter in that it can be molded while still hot to form various shapes, such as pastry cups to hold fresh berries, mousse or ice creams. It can also be cut into shapes to garnish a dessert.

For uniformly shaped garnishes, use a stencil. Cut out the desired shape from the lid of an empty food container, discarding the cut-out piece. Lay the stencil flat on a parchment paper-lined baking sheet and spread the paste very thinly to fill the space before peeling off the stencil. Repeat for desired number of garnishes. To make pastry cups, carefully press the hot, just-baked shapes into or over empty cups or ramekins and cool.

4 oz. (1/2 c.) unsalted butter
8 oz. (1 1/4 c.) sugar
1/2 tsp. vanilla extract
4 oz. egg whites (approximately 4 egg
   whites)
8 oz. (2 c.) flour

Combine all the ingredients in the bowl of an electric mixer. Using the paddle or beater attachment, beat the mixture until smooth.

Spread the mixture thinly on a parchment paper-lined or nonstick baking sheet in desired shapes and bake at 350° for 6-8 minutes until the edges begin to brown.

Remove and cool on the tray.

Variation: For a Chocolate Tuille, add 1 oz. sifted cocoa powder.

Zabaglione with Vanilla Grappa

The famous Sicilian custard with a variation. Traditionally, this dessert is served while still warm. Another way is to allow it to cool, then fold in 1/2 cup whipped cream, which gives it more of a mousse-like consistency.

Grappa is a fiery Italian drink distilled from the skins, seeds and stems left over from the wine-making process. It can also be distilled from a variety of fruits, which can give each grappa its own distinct flavour. I make the vanilla grappa by simply steeping vanilla beans in grappa. If you cannot get grappa or vanilla beans, a good fruit brandy, schnapps or eau de vie and pure vanilla extract will work well.

Combine the egg yolks, whole egg, wine and sugar in a heatproof bowl.

Place over a pot of simmering water and whisk until the mixture becomes pale yellow and thickened.

Continue to whisk until the mixture falls in a continuous ribbon when lifted with the whisk.

Beat in the vanilla grappa and cook 1-2 minutes more.

Divide into individual serving cups or glasses, drop in a few berries and garnish with a tuille (page 220) or Chocolate Pine Nut Sugar Cookie (recipe below).

5 egg yolks
1 whole egg
1/2 c. dry white wine
3 tbsp. sugar
2 tbsp. vanilla-flavoured grappa
1 c. fresh berries (optional)

Chocolate Pine Nut Sugar Cookies

These cookies make a nice textural accompaniment to crème brûlée or other custard-type desserts, or serve them with a good strong cup of coffee.

Place the sugar and butter in the bowl of an electric mixer and beat with the paddle attachment until light and fluffy. Add the egg and blend well.

Sift together the flour, cocoa powder and baking powder and combine with the toasted pine nuts.

With the mixer on low speed, slowly add the dry mixture to the bowl, mixing only until it comes together as a dough.

Remove from the bowl and knead very briefly on a lightly floured board to combine.

The dough is now ready to be rolled out and cut or can be refrigerated for up to 5 days.

To make the cookies, roll the dough out on a lightly floured board to about 1/8-inch thick.

Cut into desired shapes using a cookie cutter or with a knife. Re-roll and cut any trims, being careful not to overwork.

Place the cookies on a greased baking sheet or line the sheet with parchment paper. Sprinkle extra granulated sugar on top and bake at 350°F for 10-12 minutes or until the edges are firm.

Remove from the oven and cool on the baking sheet.

This recipe will make approximately 3 dozen 2-inch round cookies.

4 oz. (2/3 c.) granulated sugar
4 oz. (1/2 c.) unsalted butter, room temperature
1 egg
8 oz. (2 c.) sifted all-purpose flour
1 tbsp. cocoa powder
2 tsp. baking powder
2 1/2 oz. (1/2 c.) pine nuts, toasted
extra sugar for topping

Chocolate Hazelnut Torte

A deliciously rich, flourless torte that freezes well without any noticeable change in texture or flavour.

8 oz. (1 c.) unsalted butter

4 oz. (²/3 c.) sugar

1/2 c. espresso or strong coffee

8 oz. semi-sweet chocolate, chopped

4 eggs

4 oz. (approx. 1 c.) skinned hazelnuts, toasted and finely ground

Coat the insides of two 6-inch or one 9-inch springform pan with butter or nonstick spray. Line the bottom with a circle of parchment paper and set aside.

Over a pot of simmering water, melt the butter, sugar, coffee and chopped chocolate.

Stir until smooth and remove from the heat. Whisk in the eggs one at a time, then whisk in the hazelnuts.

Pour the mixture into the prepared pan.

Bake in a preheated 325°F oven for 40-50 minutes until the centre springs back when pressed. The torte will rise as it bakes and then settle again as it cools.

Cool in the pan and serve at room temperature.

To serve, dust with cocoa and cut small portions with a warm, wet knife.

Garnish with Caramel Brandied Oranges (see Honey Walnut Tart recipe, page 215) and a chocolate decoration.

Chocolate for Garnishes

For making chocolate garnishes, use semi-sweet, dark or white chocolate. The cocoa butter in chocolate consists of several different fats that melt at varying temperatures between 60°F and 115°F. If the chocolate is not tempered properly for making garnishes the result will be grainy and brittle with streaks of cocoa fat that was not heated and/or cooled properly.

For a quicker, simpler way to make the garnishes, coating or dipping chocolate may be used. It is also known as baker's chocolate. The cocoa butter has been removed or blended with other fats so that the chocolate does not have to be melted and cooled to specific temperatures before using. It is easier to use but lacks the flavour and texture of true chocolate.

Tempering Chocolate for Decorations

Cut or grate the chocolate into small pieces. Reserve 1/4 of the chocolate and place the rest in a bowl over simmering water until melted. Stir constantly to avoid overheating or burning and to prevent the chocolate from becoming grainy.

Heat the chocolate to approximately 115°F and remove from the heat.

Gradually stir in the rest of the chocolate, a little at a time, waiting for each addition to melt and incorporate before adding more.

When the chocolate is perfectly smooth and the temperature has dropped to about 82°F, hold the chocolate at this temperature while stirring for 2 minutes, then slowly warm it back up again to 85°F to 90°F.

Bittersweet Ganache on a Honey Nut Phyllo Nest

For the ganache

Place the chocolate and butter in a heatproof bowl. Bring a pot of water to a boil, turn off the heat and place the bowl over the water.

While the chocolate is melting whip the cream to soft peaks. The cream should be thickened but still a little runny, like thickened sour cream.

Remove the chocolate from the heat and stir gently until smooth. Cool slightly and stir about 1/3 of the cream into the chocolate. Combine thoroughly.

Gently fold the rest of the cream into the chocolate mixture and place in the refrigerator until set.

For the phyllo nests

Combine the nuts, seeds, spices, 2 tbsp. melted butter and 2 tbsp. honey and set aside.

Lay one sheet of phyllo on a work surface and brush with melted butter.

Top with another sheet of pastry, brush with melted butter and spread 1/3 of the nut mixture on top.

Repeat the procedure twice more, ending with the nut mixture.

Starting on one edge, roll up the phyllo very loosely to form a cylinder.

Using a very sharp knife, cut the pastry crosswise very thinly, about 1/16-inch thick.

Pile the shredded pastry loosely into 8 equal portions on a baking sheet and drizzle with any extra melted butter. Bake at 350°F for 18-20 minutes until brown and crisp.

Remove from the oven and cool on the tray.

For the orange custard

Combine 1 cup milk, the honey and orange zest in a saucepan and bring to a simmer.

Combine the cornstarch, egg yolk and 1 tbsp. milk and add to the simmering milk. Stir until the mixture comes to a simmer again.

Cook 1 minute more, remove from the heat and add the orange liqueur.

Pour into a bowl and cover the surface of the custard with plastic wrap to prevent a skin from forming. Refrigerate before using.

To assemble

Combine the rye whiskey, lemon juice and 4 tbsp. honey and set aside.

Place one nest in the centre of a serving plate and drizzle with 2 tsp. of the honey/rye whiskey mixture.

With a large soup spoon dipped in warm water, place a portion of the chilled ganache on top of the nest.

Drizzle 2-3 tbsp. of the orange custard around the plate and garnish with a little fresh whipped cream and a chocolate garnish.

For the ganache
3 oz. bittersweet chocolate, finely chopped
1 tbsp. unsalted butter
1 1/2 c. heavy cream

For the phyllo nests
1/3 c. coarsely ground toasted hazelnuts
1/3 c. coarsely ground toasted almonds
1/3 c. whole pumpkin seeds
1/2 tsp. ground cinnamon
1/2 tsp. ground ginger
1/2 c. melted unsalted butter
6 tbsp. honey
6 sheets phyllo pastry
2 tbsp. rye whiskey
2 tsp. fresh lemon juice

For the orange custard
1 c. plus 1 tbsp. milk
1 tbsp. honey
4 tbsp. minced orange zest
1 1/2 tbsp. cornstarch
1 egg yolk
1 tbsp. orange-flavoured liqueur

Sourdough Chocolate Brew Cake

An unusual combination of ingredients that produces a rich, intensely flavoured cake. The sourdough starter contributes a slight tartness to the batter and also helps to leaven the cake.

Be sure to use a good dark beer that will blend well with the richness of the coffee and chocolate.

For the sauce
1 tbsp. unsalted butter
1/2 c. brewed coffee
1/4 c. dark beer, room temperature
6 oz. semi-sweet chocolate
1/4 tsp. ground cinnamon
2 tbsp. heavy cream

For the brew cake
6 tbsp. unsalted butter
6 oz. (1 c.) brown sugar
1/4 tsp. salt
4 oz. sourdough starter (page 244)
3/4 c. dark beer
1 egg
2 tbsp. coffee flavour*
3/4 tsp. vanilla extract
3 oz. (1/2 c. plus 1 tbsp.) all-purpose flour
2 1/2 oz. cocoa powder
1 1/2 tsp. baking powder
1/2 tsp. fresh grated nutmeg
icing sugar for dusting

* To make the coffee flavour, combine 110 grams (1 1/2 c.) instant coffee crystals with 1/4 c. boiling water and 2 oz. (1/3 c.) sugar, stir to dissolve and cool. This may be used to flavour a variety of sweet or savoury dishes and will keep indefinitely in the refrigerator.

For the sauce

Combine all ingredients except the cream in the top of a double boiler placed over simmering water.

Stir until the butter and chocolate have melted and the mixture is smooth.

Stir in the cream and remove from the heat.

For the brew cake

In the bowl of an electric mixer, cream the butter, sugar and salt.

In a separate bowl, combine the sourdough starter, beer, egg, coffee flavour and vanilla extract. Set aside.

Into another bowl, sift together the flour, cocoa powder and baking powder.

On low speed, add the wet ingredients and the dry ingredients alternately, one half at a time, starting with the wet and ending with the dry.

Butter and flour an 8 x 8-inch cake pan and line the bottom with parchment paper, or use 8 individual 2 x 2 1/2-inch ring molds (page 248) lined with parchment, and fill 2/3 full.

Sprinkle the tops with the fresh grated nutmeg and bake at 325°F for 20 minutes or until a toothpick comes out clean (12-15 minutes for individual ring molds).

Dust the tops with more cocoa powder and icing sugar and serve warm (not hot) with the sauce and whipped cream.

Mini Chocolate Cheesecakes

For this recipe you will need four 4-inch springform pans. Each is enough for two generous portions or quartered, the cheesecakes can be used as part of an assorted dessert plate. The ganache topping gives a rich-looking finish.

For a variation add 1/2-3/4 cup chopped walnuts to the batter, omit the Ganache Topping and coat the sides with whipped cream and extra chopped nuts.

For the cheesecakes

Coat the pans with butter or nonstick spray and set aside.

On a lightly floured board roll the Shortcrust Dough to 1/8-inch thickness. Cut the dough to line the pans and trim the excess. Refrigerate while making the filling.

Beat together the cheese and sugar until smooth, then beat in the sour cream or yogurt.

Beat in the eggs one at a time, mixing only to combine.

Stir in the melted chocolate and vanilla extract.

Fill the pans 2/3 full and bake in a 300°F oven 40-45 minutes until the centre is slightly firm.

Remove from the oven and cool before removing from the pans.

For the ganache topping

Place the chocolate in a heatproof bowl with the butter.

Bring the cream to a simmer and pour over the chocolate.

Stir with a wooden spoon or rubber spatula until smooth and all the chocolate has melted.

Cool until the mixture has thickened but still can be poured.

Place the cheesecakes on a wire rack set on a baking sheet and pour or ladle some of the ganache over top of each cake.

Spread with a spatula to cover the tops and sides, then refrigerate to allow the chocolate to firm.

Cut the cheesecakes into desired portions using a hot, wet knife.

For the cheesecakes
10 oz. cream cheese, room temperature
4 oz. (2/3 c.) sugar
1/2 c. sour cream or yogurt
3 eggs
6 oz. melted dark chocolate
2 tsp. pure vanilla extract
Shortcrust Dough (page 263)

For the ganache topping
12 oz. dark chocolate pieces
1 tbsp. unsalted butter
1 c. heavy cream

Molten Mocha Chocolate Cakes

These are great little cakes that can be prepared ahead of time and baked at the last minute. They can be refrigerated for up to 24 hours or frozen for up to 3 weeks before baking. Bake refrigerated ramekins 9-10 minutes or frozen 14-15 minutes. The timing for these cakes is crucial. Since all ovens vary slightly it may take a few tries to achieve the results you like.

butter or nonstick spray for ramekins
1 1/2 oz. (1/4 c.), plus 3 tbsp. all-purpose
  flour
1 1/2 oz. (6 tbsp.) unsalted butter
6 oz. semi-sweet chocolate
1 tbsp. instant coffee crystals
1/4 c. cream
1/2 tsp. vanilla extract
2 large eggs
2 large egg yolks
2 oz. (1/4 c.) sugar

Coat the insides of eight 6-oz. ramekins with butter or nonstick spray and 3 tbsp. of the flour. Set aside.

In a medium-sized heatproof bowl combine the butter, chocolate, coffee crystals and cream. Set over a pot of barely simmering water and stir gently until the butter and chocolate have melted and the mixture is smooth.

Remove from the heat and whisk in the 1/4 cup flour and vanilla. Set aside.

In a medium bowl whisk together the eggs, yolks and 1/4 cup sugar at high speed until very thick and pale yellow, about 4 minutes.

With a rubber spatula gently stir 1/3 of the egg into the chocolate mixture, then fold in the rest.

Pour batter into prepared ramekins to about 3/4 full.

Place the ramekins on a baking tray and place in a preheated 400°F oven.

Bake 8-9 minutes until the edges are set and the centre is still slightly soft.

Run a small knife around the edges of the ramekins and turn over onto a plate. Let the cakes cool 2-3 minutes in the ramekins before lifting.

Dust with cocoa powder and serve with a tart fruit purée and whipped cream.

Strawberry Mascarpone Ice Cream

photo top right, page 234

Combine the milk with the vanilla bean (if using) and bring to a simmer over medium heat.

Meanwhile, beat the egg yolks and sugar in a heatproof bowl until light and fluffy.

Remove the vanilla bean from the milk, scrape out the seeds and add them to the milk.

While whisking, slowly pour the hot milk into the egg mixture.

Place the egg/milk mixture over a pot of barely simmering water and stir while heating until the mixture coats the back of a wooden spoon.

Remove from the heat and stir in the mascarpone cheese, the strawberry purée* and vanilla extract (if using).

Cool completely and chill several hours or overnight. Freeze in an ice cream maker following the manufacturer's instructions.

* To enhance the colour of the ice cream add 1/4 cup strained raspberry purée to the mixture.

> 2 c. milk
> vanilla bean split in half or vanilla extract
> 4 egg yolks
> 6 oz. (1 c.) granulated sugar
> 1 c. mascarpone cheese
> 1 c. strawberry purée, strained through a fine sieve
> 1/4 c. strained raspberry purée (optional)

> **TIP**
> The texture of the ice cream is greatly improved if the custard is cooled overnight before freezing in the ice cream maker.

Salal Berry Ice Cream

photo bottom right, page 234

Salal berries are abundant on the west coast, growing wild among the evergreens. Substitute any other wild berries that may be available in your area.

Salal berries have a unique flavour similar to blueberries but lack the acidity that makes most berries so delicious. The lemon juice in this recipe helps compensate for this. These berries produce a brilliant purple-coloured ice cream but be careful, they also stain very well.

Combine the berries, lemon juice and water in a pot and simmer until the berries are soft. Remove from the heat, cool the mixture slightly and purée in a blender or food processor. Strain through a fine sieve and refrigerate until cold.

Heat the milk to scalding but do not boil.

Combine the egg yolks, sugar and vanilla extract and whisk until smooth and pale yellow.

Slowly add about 1/4 of the hot milk to the egg mixture, stirring all the time, then add the egg mixture into the rest of the milk.

Transfer to a heatproof bowl and set it over a pot of barely simmering water.

Stir constantly until the mixture thickens and coats the back of a wooden spoon.

Remove the bowl from the heat, and stir in the cream and strained berries.

Cool to room temperature, then chill covered overnight in the refrigerator. Freeze in an ice cream maker following the manufacturer's directions.

> 16 oz. salal berries
> 2 tbsp. fresh lemon juice
> 1/4 c. water
> 2 c. milk
> 10 egg yolks
> 10 oz. (1 2/3 c.) granulated sugar
> 1/2 tsp. vanilla extract
> 2 c. heavy cream

Rum and Honey Ice Cream

photo top left, page 234

Combine the milk, cream and vanilla bean (if using) and heat to scalding.

In a heatproof bowl, beat the yolks and sugar until light and fluffy.

Remove the vanilla bean and scrape the seeds into the milk mixture.

Pour the mixture into the egg yolks while whisking rapidly.

Heat over barely simmering water, stirring constantly until the mixture coats the back of a wooden spoon.

Remove from the heat and stir in the vanilla extract (if using), the honey and the rum.

Cool completely and chill several hours or overnight.

Freeze in an ice cream maker following the manufacturer's instructions.

2 c. milk
2 c. heavy cream
1 vanilla bean cut open down the middle
  or 1 tsp. vanilla extract
7 egg yolks
4 oz. (2/3 c.) sugar
3/4 c. honey
2 tbsp. dark rum

Raspberry Frozen Yogurt

photo bottom left, page 234

Combine the honey, water, lemon juice and raspberries in a pot and cook over medium heat until the berries begin to fall apart.

Beat the yolks and while whisking add a little of the raspberry mixture, then slowly add the rest.

Strain the mixture through a fine sieve and into a heatproof bowl.

Place over a pot of barely simmering water and, stirring constantly with a wooden spoon, cook the mixture until it coats the back of the spoon.

Cool completely in the refrigerator.

Combine the yogurt and vanilla extract and whisk smooth. Set aside.

In a separate bowl whip the egg whites until frothy.

Slowly add sugar while whipping and whip until firm.

Add the raspberry mixture to the yogurt, combine well, fold in the whipped egg whites and freeze in an ice cream maker following the manufacturer's directions.

1/4 c. plus 2 tbsp. honey
1 tbsp. water
1 tbsp. lemon juice
6 oz. (1 1/4 c.) fresh or frozen raspberries
4 egg yolks
2 c. plain yogurt
1 tsp. vanilla extract
2 egg whites
2 tbsp. sugar

Pumpkin Seed Ice Cream

top left, page 237

This is an eggless ice cream, which does not require the preparation of a custard.

Whisk together all ingredients except the pumpkin seeds.

Chop half of the pumpkin seeds in a food processor or on a board with a sharp knife.

Add all the seeds to the mixture and combine well. Chill 2-3 hours or overnight.

Freeze in an ice cream maker following manufacturer's instructions.

1 1/2 c. milk
2 c. heavy cream
1/2 c. honey
1/2 tsp. vanilla extract
1/2 tsp. almond extract
1 tsp. ground ginger
1/4 tsp. grated nutmeg
5 oz. (1 c.) pumpkin seeds, toasted
1/4 tsp. salt

Pine Nut Praline and Honey Ice Cream

top right, page 237

1 c. milk
1 c. heavy cream
half a vanilla bean cut open down the middle or 1/2 tsp. vanilla extract
7 egg yolks
3 oz. (1/3 c.) honey
1 tbsp. dark rum
6 oz. (1 c.) ground Pine Nut Praline (page 261)

Combine the milk and cream in a pot. Cut the vanilla bean (if using) in half lengthwise, scrape out the seeds and add to the pot along with the pod. Scald the mixture over low heat.

In a heatproof bowl, beat the yolks and honey until light and fluffy.

Remove the vanilla bean from the milk mixture, scrape out any remaining seeds and add them back to the pot.

While continually whisking, pour the milk mixture into the egg yolks.

Place the bowl over barely simmering water and cook stirring until the mixture coats the back of a wooden spoon. Remove from the heat and stir in the vanilla extract (if using) and the rum.

Cool completely and chill several hours or overnight.

Stir in the ground pine nut praline. Freeze in an ice cream maker following the manufacturer's instructions.

Chocolate Hazelnut Ice Cream

bottom right, page 237

1 1/2 c. milk
2 c. heavy cream
3 egg yolks
4 oz. (2/3 c.) granulated sugar
1 tbsp. rum, brandy or nut-flavoured liqueur
6 oz. semisweet chocolate, chopped
5 oz. (1 c.) hazelnuts, toasted and coarsely chopped

Combine the milk and cream in a pot and scald over low heat. In a heatproof bowl beat the egg yolks and sugar together until pale yellow and fluffy.

While continually whisking, slowly pour the milk into the egg mixture and stir to combine.

Place the bowl over barely simmering water and cook stirring until the mixture coats the back of a wooden spoon. Remove from the heat, add the liqueur and chocolate and stir until the chocolate is melted through.

Add the hazelnuts and refrigerate overnight. Freeze in an ice cream maker following the manufacturer's instructions.

Vanilla Spice Ice Cream

bottom left, page 237

2 c. milk
2 c. heavy cream
1 vanilla bean split or 1 tsp. vanilla extract
8 egg yolks
8 oz. (1 1/3 c.) sugar
1 tsp. ground cinnamon
3/4 tsp. ground ginger
1/2 tsp. ground nutmeg

Place the milk and cream in a heavy-bottomed pot with the vanilla bean (if using) and bring to a simmer.

Combine the egg yolks, sugar and spices in a heatproof bowl and beat until light and fluffy.

Take the cream from the heat and remove the vanilla bean. Scrape the seeds from the bean and add to the cream.

While continually whisking the egg yolk mixture slowly pour in the cream, speeding up the pouring when about half of the cream has been added.

Cook the mixture over a pot of barely simmering water, stirring constantly until the mixture coats the back of a wooden spoon. Remove from the heat and continue to stir briefly to prevent overheating. Stir in the vanilla extract (if using).

Cool the mixture completely and chill several hours or overnight. Freeze in an ice cream maker following the manufacturer's instructions.

breads

Basic White Bread	240
Oven-Dried Tomato Bread	240
Enriched White Bread	241
Focaccia	241
Hearty Breakfast Bread	242
Olive Rolls	242
Orange and Cranberry Bread	243
Whole Grain Honey Bread	243
Sourdough Starter	244
Sourdough Bread	244
Sourdough Flatbread	245
Quick Olive Nut Bread	246
Polenta, Flax and Sunflower Seed Bread	246
Sea Bread	247

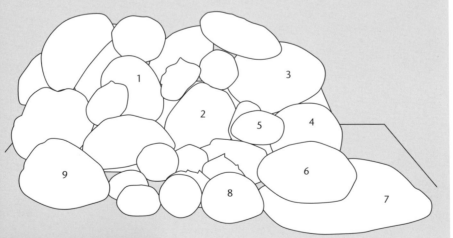

1. Polenta, Flax, Sunflower Seed Bread; 2. Whole Grain Honey Bread; 3. Basic White Bread; 4. Sourdough Bread; 5. Olive Rolls; 6. Sourdough Flatbread; 7. Focaccia; 8. Hearty Breakfast Bread; 9. Quick Olive Nut Bread

Photo: Sea Bread

breads

Basic White Bread

This is a good basic bread that can be enhanced by the addition of many favourite ingredients such as fresh herbs, whole seeds, and cheese. The shortening gives a tender crumb. For a more flavourful, softer crumb use butter and substitute milk for the water. This is enough for two 9 x 5-inch loaf pans or 24-30 rolls.

2 c. warm water
1 tbsp. dry yeast
2 tsp. granulated sugar
2 lb. (about 6 c.) bread flour
1-2 tsp. salt
1/4 c. shortening, room temperature

Note that when dry yeast is called for, I am referring to traditional, dry active yeast.

In a small bowl combine the warm water, yeast and sugar. Set aside in a warm place to dissolve the yeast, about 5-10 minutes.

Place the flour in a large bowl or the bowl of an electric mixer.

Add the dissolved yeast to the flour along with the salt and the softened shortening.

With a wooden spoon or with the dough hook of the electric mixer, mix the dough and then turn it out onto a lightly floured surface.

Knead until smooth and elastic, about 8-10 minutes, adding small amounts of extra flour if needed to prevent the dough from sticking.

Place the dough in a greased bowl and cover with plastic wrap. Set aside in a warm place until doubled in volume, about 1-1 1/2 hours.

Turn the dough out onto a lightly floured work surface and knead 8-10 minutes.

With a sharp knife or dough cutter divide the dough for loaves or rolls.

Shape and place into greased and floured loaf pans or on baking trays and set aside to rise in a warm place until almost doubled in size.

Bake in a pre-heated 375°F oven about 40 minutes for loaves and 20-25 minutes for rolls.

Remove from the pans and cool on a rack.

Oven-dried Tomato Bread

Try this bread with a variety of cold cuts and antipasti for a hearty lunch or snack. You'll thank yourself.

1 recipe Basic White Bread (above), substituting 1/4 c. extra virgin olive oil for the 1/4 c. shortening
1 c. chopped Oven-dried Tomatoes (page 250)
1/2 c. grated Asiago cheese

Place half the tomatoes into the bowl of a food processor and process to a coarse purée.

Combine with the remaining half of the tomatoes and set aside.

Follow the recipe for Basic White Bread.

Work the tomato mixture and grated Asiago into the dough after turning it out onto a work surface.

If the dough seems sticky, knead in a little more flour.

Shape as desired and bake approximately 40 minutes for loaves and 20-25 minutes for rolls.

Remove from the pans and cool on a rack.

Enriched White Bread

This bread makes great sandwiches or French toast. Add 1¹/2 cups grated aged cheddar for cheese bread. Add up to 2 cups of dried fruits or nuts for an interesting breakfast bread. The richness of the dough makes this bread a good keeper.

Combine the yeast with the warm milk and sugar and set aside in a warm spot to dissolve, about 5-10 minutes.

Place the salt and flour in a large bowl and set aside.

Break 4 eggs into the yeast mixture and whisk briefly. Pour the mixture into the flour and work in with the soft butter.

Turn out onto a lightly floured work surface and knead until smooth and elastic, about 8-10 minutes, adding more flour if needed to prevent the dough from sticking.

Place in a greased bowl, cover with plastic wrap and set aside in a warm place until doubled in size.

Divide in two, form loaves and place in greased and floured loaf pans.

Cover and set aside in a warm spot until almost doubled in volume.

Beat the remaining egg with 1 tbsp. water and brush the tops of the loaves.

Bake in a pre-heated 375°F oven for 40 minutes.

Remove loaves from pans and cool on a rack.

2 lb. (about 6 c.) bread flour
1-2 tsp. salt
2 tbsp. dry yeast
1¹/2 c. warm milk
1 tbsp. sugar
5 eggs
4 oz. (¹/2 c.) soft unsalted butter

Focaccia

Traditionally flavoured with sage, this bread is equally good with any fresh robust herb such as rosemary, basil or fresh oregano. For even more flavour, grate some Parmigiano Reggiano or Pecorino Romano on top for the last 5 minutes of baking.

Dissolve the yeast and sugar in the water.

Mix in the ¹/4 cup oil, and the salt and honey.

Add the flour and knead until smooth and elastic, about 10 minutes.

Place in an oiled bowl, cover and let rise until half doubled in volume.

Divide the dough in half. On a floured board roll each of the pieces into a rectangle roughly 10 x 12 inches and place on baking sheets dusted with cornmeal.

Combine the extra ¹/4 cup olive oil with the garlic and fresh oregano.

Brush the mixture on top of the dough and sprinkle with the coarse salt and ground black pepper.

With your fingertips make indentations over the whole surface of the dough (this helps the dough rise more evenly).

Cover and let rise until almost doubled, then bake at 350-375°F for 20 minutes.

Remove from baking sheets and cool on a rack.

1 tbsp. dry yeast
2 tsp. sugar
1¹/2 c. warm water
¹/4 c. extra virgin olive oil
2 tsp. salt
2 tbsp. honey
1 lb. 4 oz. (4¹/4 c.) bread flour
¹/4 c. extra virgin olive oil
1 tbsp. chopped garlic
2 tbsp. chopped fresh oregano
2 tbsp. coarse salt
1 tbsp. freshly ground black pepper
cornmeal for dusting the baking sheets

Hearty Breakfast Bread

1/2 c. warm water
1 c. warm milk
1 tbsp. dry yeast
2 large eggs
2 tbsp. honey
2 tbsp. molasses
1 tbsp. salt
2 oz. (1 1/4 c.) wheat bran
3 oz. (1/2 c.) cornmeal
2 oz. (3/4 c.) rolled oats
8 oz. (1 3/4 c.) whole wheat flour
2 tbsp. soft unsalted butter
12 oz. (2 1/4 c.) bread flour
1 tbsp. water
1/2 c. each oatmeal, wheat bran and
  cornmeal, combined

Combine water and milk in a large bowl or the bowl of an electric mixer. Add the yeast and dissolve.

In a separate bowl, mix one egg, honey and molasses. Add to the yeast together with the salt, bran, cornmeal, oatmeal and whole wheat flour.

Knead in the butter and bread flour, adjusting the amount of flour to produce a fairly stiff dough. Continue to knead until the dough is smooth and elastic, about 8 minutes.

Place the dough in an oiled bowl, cover and let rise until doubled.

Divide the dough into two loaves or approximately 16 rolls.

Whisk the remaining egg with the 1 tbsp. water and brush the tops of the breads.

Carefully press the breads, top side down, into the oatmeal, bran and cornmeal mixture and place on baking sheets. Cover and let rise until half doubled in size.

Bake at 400°F for 10 minutes, then 20-30 minutes for loaves, 10 minutes for rolls.

Remove from baking sheets and cool on a rack.

Olive Rolls

1 1/4 c. warm water
1 tbsp. dry yeast
pinch of sugar
2 oz. (1/2 c.) rye flour
1 lb. 2 oz. (3-3 1/4 c.) bread flour
1/3 c. extra virgin olive oil
1 tbsp. soft butter
1 tbsp. salt
3/4-1 c. black olives, pitted and coarsely
  chopped

Place the warm water and sugar in a large bowl or the bowl of an electric mixer.

Sprinkle in the yeast and set aside for 10 minutes. Add the rye flour and 1/2 cup of the bread flour. Beat until smooth.

Cover and let rise until bubbly.

Add 1/2 cup more flour, the olive oil, butter, salt and olives and beat 1 minute.

Add the rest of the flour, 1/2 cup at a time, until a soft dough is formed and it cleans the sides of the bowl.

Turn onto a floured board and knead 2 minutes until smooth and elastic.

Place in an oiled bowl, cover and let rise until doubled.

Divide the dough into 16-20 pieces and form each one into an oval-shaped roll, placing them on a floured baking sheet at least 2 inches apart.

Let rise until almost doubled.

Preheat oven to 425°F.

With floured scissors held at a 45° angle, snip the tops of the rolls 3 times down the centre.

Bake 15-20 minutes until crusty and brown.

Remove from baking sheet and cool on a rack.

Orange and Cranberry Bread

Combine the cranberries, orange zest, candied ginger and orange juice concentrate and set aside.

Follow the recipe for Enriched White Bread and after working in the soft butter, add the fruit mixture.

Knead the dough until the fruit is uniformly distributed and the dough is smooth and elastic. You may need to incorporate up to 1/3 cup extra flour to keep the dough from sticking. Continue following the directions for Enriched White Bread.

When shaping the breads make sure that there is no exposed fruit on the tops of the loaves that would burn during baking.

After brushing the tops with the whisked egg, sprinkle with poppy seeds and bake as directed.

1 recipe Enriched White Bread (page 241)
1 c. dried cranberries
3 tbsp. grated orange zest
2 tbsp. minced candied ginger
3 tbsp. orange juice concentrate
2-3 tbsp. poppy seeds

Whole Grain Honey Bread

A healthy, hearty bread with a hint of sweetness and a great chewy crust. This bread is great served with slices of strong cheese or toasted for breakfast.

The whole grains in this recipe are available at most health-food stores. Kamut is a type of wheat with a much larger kernel. If these grains are not available, others can be substituted. I've chosen these particular grains because they all cook in approximately the same time.

Place the whole grains in a dry stock pot and toast them over medium heat until lightly coloured and aromatic. Add the water, bring to a simmer and cook for 45 minutes to 1 hour until the grains are tender. Cool until tepid and strain, reserving 2 cups of the water.

Pour the reserved water in a large mixing bowl and stir in the honey and yeast.

Place in a warm spot to dissolve the yeast, about 5-10 minutes.

Add the cooked grains, oil, salt, rye flour and flax and stir until smooth.

Add 3 1/2-4 cups flour and work it in until you have a ball of dough. Divide the dough into 3 pieces.

Turn out the dough on a lightly floured work surface and knead 6-8 minutes. Add just enough flour as you knead to keep the dough from sticking to the board. Knead until smooth.

Place the dough in an oiled bowl, cover with plastic wrap and set in a warm place to rise until doubled in volume.

Divide the dough into 3 and form each piece into a round loaf. Place on a greased and floured baking sheet. Cover and let rise to 1 1/2 times the original size.

The loaves can also be baked in regular 9 x 5-inch loaf pans.

Whisk together the egg and 2 tbsp. water and set aside.

After the loaves have risen, brush with eggwash and bake in a preheated 350°F oven 40-45 minutes.

Remove from the baking sheet and cool on a rack.

1/2 c. whole wheat kernels
1/4 c. barley
1/4 c. whole kamut kernels
1/4 c. whole rye kernels
1/4 c. hulled oats
4 c. water
1/2 c. honey
1 tbsp. dry yeast
1/4 c. vegetable or extra virgin olive oil
2 tsp. salt
5 oz. (1 c.) dark rye flour
1/2 c. ground flax seed
1/4 c. whole flax seed
1 lb. 6 oz. (4-4 1/4 c.) all-purpose or bread flour
1 egg plus 2 tbsp. water

Sourdough Starter

1¹/2 tbsp. dry yeast
1 oz. (2 tbsp.) sugar
3 c. warm water
1 lb. 8 oz. (4¹/2 c.) bread flour

In a plastic, glass or ceramic container, with plenty of room for expansion, dissolve the yeast with the sugar in the water and let it sit in a warm spot until frothy. Mix in the flour, stirring to a smooth paste.

Cover with cheesecloth and let sit at room temperature at least 2-3 days. Stir down once a day as the starter ferments, stirring in any crust that forms on top.

When the starter is ready to use, remove the 1 lb. 4 oz. (2¹/4 cups) needed for the bread recipe and replenish the starter with 12 oz. (2¹/4 cups) of flour and 1 cup of warm water. Let stand for 24 hours before using; after that store the starter in the refrigerator.

Caring for the starter

If the starter is not used, add 8 oz. (1¹/2 cups) of flour and 1 cup of warm water once a week. If more than 2-3 weeks go by without using the starter, remove from the container and discard half (or give it to an appreciative friend), wash out the container and replace the starter. Add 10 oz. (2 cups) of flour and 1 cup of warm water. If the starter is left too long without replenishing, the yeast will eventually die.

Sourdough Bread

1 tbsp. dry yeast
2 c. warm water
¹/2 oz. (1 tbsp.) sugar
1 lb. 4 oz. (2¹/4 c.) sourdough starter
1 tbsp. salt
2 lb. 6 oz. (7¹/2 c.) bread flour,
    approximately
cornmeal for sprinkling on trays

Dissolve the yeast in the water and add the sugar and starter.

Add the salt and incorporate enough flour to form a firm dough.

Knead for 8-10 minutes until the dough is smooth and elastic.

Place in an oiled bowl, cover with plastic wrap and allow to rise until doubled in size.

Divide the dough into 4 loaves or approximately 36 rolls.

Shape the loaves and place on baking sheets sprinkled with cornmeal. Cover and let rise by a half.

Dust liberally with flour and score the tops in a criss-cross pattern with a very sharp serrated knife.

Have a baking pan ready on the bottom shelf of a preheated 450°F oven.

Place the loaves in the oven and immediately throw 10-12 ice cubes* onto the pan on the bottom shelf.

Bake 10 minutes, then reduce the temperature to 350°F and bake 25 minutes more for loaves and about 10 minutes for rolls.

Remove from baking sheets and cool on a rack.

* The ice creates steam that allows the bread to rise more and also forms a crisper crust.

Sourdough Flatbread

For the olive herb oil

Place the olives, herbs, garlic and olive oil in the bowl of a food processor and pulse until you have a coarse paste. Adjust the seasoning if necessary with salt and pepper and set aside.

For the dough

Place the yeast, sugar and warm water in a mixing bowl and stir to combine.

Cover with a clean towel and let stand in a warm spot until creamy, about 5 minutes.

Add the starter, milk, olive oil and salt.

With a wooden spoon or an electric mixer beat in the flour a little at a time until you have a dough that is firm and does not stick to the sides of the bowl.

Remove from the bowl and knead on a lightly floured surface until smooth and elastic, adding extra flour 1 tbsp. at a time to keep the dough from sticking.

Form the dough into a ball and place in a lightly oiled bowl. Cover and place in a warm area to rise until doubled, approximately 1 hour depending on the room temperature.

Remove the dough from the bowl and divide into 8 pieces.

Form each piece into a ball, then using a rolling pin, roll the balls into 6-inch disks.

Place the disks on two 13 x 16-inch baking sheets that have been dusted with flour.

Set aside for 10 minutes and allow to rise slightly, then bake in a preheated 400°F oven 12-14 minutes or until lightly coloured and the bread springs back when pressed.

Remove from baking sheets and brush or spoon a heaping tablespoon of olive herb oil on each flatbread. Cut into wedges and serve warm.

For the olive herb oil
1 c. pitted olives that have been packed in oil, green or black or a combination
1/4 c. fresh oregano leaves
1/4 c. fresh rosemary leaves
1/4 c. fresh chives
2 tbsp. minced garlic
1 c. extra virgin olive oil
salt and ground black pepper to taste

For the dough
1 tbsp. dry yeast
2 tsp. sugar
1 c. warm water
4 oz. (1/2 c.) sourdough starter (page 244)
1/2 c. milk
2 tbsp. olive oil
pinch of salt
1 lb. 2 oz. (3-31/4 c.) bread flour
extra flour

Quick Olive Nut Bread

When in a pinch, this is a quick, savoury bread that is at its best eaten the day it is baked.

12 oz. (3 c.) sifted all-purpose flour
3 tbsp. baking powder
1 tsp. salt
10 oz. (2 c.) whole wheat flour
2 eggs, plus 1 egg for eggwash
2 c. milk
1/4 c. extra virgin olive oil
2 c. coarsely chopped pitted olives, black or green or a combination
12 oz. (2 c.) walnuts, chopped

Preheat oven to 350°F.

Sift together the all-purpose flour, baking powder and salt.

Add the whole wheat flour.

Mix 2 eggs, milk and olive oil and combine with the flour mixture using a few quick strokes, then add the olives and nuts.

Knead gently just to incorporate the nuts and olives.

Form into two loaves and place into greased 9 x 5-inch loaf pans, or shape into round loaves and bake on a baking sheet.

Whisk the last egg with 1 tbsp. water and brush the tops of the loaves.

Bake 35-40 minutes.

Remove from pans and cool on a rack.

Polenta, Flax and Sunflower Seed Bread

2 tbsp. dry yeast
1 tbsp. sugar
1 1/2 c. warm water
1/2 c. honey
1/4 c. vegetable oil
1 egg, plus 1 egg for eggwash
1 tbsp. salt
10 oz. (2 c.) whole wheat flour
14 oz. (2 3/4 c.) bread flour
1/3 c. flax seed
1 1/2 oz. (1/4 c.) cornmeal
1/4 c. sunflower seeds

Dissolve the yeast and sugar in 1/2 cup of the water.

Combine with the rest of the water, the honey, vegetable oil, one egg and salt.

In the bowl of the mixer combine the whole wheat flour, bread flour, flax seed, cornmeal and sunflower seeds.

On low speed, add the liquid mixture to the mixing bowl.

Knead until the dough is smooth and cleans the sides of the bowl, adding more flour 1 tbsp. at a time if needed.

Place in an oiled bowl, cover and let rise until doubled.

Divide the dough into 2 loaves or into 20 rolls.

Allow to rise until half doubled, and brush with eggwash made by whisking egg with 1 tbsp. water.

Bake at 375°F for 30-35 minutes for loaves or 15-20 minutes for rolls.

Remove from pans and cool on a rack.

Sea Bread

Over 200 varieties of edible seaweeds, rich in vitamins and minerals, flourish in the cold Pacific waters off the west coast. Common varieties include sea lettuce, which makes a wonderful briny pesto, sea asparagus, sea cabbage, alaria, porphyra and egregia. I like to use various seaweeds in anything from bread to mixed salads, soups and for stuffing or rolling fish and shellfish.

Combine the warm water, yeast and honey in a mixing bowl and set in a warm place until frothy.

Stir in the beer, olive oil, seaweeds and salt. Add the cornmeal, whole wheat flour and enough bread flour to form a firm dough that cleans the sides of the bowl and is not sticky to the touch.

Place the dough on a lightly floured board and knead until smooth and elastic, about 8-10 minutes.

Place in a lightly oiled bowl, cover with a damp cloth or plastic wrap and set aside to rise until doubled in size, approximately 1 hour.

Remove from the bowl and knead briefly on a lightly floured board. Divide dough into 4 pieces. Form each piece into a ball, then roll into an oval about 8-10 inches by 4-5 inches wide.

With your hands, flatten and push out the dough to about 1- to 1¹/₂-inches thick and irregularly shaped.

Place two loaves each on two 12 x 16-inch baking sheets dusted with cornmeal, cover and allow to rise to about 1¹/₂ times.

With a pair of sharp scissors dipped in flour, make random cuts into the edges of the dough at different lengths to resemble fronds of seaweed.

Brush with eggwash and sprinkle with coarse sea salt.

Bake in a 375°F oven for 20-30 minutes. Remove from baking sheets and cool on a rack.

Serve, if desired, with Sea Lettuce Pesto (page 252).

1/2 c. warm water
1 tbsp. dry yeast
2 tbsp. honey
12 oz. (1¹/₂ c.) beer, room temperature
2 tbsp. extra virgin olive oil
2 c. assorted fresh seaweeds, coarsely chopped
2 tsp. sea salt
6 oz. (1 c.) yellow cornmeal
5 oz. (1 c.) whole wheat flour
1 lb. 4 oz. (3¹/₄-3¹/₂ c.) bread flour
eggwash made with 1 egg and 2 tbsp. water
coarse sea salt to sprinkle on the bread

Rings and Molds

Throughout this book you will encounter recipes that call for the use of metal rings or molds. The rings are lined with various types of dough for the production of tarts, coated with oil and placed in poaching water to hold the shape of a poached egg or they are filled with assorted items for presentation. Although I use metal rings, preferably stainless steel, they can also be of food grade plastic.

I prefer metal because it allows me to bake items as well as use the rings solely for presentation.

Any good-sized kitchen supply store should carry at least some rings or molds in a variety of shapes and sizes and in plastic and/or metal.

It is possible to cut your own rings from plastic pvc pipe, which is what is used for potable water lines in homes.

It is also possible to have the rings cut from stainless steel piping by a sheet metal shop, which is where most of mine have come from. The advantage of going to a sheet metal shop is that you can have your rings cut to any size from pipe or even have them custom sized and shaped from sheet metal. This will be a little more costly than if you were to buy from a kitchen store, but they will also be much more durable. Having them made to size and shape allows for the variety of presentations that you see in this book.

basics

Preserved Lemons	250
Oven-dried Tomatoes	250
Tomato Sauce	251
Basil Garlic Mayonnaise	251
Gorgonzola Walnut Cream	251
Sea Lettuce Pesto	252
Cilantro Pumpkin Seed Pesto	252
Basil Pesto	252
Wild Berry and Honey Vinegar	253
Nasturtium Vinegar	253
Chive and Rosemary Garlic Oil	253
Pumpkin Seed and Cilantro Oil	253
Coriander Chips	254
Crispy Parsnip Strips	254
Croutons	255
Pumpkin Seed Crisps	255
Parmesan Crisps	255
Brown Meat Stock, White or Clear Meat Stock, Fish Stock, and Vegetable Stock	256
Quick Smoked Trout (or Chicken)	257
Dessert Sauces	258
Chocolate Sauce	258
White Chocolate Sauce	258
Caramel Sauce	258
Raspberry Sauce	259
Black Currant Sauce	259
Gummi Berry Sauce	259
Rhubarb Sauce	259
Almond Sheet Cake	260
Brandied Vanilla Custard	260
Lemon-Lime Curd	260
Pine Nut Praline	261
Caramel Sugar Garnish	261
Sugared Lemon and Lime Slices	262
Cinnamon Sugar	262
Spiced Sugar	262
Almond or Hazelnut Filling	262
Shortcrust Dough	263
Basic Pie Dough	263
Pâté Dough	263

Photo: Preserved Lemons

basics

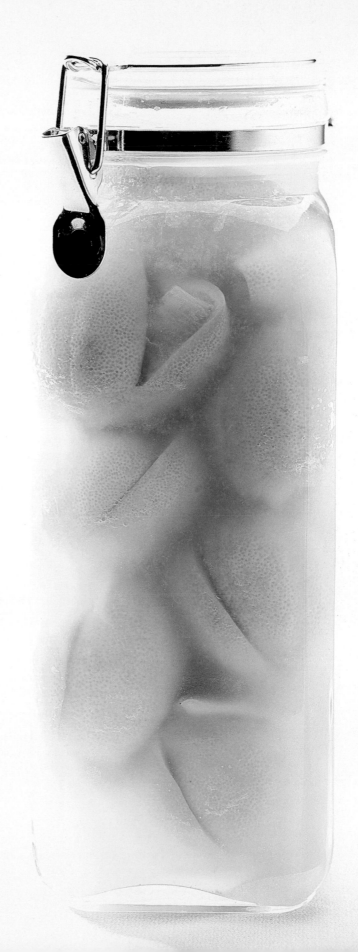

Preserved Lemons

Preserved lemons are an important part of North African cooking. They are used in a variety of dishes but are an indispensable ingredient in tagines, which are a type of spicy meat and vegetable stew usually made with lamb. They are also used in lemon chicken and olive recipes. The preserved lemons work well with many other dishes and add a wonderful lemon intensity to rice or couscous, salads, and roasted or grilled fish. The preserved lemon has a pungent flavour without being too salty since they are rinsed before using.

about 12-14 organic lemons
1 c. coarse salt
1 sterile 2-quart jar

Wash the lemons well and dry. Cut into quarters to within a half inch of the base and gently spread open.

Cover the bottom of the jar with a thin layer of salt. Pack the inside of a lemon with salt and press into the bottom of the jar.

Repeat this with the rest of the lemons, sprinkling salt in between, and packing them in tightly. This will release some of the juice from the lemons, which will eventually cover the fruit once the jar is full.

Once you have packed in as many lemons as will fit, squeeze extra lemons and add the juice to the jar to ensure they are completely covered, leaving a small air space at the top.

Store for at least two weeks at room temperature in a dark place before using. Refrigerate after opening. The preserved lemons will keep at least one year.

To use, remove a lemon from the jar with a utensil and rinse off the excess salt. Remove the soft flesh if desired and dice or slice the rind. After a while you may notice a cloudy sediment at the bottom of the jar. This is only lemon that has been dissolved by the salt and is harmless.

Oven-dried Tomatoes

8 medium-sized ripe Roma or plum
   tomatoes
2 tbsp. finely minced fresh garlic
1/2 c. chopped fresh oregano
1/2 c. chopped fresh basil
salt and ground black pepper to taste

Core out the stem end of the tomatoes and slice into 1/2-inch slices. Combine in a bowl with the rest of the ingredients.

Place the tomato slices on a 12 x 16-inch baking sheet with a small meshed rack to fit, being careful not to crowd them.

Distribute any of the remaining seasoning in the bowl among the slices and place in a preheated 175-200°F oven. Dry the tomatoes for 4-5 hours. They should be dry but still pliable, like dried fruit.

Remove from the oven and cool.

When cooled the tomatoes can be stored in the refrigerator for up to 2 weeks as is, or covered with olive oil and used as an antipasto.

Tomato Sauce

Heat the olive oil in a 2- to 3-quart sauce pan until a light haze forms.

Add the onions and cook until soft but not brown.

Add the garlic and chili flakes and cook 30 seconds or until aromatic.

Add the oregano and basil and cook 30 seconds, then add the tomatoes, tomato paste, salt and a few grindings of pepper.

Reduce heat to low and simmer approximately 30-40 minutes, stirring occasionally.

Serve as is or pass through a sieve or food mill.

Adjust the seasoning if needed.

3 tbsp. extra virgin olive oil
1/2 c. finely chopped onion
1tbsp. minced garlic
1/2 tsp. red chili flakes
1 tbsp. dried oregano
1 tbsp. dried basil
3 c. peeled plum tomatoes, coarsely chopped
4 tbsp. tomato paste
1 tsp. salt
freshly ground black pepper

Basil Garlic Mayonnaise

Place all the ingredients except the oil, salt and pepper in the bowl of a food processor or blender.

With the motor running, very slowly pour in the olive oil. It is important not to add the oil too quickly at first or the mayonnaise will not emulsify and the oil will separate from the rest of the ingredients.

As the mayonnaise begins to thicken add the oil a little faster until the mixture is thick. It will be a little thinner than a commercial type of mayonnaise.

Add the salt and ground black pepper, adjust the seasoning if necessary and refrigerate.

2 egg yolks
2 tbsp. fresh lemon juice
2 tsp. minced fresh garlic
1 c. loosely packed fresh basil leaves
1 tbsp. Dijon mustard
1 1/4 c. (approximately) extra virgin olive oil
1/4 tsp. salt
1/4 tsp. freshly ground black pepper

Gorgonzola Walnut Cream

Although intended for pasta or gnocchi, this sauce also goes well with grilled meats, especially beef. It also works well as a warm dip accompanied by an assortment of seasonal vegetables as a first course.

Heat the olive oil on medium heat and add the walnuts. Cook stirring until lightly toasted and aromatic.

Add the onions and cook 1-2 minutes, then stir in the garlic.

Cook 30 seconds, then add the wine and reduce by half.

Add the cream, bring to a low boil and reduce for 3-4 minutes.

Add the cheese and stir to partially melt through.

Add the basil, season to taste and toss with fresh cooked noodles or gnocchi.

1 tbsp. extra virgin olive oil
1/2 c. coarsely chopped walnuts
1/2 small onion, minced
2 garlic cloves, finely minced
1/4 c. dry white wine
1 c. heavy cream
2 oz. Gorgonzola cheese
1/4 c. chopped fresh basil
salt and freshly ground black pepper to taste

Sea Lettuce Pesto

This is a great sauce with which to surprise your unsuspecting guests. They'll never guess what the main ingredient is. Use it as an uncooked sauce with any variety of fish or shellfish or even grilled chicken. It makes a great dip for chilled poached prawns or shrimp, or can be tossed with hot pasta immediately before serving.

Sea lettuce is a common seaweed on the west coast. It has a vivid bright green colour and looks like giant leaves of lettuce. The texture is slightly crunchy. It should be harvested off the rocks at low tide. The sea lettuce that you may see washed up on the beach is past its prime and should not be collected. Although practically all seaweeds on the west coast (approximately 200 varieties) are edible, be sure that you have the advice of a reputable picker if you decide to harvest your own.

3 c. fresh sea lettuce, rinsed, drained well
   and coarsely chopped
2 large garlic cloves, peeled
1 tbsp. grated lemon zest
3 tbsp. fresh lemon juice
1 tbsp. honey
1/3 c. toasted skinned hazelnuts
1 1/4 c. sunflower oil (approximately)
salt and freshly ground pepper to taste

Combine all the ingredients except the oil, salt and pepper in the bowl of a food processor.

With the motor running add about half the oil and continue to add slowly until the pesto has reached the desired consistency.

Season to taste with salt and pepper.

Be careful not to overprocess. This may cause the pesto to become bitter.

Cilantro Pumpkin Seed Pesto

Try this on grilled chicken breast or pork chops or omit the cheese and serve on fish. Top with extra grated cheese and place under a broiler for a few minutes. It also goes well with grilled or steamed green vegetables.

1 large garlic clove, peeled
1 bunch of fresh cilantro, coarsely chopped
1/3 c. unsalted green pumpkin seeds
1/3 c. extra virgin olive oil
1/4 c. grated Parmigiano Reggiano or
   Pecorino Romano cheese
fresh lemon or lime juice to taste
salt and freshly ground pepper to taste

Combine all ingredients in the bowl of a food processor.

Process in short intervals until the pesto has reached the desired consistency, adding more extra virgin olive oil if necessary. Stir in lemon or lime juice to taste and season if necessary with salt and pepper.

Basil Pesto

Everybody who enjoys food, especially Italian food, knows basil pesto. Pesto, which in Italian means ground, as in a paste, can refer to a variety of sauces made in the same way as the more familiar basil version. Traditionally made in a mortar and pestle, a food processor works well also. Usually served with freshly cooked pasta, this sauce can also be used to dress fresh grilled vegetables or meats, on salads or to garnish vegetable soup just before serving. You can also make it without the cheese and serve with grilled or poached shellfish.

2 c. fresh basil leaves
1/3-1/2 c. lightly toasted pine nuts
3-4 cloves garlic, peeled
1-2 tsp. coarse salt
1/3 c. grated Parmigiano Reggiano or
   Pecorino Romano or combination
1/2 c. extra virgin olive oil

Place the basil, pine nuts, garlic, salt, cheese and a little oil in the bowl of a food processor. Process to a smooth paste. Scrape down the sides if necessary and blend in the rest of the oil.

Thin if necessary with 2-3 tbsp. of water.

Variation: To make Arugula Pesto, substitute arugula for the basil, and walnuts for the pine nuts.

Wild Berry and Honey Vinegar

This uniquely flavoured vinegar can be used in small amounts to add a distinctive edge to salad dressing. I would recommend diluting it with an equal amount of plain white wine vinegar. My favourite way to use it is for flavouring rich savoury sauces, such as in my Pheasant Breast with Garlic Potato Crust (page 170) and for game meats such as venison. Try making this with a combination of seasonal berries or do batches of individual varieties of berries.

Combine the berries and vinegar in a stainless steel pot and heat to 180°F. Pour into a non-corrosive container and cool. Cover and allow to sit undisturbed in a cool room for 2 weeks.

Strain through several layers of cheesecloth without pressing. Return the mixture to a pot and stir in the honey. Warm the liquid to 180°F.

Pour into hot sterile bottles and cap. This will make about six 8-oz. bottles.

1 lb. berries (e.g., salal berries, Oregon grape, blackberries)
1 quart white wine vinegar
1 lb. honey

Nasturtium Vinegar

Fill a 4-quart glass jar with a non-corrosive lid with washed and dried fresh nasturtium flowers. Add white wine vinegar to cover the flowers and place the lid on the jar.

Let stand in a cool dark place for 2 weeks. The vinegar will take on the colour of the flowers used. Strain through several layers of cheesecloth and bottle. The vinegar will keep for 1 year.

Chive and Rosemary Garlic Oil

In a small saucepan, heat 1/2 c. olive oil with the sliced garlic on medium heat until the garlic is soft and the edges begin to colour slightly.

Remove from heat and pour into a heatproof bowl. Add the other 1/2 cup olive oil and cool slightly.

Bring a pot of lightly salted water to a boil. Have a bowl of ice water ready at the side. Drop the herbs into the boiling water and cook for 15 seconds. Immediately remove the herbs from the water and immerse in the ice water. Cool completely and remove.

Squeeze the herbs dry, place into a blender and pour the oil and garlic in. Process to a fine purée. Pour into a strainer lined with cheesecloth and set aside to drip through. For a clear oil, do not press on the mixture, or it will become cloudy.

Pour into a small jar or squeeze bottle and refrigerate. Bring to room temperature before using.

1 c. extra virgin olive oil
4 large garlic cloves, sliced
1/4 c. fresh rosemary leaves
3/4 c. fresh chives

Pumpkin Seed and Cilantro Oil

On low to medium heat, warm 1/4 c. of the oil with the garlic. Add the pumpkin seeds and sauté for 2 minutes, until lightly toasted.

Remove from heat and cool. Add the rest of the oil and set aside.

Bring a pot of lightly salted water to a boil. Have a bowl of ice water ready at the side. Drop the cilantro and spinach leaves in the boiling water and cook for 10 seconds. Immediately remove from the water and immerse in the ice water. Chill completely and remove.

Squeeze the herbs dry, place in a blender and add the reserved oil mixture. Process to a fine purée. Strain through a fine strainer or cheesecloth. For a clear oil, do not squeeze or press the purée too much or it will be cloudy.

Pour into a small jar or squeeze bottle and refrigerate. Bring to room temperature before using.

3/4 c. extra virgin olive oil
2 garlic cloves
1/2 c. pumpkin seeds
1 c. fresh cilantro leaves
1/2 c. spinach leaves
1/2 tsp. salt
1/2 tsp. freshly ground black pepper

Coriander Chips

This recipe makes many more chips than you will need to garnish a soup or side dish. Fortunately they also make a nice snack so they most likely will not have to be stored too long. Try experimenting with different herbs and spices to suit particular dishes you may want to serve them with.

1½ oz. (¼ c.) corn flour
1½ oz. (¼ c.) cornmeal
½ c. plus 2 tbsp. all-purpose flour
½ tsp. freshly ground black pepper
1 tsp. ground coriander
2 tsp. paprika
3 egg whites
1 tbsp. extra virgin olive oil
2 tbsp. whole coriander, crushed with
   the back of a knife
1 tbsp. (approximately) coarse salt

Reserve one egg white, the salt and the crushed coriander seeds and place the rest of the ingredients in the bowl of a food processor.

Pulse until the mixture forms a ball.

If the mixture seems dry and does not form a ball, add 1 tbsp. water.

Remove from the bowl and divide into 4 pieces.

Using a pasta machine or a rolling pin, roll each piece into a long sheet to fit your baking tray. The dough needs to be rolled out very thinly or it will not crisp when baked.

Line the baking tray with parchment paper and lay a sheet of dough on top.

Using a pastry wheel dipped in flour, cut the sheets into desired shapes.

Whisk the reserved egg white with 1 tbsp. water and lightly brush on top of the dough.

Press some of the crushed coriander seed into the cut-out chips, then sprinkle with coarse salt.

Bake at 350°F for 8-10 minutes.

Allow to cool on the tray.

Crispy Parsnip Strips

This recipe is more about the method than the specific ingredients. It works well with strips of beets or other root vegetables such as carrots. Use the crispy strips as a garnish or as a snack just on their own.

A countertop deep fryer works best, but you can also use a pot on the stove. Be sure the pot is large enough to hold the ingredients and never fill the pot more than halfway with oil.

vegetable oil for deep-frying
2 medium-sized parsnips
juice of ½ lemon
2-3 tbsp. cornstarch
freshly ground black pepper
salt

Heat the oil to 350°F.

Peel the parsnips and trim the ends. With a sharp peeler cut as many thin strips as possible from both parsnips.

Stack the strips on top of each other and with a sharp knife cut the strips lengthwise, approximately ½-inch wide.

Place the cut strips in a bowl and add the lemon juice, cornstarch and some ground black pepper.

Working with small amounts at a time shake the excess starch from the strips and place in the hot oil.

Gently move the strips in the oil to prevent them from sticking to each other and fry until golden coloured and crisp.

Remove with a slotted spoon or a sieve and place on clean towels to drain. Season with salt while still hot.

Serve immediately.

Croutons

With a 2-inch round cutter, cut 2-3 croutons from each slice of bread.

Coat a baking sheet with the olive oil and season with the salt and pepper.

Place the croutons on the sheet and turn to coat both sides with oil.

Bake in a 375°F oven until toasted and crisp.

6-8 slices of firm white or whole wheat sandwich bread
1/4 c. extra virgin olive oil
1/2 tsp. each salt and freshly ground black pepper

Pumpkin Seed Crisps

Combine all but the ground pumpkin seeds in an electric mixer and beat until smooth.

Add the ground seeds and mix to combine.

To shape the crisps, take a small spatula and spread the mixture very thinly on a parchment paper-lined baking sheet into desired shapes. Bake at 350°F for 6-8 minutes until the edges are browned.

Cool on the tray and use as a dessert garnish.

2 tbsp. unsalted butter
2 oz. (1/3 c.) granulated sugar
1/4 tsp. vanilla extract
1 egg white
2 oz. (1/2 c.) all-purpose flour
1 oz. (1/4 c.) unsalted pumpkin seeds, toasted and ground

Parmesan Crisps

These are very tasty crisps that can be used to garnish a variety of savoury dishes. They can be made with any of your favourite hard aged cheeses, such as Pecorino, Asiago or even cheddar. Also try adding minced herbs. The crisps can be made any size and while still hot can be formed into small cups to hold salads or other fillings. Be sure to make a few extras for "testing."

One and a half cups of grated cheese will yield about eight 2-inch crisps.

Heat a nonstick pan on low to medium heat.

Grate the parmesan or selected cheese and place mounds on the hot pan. Spread into rough 2-inch rounds with your fingers.

Cook until the cheese begins to bubble. With a spatula, carefully turn the crisps over to cook the other side. Cook until golden, remove and place on paper towels to cool. They will be soft but will crisp up as they cool.

The crisps can also be made on a nonstick baking sheet and baked at 350°F until golden.

Remove and allow to cool on the baking sheet.

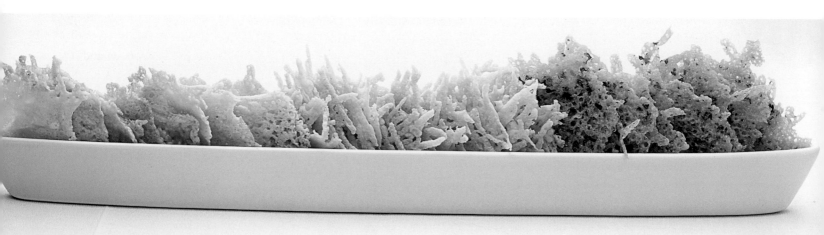

Brown Meat Stock

Yields about 3 cups

Use this recipe with different types of bones (beef, poultry, lamb, pork, veal) to make a base for a variety of sauces or soups. Because of the time it takes to make, it is worthwhile to make larger batches and freeze in portions that may be used later.

2 lbs. bones cut into 2- to 3-inch pieces

1 c. each rough chopped celery, peeled carrot and onion

4-6 garlic cloves, crushed

2 tbsp. tomato paste

2 tbsp. all-purpose flour

6 c. water

2 bay leaves

2 tsp. black peppercorns

Rinse the bones well in 2 or 3 changes of cold water. Place them in a roasting pan and roast in a 400°F oven for approximately 1 1/2 hours until well browned, turning them halfway through.

Add the vegetables to the roasting pan and roast for 20 minutes more. Add the tomato paste, spreading it around the bones, then sprinkle the flour on top and roast 20 minutes more until the flour has started to brown. (The flour helps to give body to the sauce. It can be omitted.)

Remove from the oven and place the contents in a 3-4 quart stock pot and add the water, the bay leaves and peppercorns. Bring to a simmer and cook on low heat for at least 4 hours and up to 8 hours.

Add water during the cooking if necessary to keep the bones covered.

Strain the stock through a colander to remove the large pieces and then through a fine sieve or cheesecloth. Skim any fat or foam off the top or place the stock in the refrigerator overnight and then remove the hardened fat.

White or Clear Meat Stock

Follow the basic recipe for Brown Meat Stock (recipe above), except skip the roasting process and place rinsed bones in a stock pot. Cover with cold water and bring to a simmer. Skim off any impurities that come to the surface, then add the vegetables (omitting the tomato paste and flour).

Fish Stock

Yields about 4 cups

1 1/2 lbs. fish bones and trim

1/2 c. each diced celery, peeled carrot and onion

2-3 peeled and crushed garlic cloves

1 small bunch fresh parsley

3-4 sprigs fresh thyme

1 crushed bay leaf

2 tsp. black peppercorns

5 c. cold water

Rinse the bones in two to three changes of cold water and place into a stock pot.

Bring to a simmer and after 5-10 minutes skim off any impurities that rise to the top.

Add the rest of the ingredients and simmer on low heat for 45-60 minutes.

Strain through a colander and then through a fine meshed sieve or cheesecloth and store in desired portions.

Variation: *Try adding fennel tops, fresh basil, dill or lemon zest to give a more distinctive flavour to this stock.*

Vegetable Stock

Yields about 4 cups

2 tbsp. vegetable or olive oil

1 c. each diced celery, peeled carrot and onion

2-3 peeled crushed garlic cloves

1/2 c. crushed fresh tomato or 1 tbsp. tomato paste (optional)

1 small bunch of parsley

2 tsp. whole black peppercorns

4 c. cold water

Heat the oil in a small stockpot on medium to low heat and add the diced vegetables and garlic.

Cook stirring for 2 minutes, without colouring the vegetables, then add the fresh tomato or tomato paste (if using).

Stir to combine and add the cold water and herbs. Simmer 30-40 minutes and strain through a fine meshed sieve or cheesecloth.

Quick Smoked Trout (or Chicken)

There is no substitute for the distinct flavour of a slowly smoked fresh trout fillet. This recipe is designed for those who do not have the space or equipment but would still like to produce that much sought-after flavour. The ice water in the recipe speeds up the making of the brine.

This method can also be used to quick smoke other types of fish, shellfish or chicken.

Combine the salt, sugar and 1 cup water in a non-corrosive pot and bring to a boil, stirring until the contents have dissolved.

Remove from heat and pour into a stainless steel, glass or enamel container large enough to hold the rest of the water and the trout fillets.

Add the ice water and refrigerate until cold. Add the trout fillets and refrigerate 2-4 hours.

Remove the trout fillets from the brine, then rinse and pat dry.

The brine can be strained through cheesecloth and used for more trout or frozen to be used at a later date. Do not reuse the brine more than once.

Prepare the wok by lining it and the lid with the aluminum foil.*

Place the wood chips in the bottom of the wok, cover with the lid and heat on medium high until the chips begin to smoke. Remove the lid.

Spray the rack with a nonstick coating and place it in the wok so that it sits above the wood chips. Lay the trout fillets on the rack and replace the lid.

Turn the heat down to low and smoke the trout about 1 hour, until the meat is firm. You may have to monitor the heat to make sure it does not get too hot too quickly, otherwise the trout will cook before it can absorb the smoke flavour.

Remove and cool before refrigerating.

* If you have an old wok to dedicate just for smoking you may eliminate this step.

1/4 c. pickling salt
1/4 c. brown sugar
1 c. water
1 c. ice water
6 boneless fresh trout fillets, approximately 5-6 oz. each

Equipment for smoking
12-inch Chinese wok with a tight-fitting lid
aluminum foil to line the wok and lid
about 1 c. hardwood chips for smoking (e.g., alder, hickory, cherry) soaked in warm water for 30 minutes and drained
one 10- to 11-inch round metal rack

Dessert Sauces

Sweet sauces add colour, texture and flavour to desserts. Chosen well and used minimally they increase the overall enjoyment of the dish. They also help elevate the appearance of the finished dish for a special occasion. They are easy to make and usually keep well in the refrigerator.

To enhance the look of the sauce even further, add a contrasting line made of plain yogurt or sour cream thinned with milk to the plated sauce. The yogurt should be the same consistency as the sauce so that they do not run into each other. Using a spoon or a squeeze bottle, place dots or lines of yogurt in the main sauce and pull a knife through it to get that "restaurant look."

The following are just a few of the dozens of sauces that can be used to enhance your desserts. Try experimenting with the ingredients to create your own. These recipes are flexible, especially the fruit-based sauces in which almost any seasonal fruit can be used.

Chocolate Sauce

1 c. heavy cream
8 oz. semi-sweet chocolate chips
1 tbsp. brandy
2 tbsp. brewed coffee

Heat the cream to a simmer and pour it over the chocolate chips.

Add the brandy and coffee and stir until smooth and the chocolate is completely melted.

Cool and adjust the consistency of the sauce if necessary with a little extra cream or milk.

White Chocolate Sauce

1 c. heavy cream
6 oz. white chocolate, chopped
2 tbsp. sambuca

Heat the cream to a simmer and pour it over the chocolate. Stir until smooth and the chocolate is completely melted, then add the sambuca.

Cool and adjust the consistency of the sauce with a little extra cream or milk.

Caramel Sauce

For chocolate caramel sauce add 2 oz. chopped dark chocolate after adding the cream and stir until melted.

8 oz. (1 1/3 c.) sugar
1/4 c. water
1/4 tsp. cream of tartar or 1 tsp. fresh
  lemon juice
1 c. heavy cream
2 tbsp. unsalted butter
1/2 tsp. vanilla extract

In a heavy-bottomed saucepan combine the sugar, water and cream of tartar or lemon juice.

Place on medium heat and bring to a boil.

With a pastry brush and cold water, wash down the side of the pan to remove any sugar crystals. (Alternatively you can cover the pan with a lid for 2-3 minutes and the steam will wash down the sides of the pan.)

Boil the sugar uncovered without stirring until it begins to take on colour. At this point you must pay careful attention as it will caramelize quickly.

Swirl the pan to even the browning but do not stir.

When the sugar is a light mahogany colour remove from the heat and very slowly add the cream while whisking. It will boil up if you add the cream too quickly.

Whisk in the butter and the vanilla extract and pour into a bowl to cool.

The sauce will thicken as it cools. At this point it can be thinned to desired consistency with extra cream or milk.

Raspberry Sauce

Combine the berries, sugar and water in a saucepan and bring to a boil.

Simmer until the berries begin to fall apart and stir in the dissolved cornstarch.

Continue to stir and bring the mixture to a boil again, then simmer for about 1 minute to cook out the starch.

Remove from the heat and press the mixture through a fine sieve and cool, stirring frequently to prevent a skin from forming.

Chill in the refrigerator until ready to use.

12 oz. (2 c.) fresh or frozen raspberries
1/3 c. sugar
1/2 c. water
1 tbsp. cornstarch dissolved in 2 tbsp. water

Black Currant Sauce

Follow the directions for Raspberry Sauce (recipe above).

12 oz. (2 c.) black currants
2/3 c. sugar
1/2 c. water
1 tbsp. cornstarch dissolved in 2 tbsp. water

Gummi Berry Sauce

Gummi berries are another one of those bushes I inherited from my father. The Italian name for them is crugnali. The berries we have are red, but my father says that in Italy they grow wild and are black, with a hard pit instead of a soft one. The fruit has a stem similar to a cherry but is oblong instead of round, growing on a large bush that can reach 10-12 feet in height and width. The flavour is somewhere between a raspberry and sour cherry. Through a bit of informal research with a local nursery I learned they are native to Asia.

Follow the directions for Raspberry Sauce (above).

14 oz. (2 1/4 c.) fresh or frozen gummi berries
2 oz. (1/4 c.) fresh or frozen raspberries
1/3 c. sugar
1/2 c. water
1 tbsp. cornstarch dissolved in 2 tbsp. water

Rhubarb Sauce

This sauce is good served warm or cold with vanilla ice cream. The tartness of the sauce also helps to cut through the richness of a custard-based dessert.

Combine all ingredients except the 2 tbsp. orange juice and cornstarch in a small pot and bring to a simmer.

Cook until the liquid has reduced by a quarter and the rhubarb is soft and has begun to break down.

Dissolve the cornstarch in the 2 tbsp. of orange juice and stir into the rhubarb mixture.

Bring back to a simmer and cook for 1 minute.

Remove from the heat and allow to cool slightly. Pour into a food processor or blender and purée until smooth.

Strain through a fine mesh sieve before serving.

12 oz. (2 c.) diced fresh or frozen rhubarb
4-5 large strips of lemon zest
1/2 c. sugar
1 tsp. ground cinnamon
1/2 tsp. ground nutmeg
2/3 c. plus 2 tbsp. orange juice
2 tsp. cornstarch

Almond Sheet Cake

Substitute any assortment of nuts in this recipe for variation and/or add up to 3 tbsp. sifted cocoa powder for a chocolate nut sheet cake.

1/2 c. ground blanched almonds
3 oz. (3/4 c.) sifted icing sugar
1/2 oz. (2 tbsp.) flour
2 eggs
1/2 oz. (1 tbsp.) melted butter
1/2 tsp. almond extract
3 egg whites
1 tbsp. granulated sugar
21/2 oz. (1/2 c.) lightly toasted sliced almonds (optional)

Whisk together the almonds, icing sugar and flour. Then whisk in the eggs, melted butter and almond extract.

Whip the egg whites until frothy, and while still beating, slowly add in the sugar and beat until stiff.

Fold the egg whites into the almond and flour mixture until evenly combined.

Spread the toasted almonds (if using) evenly over the bottom of a parchment paper-lined 12 x 18-inch baking sheet. Pour the batter over the almonds and spread evenly with a spatula.

Bake in a preheated 375°F oven for 8-10 minutes or until lightly coloured and the centre is firm.

Remove from the oven and cool on the tray.

Brandied Vanilla Custard

This versatile custard can be used as a filling for tarts or to accompany fresh berries or fruit. It can also be thinned for use as a sauce. Traditionally, custard sauces are thickened by egg yolks. The addition of cornstarch makes this is a quicker, more fail-safe method.

21/4 c. milk
4 tbsp. sugar
1 vanilla bean split or 1 tsp. vanilla extract
3 tbsp. cornstarch
2 large egg yolks
2 tbsp. brandy

For variation: Substitute 2 tbsp. orange concentrate for the vanilla and brandy to make an orange custard.

Place 2 cups of the milk, 3 tbsp. sugar and vanilla bean (if using) into a saucepan and bring to a boil.

Combine 1 tbsp. sugar and the cornstarch, then whisk in the egg yolks and remaining 1/4 cup milk.

As the milk comes to a boil pour in the egg mixture while continually stirring. Bring back to a simmer for 1-2 minutes to cook out the starch.

Remove from the heat, take out the vanilla bean (if using), and add the brandy. If not using the vanilla bean add the extract.

Pour into a clean bowl and cover with plastic wrap.

Cool and thin to desired consistency with extra milk before using.

Lemon-Lime Curd

This makes an intensely flavoured curd that can be used as a filling for tarts, layered cakes or rolled into a sponge cake jelly-roll style. Before the mixture is completely chilled and not too firm, fold in 1/2 cup whipped cream to make a lighter filling or an easy citrus mousse. The curd is also delicious partnered with fresh fruit.

3 tbsp. all-purpose flour
3/4 c. sugar
5 egg yolks
grated zest of 1 lemon
grated zest of 1 lime
1/2 c. fresh lemon juice
1/4 c. fresh lime juice
1/2 c. water
3 tbsp. unsalted butter

In the top of a double boiler, off the heat, whisk together the flour and sugar, then whisk in the egg yolks. Add the rest of the ingredients, except the butter, and stir together.

Place over simmering water and stir with a wooden spoon or spatula until the mixture thickens. This may take 10 minutes or more.

Remove from the heat and whisk in the butter.

Pour the curd into a clean bowl and cover with plastic wrap or waxed paper to prevent a skin from forming on the top.

Cool and store in the refrigerator for up to a week.

Pine Nut Praline

Combine the sugar, water and cream of tartar or lemon juice in a heavy-bottomed pot or saucepan.

Stir to mix and then bring to a boil over medium to high heat.

With a pastry brush and cold water, clean the inside of the pan of any sugar that may cling to the side (this helps prevent crystallization of the mixture).

Continue to cook the mixture without stirring until the sugar begins to colour. At this point you can lift the pan and swirl the mixture to even the browning.

While the sugar is cooking, line a tray with parchment or baker's paper.

When the sugar has reached a golden brown colour it is ready.**

Remove from the heat and stir in the pine nuts.

Pour the mixture onto the prepared tray and spread by tilting it from side to side. Set aside to cool.

To use for a flavouring in ice cream, mousse or other fillings, break into small pieces and grind to desired consistency in a food processor or with a rolling pin between two sheets of parchment paper.

The praline can also be used as a garnish for desserts or dipped in chocolate to eat as is. In this case I recommend rolling the mixture while still warm and pliable between two sheets of parchment to get it quite thin, and then scoring heavily with a sharp knife. When cool, break the praline along the score lines.

1¹/2 c. granulated sugar
¹/4 c. water
¹/4 tsp. cream of tartar or 1 tsp. fresh lemon juice
6 oz. (1¹/4 c.) pine nuts*, toasted (substitute any variety of nuts or seeds)

TIP

*To toast nuts or seeds place on a baking tray and into a 375°F oven for 8-10 minutes, stirring 2-3 times to even the browning. Remove and cool.

**The sugar can be cooked to suit your taste – the darker it becomes the less sweet it will be and less sticky when eating on its own. Experiment a few times to get the results you prefer.

Caramel Sugar Garnish

Line a 9 x 13-inch baking tray with parchment paper and set aside.

In a heavy bottomed saucepan combine the sugar, water and cream of tartar or lemon juice. Place over medium heat and bring to a boil.

With a pastry brush and cold water wash down the sides of the pan to remove any sugar crystals. Alternatively, cover the pan with a lid for 2-3 minutes and the steam will wash the sugar crystals from the sides of the pan.

Boil the sugar uncovered without stirring until the mixture begins to colour.

At this point you must pay careful attention, as the sugar will colour quickly.

Swirl the pan to even the browning but do not stir.

When the sugar is a light mahogany colour remove the pan from the heat and add the pine nuts. Carefully pour the sugar onto the lined tray. Before the mixture cools, pick up the tray and tilt it from side to side to obtain an even, thin layer of sugar. Score with a sharp knife into desired shapes or allow to cool and break into random pieces to use as a dessert garnish.

4 oz. (²/3 c.) sugar
¹/4 c. water
pinch of cream of tartar or 1 tsp. fresh lemon juice
2-3 tbsp. toasted pine nuts (optional)

Sugared Lemon and Lime Slices

Use this method for any type of citrus. The slices make a wonderful garnish and can also be chopped or ground to use as a flavouring for fillings or sauces. Try to use organic fruit if possible. In either case make sure to wash it well. These can be made in advance and will store for several weeks.

1 c. sugar plus extra for coating
1 c. water
2 lemons
2 limes

Combine the sugar and water in a 1-quart pot and bring to a simmer to dissolve the sugar.

Cut the lemons and limes into thin slices and place in the syrup.

Simmer very gently for 10 minutes, then remove from the heat.

With tongs or a fork gently remove the slices one by one and place on paper towels to absorb any extra syrup.

Prepare a tray with extra sugar and place the slices on top of the sugar, turning to coat both sides.

Remove the slices from the sugar and place on a parchment-lined baking sheet.

Place in a preheated 250°F oven for 3-4 hours to dry.

The slices should be dry but still pliable, like dried fruit, when done.

Let the slices dry, uncovered, at room temperature for 3-4 more hours or overnight, then store in an airtight container.

Cinnamon Sugar

Combine 1/4 c. ground cinnamon and 1 1/4 c. granulated sugar. Store in an airtight container.

Spiced Sugar

1 c. granulated sugar
1 tbsp. ground cinnamon
1 tbsp. ground ginger
1 tsp. ground nutmeg

This mixture can be used to add an extra flavour punch in anything cinnamon sugar would be used for.

Sift together all ingredients. Store in an airtight container.

Almond or Hazelnut Filling

A common filling with many applications.

Spread onto the bottom of a sweet pastry shell and bake before topping with fresh fruit, or fill phyllo pastry pockets along with berries or fruit. The nuts can be either blanched or left with the skins on. Vary the nuts for different flavour. Toasted nuts will produce a coarse texture and fuller flavour.

4 oz. (1/2 c.) unsalted butter, room temperature
2 oz. (1/3 c.) sugar
pinch of salt
3 eggs
1 tsp. almond or vanilla extract
8 oz. (1 3/4 c.) ground almonds or hazelnuts

Cream together the butter, salt and sugar. When the mixture is light and airy, beat in the eggs one at a time. Add the extract.

Add the ground nuts all at once and beat until smooth.

Shortcrust Dough

A versatile dough that has many applications. The butter and sugar make this dough very tender with the texture of shortbread. Use it for sweet tart shells, baked cheesecake bottoms or for simple cookies. Try adding some ground nuts, spices or cocoa powder for variation.

Cream together the butter and sugar.

Beat in the eggs one at a time, scraping down the sides to combine thoroughly.

Sift together the flour and baking powder.

Add the flour mixture and beat or fold in only until combined.

Remove from the bowl and knead very briefly on a lightly floured board.

Form into a ball and flatten. Wrap in plastic and chill 1 hour before rolling.

8 oz. (1 c.) unsalted butter, room temperature
8 oz. (1 1/3 c.) sugar
2 eggs
1 lb. 4 oz. (4 c.) all-purpose flour
1 tbsp. plus 2 tsp. baking powder

Basic Pie Dough

This amount will make three 9-inch pie shells without tops. It can also be used for tart shells or for sweet or savoury filled pastries.

Place the flour, butter, salt and sugar (if using) into a bowl.

Using a pastry cutter or your fingers work the butter into the flour until pea-sized.

Add the ice water one tablespoon at a time and work in carefully until the dough comes together without being crumbly or sticky. To test the dough, squeeze a small amount in your palm. If it is still too crumbly, add a little more ice water.

Gather the dough into a ball and flatten. Wrap in plastic and chill at least 1 hour or overnight before rolling.

To make the dough in a food processor place all ingredients except ice water into the work bowl and pulse for two-second intervals to work in the butter.

When the butter is worked in add ice water 1 tbsp. at a time until the dough begins to come together. Test and add more water if necessary.

14 oz. (2 1/2 c.) all-purpose flour
8 oz. (1 c.) cold unsalted butter, cut into small cubes
1 tsp. salt
1 tsp. sugar (optional)
up to 1/4 c. ice water

Pâté Dough

Place the butter, shortening, flour, salt and sugar (if using) into the bowl of a food processor and pulse until the fat is evenly distributed but still in pieces 1/4-1/2 inch in size.

Add the beaten egg and pulse briefly to combine.

Add ice water to moisten the dough slightly to hold together. This may take only 1-2 tbsp.

Remove the dough from the bowl and on a lightly floured board, knead very briefly and flatten into a disk. Wrap in plastic wrap or waxed paper and refrigerate for 30 minutes before rolling out.

2 oz. (1/4 c.) cold unsalted butter
2 oz. (1/4 c.) cold shortening (preferably lard)
8 oz. (2 c.) all-purpose flour
1/4 tsp. salt
1/2 tsp. sugar (optional)
1 egg, lightly beaten
ice water

index

Almond
Almond or Hazelnut Filling 262
Almond Plum Cake with Spiced
   Merlot Plum Sauce 203
Almond Sheet Cake 260
Pear and Almond Strudel 12
Apple
Apple Frisée Salad 110
Apple Turnovers 11
Apple, Rosemary and Sage Risotto 131
Candied Trout with Seared Apple
   and Fresh Mint 43
Green Apple and Honey Sorbetto 143
Warm Apple Crêpe with Caramel
   Orange Sauce 30
Apricots
Apricot and Sunflower Seed
   Yogurt Cheese 6
Asparagus
Ricotta Flan with Prosciutto
   Wrapped Asparagus 20
Sea Asparagus Salad 95
Seared Tuna Medallions with Pickled
   Summer Squash, Cucumber and
   Sea Asparagus 100
Basil
Basil Garlic Mayonnaise 251
Basil Pesto 252
Whole Seed-Crusted Fish Fillet with
   Basil Lemon Butter Sauce 160
Beans
Beer Braised Oxtail with White
   Beans and Chick Peas 194
Chilled Fava Bean Soup with Snow
   Pea and Preserved Lemon Salad 54
Smoked Trout and Green Bean Salad 78
White Beans with Prosciutto
   and Roasted Pepper Salad 107
Beef
Beer Braised Oxtail with White
   Beans and Chick Peas 194
Braised Veal Shank (Osso Buco) 196
Mushroom Crusted Beef Tenderloin
   with Gorgonzola Onion Stuffing 177
Berries
Black Currant Sauce 259
Fresh Berry and Almond Tarts 8
Fresh Berries with Honey and Mint 4
Gummi Berry Sauce 259
Gummi Berry Sorbetto 144
Orange and Cranberry Bread 243
Merlot and Sun-dried Cranberry Sauce 187
Raspberry Sauce 259
Salal Berry Ice Cream 233

Salal Berry Rice Pudding with
   Caramel Pears 220
Pheasant Breast with Garlic Potato
   Crust and Salal Berry Sauce 170
Raspberry Frozen Yogurt 205
Strawberry Mascarpone Ice Cream 233
Wild Berry and Honey Vinegar 253
Breads 15, 16, 238-247
Cake
Almond Plum Cake with Spiced
   Merlot Plum Sauce 203
Almond Sheet Cake 260
Corn Cake 116
Fennel Polenta Cake 118
Hazelnut Fig Cake 216
Molten Mocha Chocolate Cakes 232
Plum Cake (Coffee Cake) 204
Sourdough Chocolate Brew Cake 228
Chard, Swiss
Island Spot Prawns with Prawn Roe
   Emulsion and Swiss Chard Flan 86
Rolled Smoked Salmon and
   Swiss Chard Omelet 26
Swiss Chard Risotto 131
Cheese
about 52
Apricot and Sunflower Seed
   Yogurt Cheese 6
Crab and Mascarpone Parfait 85
Gingersnaps with Mascarpone Filling 208
Gorgonzola Walnut Cream 251
Herb-Crusted Goat Cheese with
   Rainbow Tomato Salad 77
Lemon, Fig and Raisin Cheese Tart 213
Mini Chocolate Cheesecakes 231
Mushroom Broth with Chicken
   Gorgonzola Dumplings 58
Mushroom Crusted Beef Tenderloin
   with Gorgonzola Onion Stuffing 177
Mushroom, Ricotta and Sun-dried
   Tomato Strudel 47
Oyster Turnover with Fennel and
   Mascarpone Cream 91
Parmesan Crisps 255
Polenta with Parmesan and
   Fresh Herbs 135
Ricotta and Fresh Fruit Crêpe with
   Yellow Plum Sauce 33
Ricotta Flan with Prosciutto Wrapped
   Asparagus 20
Ricotta Lemon Ravioli with
   Mascarpone Lemon Cream 122
Roasted Beet Salad with Fresh Greens
   and Goat Cheese 81
Salmon, Fennel and Goat Cheese Tarts 41
Smoked Sablefish and Mascarpone Pâté
   with Warm Potato Arugula Salad 103
Smoked Tomato Soup with Gorgonzola
   Vegetable Dumplings 61

Soft Goat Cheese with Toasted
   Pine Nuts and Honey 5
Strawberry Mascarpone Ice Cream 233
Roasted Eggplant and Fennel Tart with
   Fresh Goat Cheese and
   Thyme-Scented Honey 108
Cheesecake
Lemon, Fig and Raisin Cheese Tart 213
Mini Chocolate Cheesecakes 232
Chips, Crisps and Croutons 254-255
Chocolate
about 198, 224
Bittersweet Ganach on a
   Honey Nut Phyllo Nest 227
Chocolate Crème Brûlée 210
Chocolate Crescents 10
Chocolate Fig Bread 16
Chocolate Hazelnut Torte 224
Chocolate Pine Nut Sugar Cookies 223
Chocolate Sauce 258
Chocolate-Hazelnut Ice Cream 236
Hazelnut, Cherry and Chocolate Pouches
   on Orange Custard Sauce 212
Lemon-Lime and White Chocolate
   Éclairs with Mint and Citrus Salad 200
Molten Mocha Chocolate Cakes 232
Raspberry, Fig and White Chocolate
   Bread Pudding 219
Sourdough Chocolate Brew Cake 228
White Chocolate Sauce 258
Coffee
Chocolate Hazelnut Torte 224
Espresso Pork Tenderloin 185
Molten Mocha Chocolate Cakes 232
Sourdough Chocolate Brew Cake 228
Crêpes and Pancakes
Curried Chicken Pancake 51
Dessert or Breakfast Crêpes 30
Ricotta and Fresh Fruit Crêpe with
   Yellow Plum Sauce 33
Warm Apple Crêpe with Caramel
   Orange Sauce 30
Seedy Little Pancakes
   with Sour Cherry Sauce 37
Smoked Salmon Crêpe 95
Desserts 198-236
Dessert Sauces 258-260
Egg
Baked Eggs with Pancetta
   and Mushrooms 19
Poached Egg, Fennel Sausage and
   Roasted Potatoes 25
Savory French Toast with Smoked
   Chicken Scrambled Eggs and
   Honey Balsamic Vinegar Syrup 29
Individual Sausage, Potato
   and Onion Frittata 22
Eggplant
Penne with Sausage and
   Roasted Eggplant 123

Roasted Eggplant and Fennel Tart
  with Fresh Goat Cheese and
  Thyme-Scented Honey   108

Fennel
Fennel and Black Olive Salad   99
Fennel Polenta Cake   118
Oyster Turnover with Fennel and
  Mascarpone Cream   91
Poached Egg, Fennel Sausage and
  Roasted Potatoes   25
Roasted Eggplant and Fennel Tart
  with Fresh Goat Cheese and
  Thyme-Scented Honey   108
Salmon, Fennel and Goat Cheese Tarts   41
Tuna Carpaccio with Fennel and
  Black Olive Salad   99

Figs
Chocolate Fig Bread   16
Fresh Fig Sorbetto   140
Hazelnut Fig Cake   216
Lemon, Fig and Raisin Cheese Tart   213
Poached Dried Figs in Riesling Wine   6
Raspberry, Fig and White Chocolate
  Bread Pudding   219

Fish
Whole Seed-Crusted Fish Fillet with
  Basil Lemon Butter Sauce   160
Cod (and Salt Cod)
Braised Ling Cod in White Wine
  Tomato Broth   148
Codfish Cakes with Fresh Coriander
  and Mint   104
Salmon Fillet with Baccala (salt cod)
  Salad   44
Halibut
Baked Halibut Fillet with Fresh Herb
  and Lemon Salad and Yukon Gold
  Potatoes   155
Halibut Fillet with Spiced Scallops
  and Tomato Olive Sauce   151
Red Snapper
Red Snapper Fillet in Phyllo Pastry   156
Sablefish (Black Cod)
Braised Sablefish with Leeks and
  Poached Oysters   149
Smoked Sablefish and Mascarpone Pâté
  with Warm Potato Arugula Salad   103
Salmon
Citrus Marinated Salmon and Tuna   41
Rolled Smoked Salmon and
  Swiss Chard Omelet   26
Salmon Cakes with Dungeness
  Crab Salad   96
Salmon Fillet with Baccala Salad   44
Salmon Fillet with Pear Cider Sauce
  and Asian Pear Salad   159
Salmon, Fennel and Goat Cheese Tarts   41
Salmon, Prawn and Scallop Timbale   152
Smoked Salmon Crêpe   95
Spiced Scallops in a Smoked
  Salmon Broth   92

Trout
Candied Trout with Seared Apple
  and Fresh Mint   43
Poached Trout Fillet with Cilantro
  Citrus Sauce   150
Quick Smoked Trout (or Chicken)   257
Smoked Trout and Green Bean Salad   78
Trout Fillet with Roasted
  Mediterranean Salad   163
Tuna
Citrus Marinated Salmon and Tuna   41
Prawn and Tuna Cocktail   82
Seared Tuna Medallions with
  Pickled Summer Squash,
  Cucumber and Sea Asparagus   100
Tuna Carpaccio with Fennel and
  Black Olive Salad   99

Flowers, Edible
about   72
Nasturtium Vinegar   253

Garlic
about roasting garlic   62
Aioli   104
Basil Garlic Mayonnaise   251
Chanterelle Mushrooms with
  Roasted Chestnuts and Garlic   116
Chive and Rosemary Garlic Oil   253
Couscous with Roasted Garlic
  and Pine Nuts   135
Crab and Corn Soup with Sorrel
  and Roasted Garlic Oil   62
Pheasant Breast with Garlic Potato
  Crust and Salal Berry Sauce   170
Potato, Cauliflower and Roasted
  Garlic Purée   118

Gnocchi
Gnocchi   136
Saffron Gnocchi in a Seafood Broth   68

Hazelnut
Almond or Hazelnut Filling   262
Avocado Hazelnut Semifreddo   204
Chocolate Hazelnut Torte   224
Chocolate-Hazelnut Ice Cream   236
Hazelnut Cinnamon Rolls   13
Hazelnut Fig Cake   216
Hazelnut, Cherry and Chocolate
  Pouches on Orange Custard Sauce   212

Ice Cream
Chocolate-Hazelnut Ice Cream   236
Pine Nut Praline and Honey Ice Cream   236
Pumpkin Seed Ice Cream   235
Rum and Honey Ice Cream   235
Salal Berry Ice Cream   233
Strawberry Mascarpone Ice Cream   233
Vanilla Spice Ice Cream   236

Lamb
Braised Lamb Shanks with
  Winter Vegetables   181
Wild Mushroom Crusted Lamb Loin   178

Lemon
Baked Halibut Fillet with Fresh Herb
  and Lemon Salad and Yukon
  Gold Potatoes   155
Lemon Sorbetto   141
Lemon, Fig and Raisin Cheese Tart   213
Lemon-Lime and White Chocolate
  Éclairs with Mint and Citrus Salad   200
Lemon-Lime Curd   260
Preserved Lemons   250
Rhubarb Lemon-Thyme Granita   144
Ricotta Lemon Ravioli with
  Mascarpone Lemon Cream   122
Sugared Lemon and Lime Slices   262
Whole Seed-Crusted Fish Fillet with
  Basil Lemon Butter Sauce   160

Mayonnaise
Aioli   104
Basil Garlic Mayonnaise   251

Mushroom
Baked Eggs with Pancetta and
  Mushrooms   19
Chanterelle Mushrooms with Roasted
  Chestnuts and Garlic   116
Mushroom Broth with Chicken
  Gorgonzola Dumplings   58
Mushroom Crusted Beef Tenderloin
  with Gorgonzola Onion Stuffing   177
Mushroom, Ricotta and Sun-dried
  Tomato Strudel   47
Parsnip Soup with Chanterelle
  Mushrooms   71
Pickled Wild Mushrooms   40
Pork Medallions with Wild
  Mushrooms   185
Roasted Breast of Game Hen with
  Mushroom and Walnut Stuffing   165
Wild Mushroom Crusted Lamb Loin   178
Wild Mushroom Risotto   133

Oils and Vinegars, Flavoured   57, 149, 253
Olive
Deep Fried Olives   44
Fennel and Black Olive Salad   99
Halibut Fillet with Spiced Scallops
  and Tomato Olive Sauce   151
Olive Rolls   242
Quick Olive Nut Bread   246
Tuna Carpaccio with Fennel and
  Black Olive Salad   99

Pasta   120-130
Pastry/Doughs
Basic Pie Dough   263
Pâté Dough   263
Pâté à Choux (Cream Puff Paste)   201
Shortcrust Dough   263
Sourdough Starter   244
Tuille Paste   222

Peppers
White Beans with Prosciutto and
  Roasted Pepper Salad   107

Pesto
Basil Pesto 252
Cilantro Pumpkin Seed Pesto 252
Poached Prawn with Cucumber
and Parsley Pesto 43
Sea Lettuce Pesto 252
Smoked Chicken Ravioli with
Cilantro Pumpkin Seed Pesto 126

Polenta
Fennel Polenta Cake 118
Polenta Crostini 48
Polenta with Parmesan and Fresh Herbs 135
Polenta, Flax and Sunflower
Seed Bread 246

Pork
Baked Eggs with Pancetta and
Mushrooms 19
Crusted Pork Loin Chop with
Caramel Honey and Orange Sauce 182
Espresso Pork Tenderloin 185
Pork Tenderloin Medallions with Merlot
and Sun-dried Cranberry Sauce 187
Prosciutto and Melon Soup 57
Prosciutto Wrapped Prawns 75
Ricotta Flan with Prosciutto
Wrapped Asparagus 20
Smoked Pork Hock, Rabbit and
Chervil Terrine 110
Venison Medallions with Pork and
Venison Sausage 189
White Beans with Prosciutto and
Roasted Pepper Salad 107

Poultry
Chicken
Curried Chicken Pancake 51
Molded Chicken Cannelloni "Stack" 129
Mushroom Broth with Chicken
Gorgonzola Dumplings 58
Savoury French Toast with Smoked
Chicken Scrambled Eggs and
Honey Balsamic Vinegar Syrup 29
Smoked Chicken Ravioli with
Cilantro Pumpkin Seed Pesto 126
Duck
Braised Duck Leg 169
Game Hen
Pan Roasted Game Hen with
Honey Brandy Glaze 166
Roasted Breast of Game Hen with
Mushroom and Walnut Stuffing 165
Pheasant
Pheasant Breast with Garlic Potato
Crust and Salal Berry Sauce 170
Turkey
Roast Turkey Breast with
Dried Fruit Stuffing 174
Stuffed Turkey Cutlet with
Quince and Cranberries 173

Rabbit
Roast Rabbit with Italian Sausage
and Bacon 191
Smoked Pork Hock, Rabbit and
Chervil Terrine 110

Rhubarb
Rhubarb and Berry Compote 5
Rhubarb Lemon-Thyme Granita 144
Rhubarb Sauce 259
Rhubarb with Red Wine and Rosemary 119

Rice, Risotto
about, 120
Apple, Rosemary and Sage Risotto 131
Mussel Risotto 133
Salal Berry Rice Pudding with
Caramel Pears 220
Swiss Chard Risotto 131
Wild Mushroom Risotto 133

Ricotta
Mushroom, Ricotta and Sun-dried
Tomato Strudel 47
Ricotta and Fresh Fruit Crêpe with
Yellow Plum Sauce 33
Ricotta Flan with Prosciutto
Wrapped Asparagus 20
Ricotta Lemon Ravioli with
Mascarpone Lemon Cream 122

Sausage
Homemade Sausages 190
Individual Sausage, Potato and
Onion Frittata 22
Penne with Sausage and Roasted
Eggplant 123
Poached Egg, Fennel Sausage and
Roasted Potatoes 25
Roast Rabbit with Italian Sausage
and Bacon 191
Venison Medallions with Pork
and Venison Sausage 189

Shellfish
Clams
Mussel, Clam and Roasted Corn
Chowder 65
Crab
Crab and Corn Soup with Sorrel
and Roasted Garlic Oil 62
Crab and Mascarpone Parfait 85
Salmon Cakes with Dungeness
Crab Salad 96
Oysters
Braised Sablefish with Leeks and
Poached Oysters 149
Oyster Soup with Fresh Mint 67
Oyster Turnover with Fennel and
Mascarpone Cream 91
Mussels
Mussel Risotto 133
Mussel, Clam and Roasted Corn
Chowder 65

Prawns and Shrimp
Grilled Prawns with Beet and Orange
Slaw and Pickled Red Onion 88
Island Spot Prawns with Prawn Roe
Emulsion and Swiss Chard Flan 86
Poached Prawn with Cucumber
and Parsley Pesto 43
Prawn and Tuna Cocktail 82
Prosciutto Wrapped Prawns 75
Scallops
Halibut Fillet with Spiced Scallops
and Tomato Olive Sauce 151
Salmon, Shrimp and Scallop Timbale 152
Spiced Scallops in a Smoked
Salmon Broth 92
Soups 52-71
Stocks
Brown Meat Stock, White or Clear
Meat Stock, Fish Stock and
Vegetable Stock 256

Tomato
Braised Ling Cod in White Wine
Tomato Broth 148
Egg Noodles with Tomato and
Fresh Herbs 130
Halibut Fillet with Spiced Scallops
and Tomato Olive Sauce 151
Herb-Crusted Goat Cheese with
Rainbow Tomato Salad 77
Mushroom, Ricotta and Sun-dried
Tomato Strudel 47
Oven-Dried Tomato Bread 240
Oven-dried Tomatoes 250
Smoked Tomato Soup with
Gorgonzola Vegetable Dumplings 61
Tomato Rosemary Granita 144
Tomato Sauce 251

Vegetables
Braised Curly Endive 117
Braised Lamb Shanks with
Winter Vegetables 181
Gratin of Fresh Greens 117
Grilled Summer Vegetable Terrine 113
Leek and Potato Tarts 49
Venison
Venison Medallions with Pork
and Venison Sausage 189
Yogurt
Apricot and Sunflower Seed
Yogurt Cheese 6
Raspberry Frozen Yogurt 235

Zabaglione with Vanilla Grappa 223